Row 1, left to right: Babe Hiskey, Ben Hogan, Bert Weaver, Bert Yancey.

Row 2, left to right: Billy Casper, Bob Rosburg, Bobby Nichols, Bruce Crampton.

Row 3, left to right: Chi Chi Rodriguez, Chuck Courtney, Dave Ragan, Dean Refram.

Row 4, left to right: Don Bies, Doug Sanders, Dow Finsterwald, Frank Beard.

Row 5, left to right: Frank Boynton, Gary Player, Gene Littler, George Bayer.

THE AGE OF PALMER

PRO GOLF IN THE 1960s, ITS GREATEST ERA

Patrick Hand

The Age of Palmer: Pro Golf in the 1960s. Its Greatest Era

Printed in the United States of America
Hardcover ISBN: 978-1-959096-41-2
Paperback ISBN: 978-1-959096-42-9
Ebook ISBN: 978-1-959096-43-6
Library of Congress Control Number: 2023933167

Canoe Tree Press

4697 Main Street
Manchester Center, VT 05255
Canoe Tree Press is a division of DartFrog Books

Table of Contents

When Palmer won his second Masters in 1960, it just perked up every antenna and it was like, "Whoa, what do we have here?" All of a sudden, you got Arnold Palmer. You knew who he was going to be. You could just tell it. He had that swagger, and he had the gallery. They loved him. We loved him. Television thought, "This is it. This is our ticket into big-time golf and big-time money." And they were right. He had that look. All the women were in love with him. They wanted to go straight to the motel room. Sex appeal sells, and he had it.
—Frank Beard, 2021

"I'll tell you, I would much rather have played in my time than play in this time now, Guys used to travel together. We used to all go out to dinner together. We stayed in private homes. My wife and I with our children, I remember in Milwaukee staying with a family there. You would never dream of doing that today. We used to bring a member out onto the practice tee and give him a lesson. We had jokes. It was a different world altogether. It was a great time, I must say."
—Gary Player, 2022

Preface

My first experience with golf in the 1960s came before my earliest memory. My Dad reports I pointed and exclaimed, "There's Arner Parmer!" one weekend afternoon as he watched golf on a black-and-white television in the railroad apartment we inhabited in Yonkers, New York. It must have been 1961, when I was 3 years old.

Several years later, Major League Baseball (particularly the awful early New York Mets), and to a lesser degree professional football, basketball and hockey captivated my attention as a young sports fan. Willie Mays, Fran Tarkenton, Wilt Chamberlain, and Gordie Howe were my early sports benchmarks. From reading the sports pages of the *New York Herald Tribune* and the *Daily News*, the names of Arnold Palmer and Jack Nicklaus were familiar to me, but only because of the frequency with which they appeared while I worked my way down to the box scores.

I remember the day it changed. My Dad was watching a golf tournament on television during the summer of 1968. It was the American Golf Classic at the Firestone Country Club in Akron, Ohio. At the end of 72 holes, Jack Nicklaus was tied with Frank Beard and Lee Elder. I learned the term "sudden-death playoff." Beard dropped out after the first playoff hole when he parred while Nicklaus and Elder birdied. On 17, Elder was poised to win, but Nicklaus holed a 15-footer to save par after hitting his approach in a bunker. The second time they played 17, Elder just missed a 15-foot putt before Nicklaus holed an eight-footer to win.

At the time, I had no idea of the significance of what had transpired. Black baseball, football and basketball players were in abundance, and I did not give a thought to Lee Elder—a Black golfer—being locked in a duel with Nicklaus, other than, unlike Nicklaus, I had never heard of him, and I assumed he was the underdog. What I came away with after watching the five-hole playoff was that golf could be as exciting a spectacle as the team sports I followed.

The following Wednesday evening, my Dad asked if I wanted to go with him and my grandmother to the Westchester Classic the following day. I happily accepted the invitation. We arrived early at the Westchester Country Club in Rye, New York, on a sunny, cool Thursday morning for the first round. After parking the car, I gaped in awe at the massive clubhouse that loomed over the grounds.

Ingrained in my memory more than half a century later is my first glimpse of golf in person. At the par-3 10th hole, Rives McBee, Dean Refram and Bob Stanton were starting their rounds. Few spectators watched them. They hit their shots and walked to the green. I saw Refram hold the putter in front of him and close one eye to plumb bob, which to me looked odd. We then walked to catch up with the featured morning threesome of Palmer, Kermit Zarley and Bert Weaver.

Much later, I learned that McBee was then a struggling 29-year-old from Texas who was in his second full season on the tour. He had won less than $6,000 during the year. In 1968, the Westchester Classic's purse of $250,000 was by far the biggest of the year, with $50,000 to the winner (adjusted to today's dollars, the total payout would be $2,132,500; for 2022-2023, the *smallest* PGA Tour purse is $3,800,000). Thus, it offered McBee the chance for a decent payday. After an opening round 69, McBee eagled the 18th hole on Friday for a 66 that left him two shots back of leader Bob Murphy. It also put him in a threesome with Nicklaus and 48-year-old Julius Boros (fresh off his victory at the PGA Championship a month earlier) for the third round on Saturday.

I caught up with McBee at his home in Irving, Texas, to talk about his long-ago round with the future members of the World Golf Hall of Fame. He remembered it with clarity, particularly how he was visibly upset in the early going:

They couldn't have been nicer guys to play with. I bogeyed the first hole. I get around to the third hole. I double-bogeyed it and I was 3 over after three holes.

Jack came over and told me, "Settle down. Now, you've got 15 holes and a lot of birdie holes from here to the clubhouse, but just settle down and play like you're capable of. Don't throw a good round away." And Julie said the very same thing. He said, "Young man, you played too good to get to this point. Don't throw it away, settle down. Make you some birdies from here to the clubhouse and see if you can't get it back."

I made five birdies from there to the clubhouse and shot, I think a 70, and I could have shot 90 if they hadn't come over and patted me on the back and told me to calm down. Both of them said the same thing in just a little bit different way. And they did a good job of it.

Boros would win the Westchester Classic the next day. Nicklaus and Murphy tied for second. McBee remained steady and tied for sixth, earning $9,000, 60 percent of the $15,003 he would take home for the year.

In the 1950s, the PGA tour's biggest stars were Ben Hogan, Sam Snead, Jimmy Demaret, Doug Ford, and Cary Middlecoff. They were among the greatest to ever play the game. Many played with a flair, and some (like Snead and Demaret) had colorful personalities. However, they are remembered today mostly through black-and-white—often grainy—photographs and videos. As few tournaments were televised, fans mostly had to be content with following pro golf in newspapers.

In the 1960s, golf became colorized, both on television and in glossy magazines such as *Sports Illustrated* and *Golf Digest*, through which golf fans saw a new generation of stars such as Palmer, Nicklaus, Gary Player, Billy Casper, Doug Sanders and Tony Lema. They saw them competing at Augusta National, Westchester and other venues on the East Coast and the Midwest, and in sun-splashed tournaments in Florida and the California desert. 1960s golf had a different, livelier vibe than before.

But pro golf still had a long way to go before it evolved into the game we know today, with 18-hole TV coverage and purses running into eight figures. In the 1960s, many tournaments were not telecast at all, and for those that were only the last several holes were shown, and only on weekends and in two-hour increments at most. "The leaders soon will be in range of our television cameras" often was heard from the likes of Jim McKay and Chris Schenkel. As in the present day, there were tournaments bearing the name of a commercial sponsor (e.g., the Lucky Lager Open in San Francisco and the Thunderbird Classic in Metropolitan New York), but most simply went by geographic names like the Los Angeles Open, the Pensacola Open, and the Portland Open.

Some of the pros I talked to marveled at the immaculate conditions with which present-day players uniformly are blessed, free of metal spike marks on the green and fairway divots that were part of the tour experience in the 1960s. Some tournaments back then were played on lush, well-manicured courses with comfortable clubhouses like those at Augusta National, Colonial, Doral, and Westchester. But many were played at public venues such as Rancho Park in Los Angeles, Harding Park in San Francisco, and the Keller Golf Course in St. Paul, where the fairways were lined with divots from weekenders, where the metal lockers in the clubhouse were small and the showers cramped.

The notion that, one day in the distant future, Saudi interests would pay golfers nine-figure bonuses to stars to join the upstart LIV tour was unimaginable. Consider that, by 1959, Palmer had 10 tour victories to his name. In 1958, he won the Masters and was the leading money winner with earnings of $42,608. Adjusted to 2023 dollars, that comes to about $436,732, which is exactly what Paul Barjon earned in 2021-2022 to finish 168th on the PGA Tour money list. Thus, when Palmer—then 29-years-old and with a young family to support—was offered the full-time job as the head professional at the new Laurel Valley Golf Club in Ligonier, Pennsylvania near his home, he seriously considered before turning it down.

In 1962, after Palmer had burst onto the national scene, the tour calendar still was littered with stops—such as those in Tucson, Baton Rouge, and Beaumont, Texas—with $20,000 purses.

Lafayette, Louisiana offered $17,500, Mobile, Alabama $11,500. Even in 1962, this was chump change.

Palmer and Nicklaus obtained pilot's licenses and flew private planes to tournaments, but they were the exceptions. Pros who were successful but not at the top of the pyramid car-pooled to tournaments, shared motel rooms, and ate in cafeterias. They had a middle-class lifestyle, not much different than many of the fans who attended the tournaments. Even after Gary Player had established himself as one of the top players in the world, he traveled to some tournaments in a Greyhound bus. Fans saw the pros against a verdant backdrop of fairways and greens, not at night in a wood-veneer panel motel room, hoping the clerk would remember to put through their wake-up call.

I won't claim that today's pros love golf any less than those who played in the 1960s, but back then most of the pros *really* had to love the game just to deal with the mundane stress of tour life off of the course for the limited financial rewards that were available. The retired golf pros I interviewed (all in their 70s, 80s, or 90s, and several passed away prior to publication) talked almost as much about the fellowship and camaraderie they had with their peers as about their games.

Yet, the 1960s was pro golf's greatest decade, and it takes nothing away from Snead, Hogan, Walter Hagen, Byron Nelson, Nick Faldo, Greg Norman, Tiger Woods, Phil Mickelson, Jon Rahm, Scottie Scheffler and all the other stars past and present to state this. Palmer was not the greatest golfer ever (though from 1960-1962 he was the greatest of his time), but he was the greatest golf *personality* ever. When Nicklaus and Player joined him at the top, golf had its Big Three.

Photo 1: *Palmer, Player, and Nicklaus, 1962. (Professional Golfers Career College.)*

During the 1960s, Nicklaus won seven major championships, Palmer six, and Player four. Some of Billy Casper's contemporaries think he was as good, if not better. Casper won only one major in the 1960s but had a total of 33 tour victories (compared to Palmer's 43 Nicklaus's 30, and Player's 10). A second tier of great players, including Frank Beard, Chi Chi Rodriguez, Bob Goalby, and Bobby Nichols, could beat the Big Three any given week they all competed.

With the exception of Tiger Woods, never before or since did golf have a star that captivated the public like Palmer, who arrived at his peak early in the 1960s but remained pro golf's dominant figure even as his skills diminished as the decade went on. Palmer's good looks, charisma and go-for-broke style fueled the rise of televised golf, increased the amount of the weekly purses, and put more money in the pockets of his fellow pros, just as Woods would do 35 year later. But there was a remoteness with Woods, whereas Palmer embraced the adulation of his fans. Palmer smiled and made eye contact with hundreds every round, making each one a fan for life if they weren't already. In his book "A Life Well Played," he wrote that an autograph should be "a personal experience, a memento on which you can't put a price." After his rounds, he signed countless autographs, every one of them legible.

Someday, if not already, somebody will write a book about golf in the late 1990s and early 2000s, when Woods, Phil Mickelson and Ernie Els battled one another. They never were referred to as golf's Big Three. Woods was dominant, and Mickelson, Els and others fought over table scraps, particularly in the frequent weeks that Woods did not play. In the 1960s, the Big Three were much more of a presence than Woods, Mickelson and Els ever were. Rare was the week when none of the Big Three or Casper appeared, even at the smaller events.

A handful of players whose careers dated back to the 1930s continued to be part of the scene in the 1960s. Snead, whose first tour win was in 1937, turned 48 in 1960 and won four times during the decade. His age-contemporary, Ben Hogan, who slowly drifted away from regular tour play after recovering from the serious injuries he suffered in a 1949 car crash, played in the Masters seven times and the U.S. Open four times in the 1960s, with four top-10 finishes; he never missed the cut in either of those major tournaments in the 1960s.

A library can be furnished with books about the 1960s – technologically, politically, militarily, musically, morally, and culturally. The decade started with the newly-selected Mercury Seven astronauts training for launch into earth orbit and ended with astronauts walking on the surface of the moon. The top Billboard song of 1960 was "Theme from a Summer Place" by the Percy Faith Orchestra, and at the end of 1969 "Come Together" by the soon-to-disband Beatles (who in 1960 were looking for a drummer and were four years from appearing on the landscape in America) was at the top of the charts. In 1960, few Americans had ever heard of Vietnam, and by 1969 the war there was dividing generations.

Pro golf did see major cultural change. In 1960, the PGA of America—which ran the tour—was only open to members of the Caucasian race. By 1969, African-Americans Elder, Charlie Sifford and Pete Brown were tour mainstays. By the end of the decade, the touring pros had revolted against the PGA of America and taken over management of the tour. But pro golf never became chic. At the end of the decade, hair on the younger stars still was safely above the collar. If the tour had a soundtrack, it would have been Dean Martin and maybe Herb Alpert, but definitely not Bob Dylan or the Rolling Stones. Pros who wanted to get high did it on high-balls. Nobody got busted for drugs.

This book is not intended to be an encyclopedia of pro golf in the 1960s, though you will read about great championships and players (women's professional golf in the 1960s, when LPGA stars like Mickey Wright and Kathy Whitworth were at their peak, is deserving of its own book but is not covered here). The focus is on the American tour, but events in Europe, Australia, Africa, and Central America are covered as well. You will read the stories of famous players, and others not as well-known, about great times at long-forgotten events. Drives between tournaments. Cookouts in motel parking lots and drinks at hotel bars. Games of cards and unusual bets. Pranks. All of which made the 1960s golf's greatest era, and worth revisiting.

A note about the interviews

All of the interviews from which excerpts are reproduced were conducted in 2021 and 2022. For the most part, they are verbatim, without editing for style, although many are condensed. Stories that obviously are embellished are printed as they were told. Only when the interview subject has misstated a fact (such as the year of a tournament, or the hole on which a score was made), is a corrective edit inserted.

Prelude: 1959 Buick Open

Photo 2: Art Wall. (*Creative Commons*)

In 1959, 35-year-old Art Wall, Jr. was the undisputed player of the year. He won four tournaments, including the Masters, as well as the Vardon Trophy awarded to the player with the lowest scoring average (70.35), and the money title ($53,123).

Wall typified the 1950s touring pro. He was born in a small town near Scranton, Pennsylvania, caddied in his youth, and served in the U.S. Army Air Corps in World War II. Somewhat atypically for pros of his era, after the war he attended college at Duke University, graduating with a business degree in 1949. He was quiet, serious, and almost completely colorless. Even after Wall birdied five of the last six holes at the 1959 Masters to shoot 66 to beat Cary Middlecoff by a stroke, a golf fan of the era might not have been able to pick him out of a lineup.

On July 6, 1959, Wall won the Buick Open at the Warwick Hills Country Club in Flint, Michigan, for his final victory of the year, in a playoff over defending PGA Champion Dow Finsterwald. Wall earned $9,000, a hefty winner's check at the time. Others in the top-10 were stalwarts Middlecoff, Jerry Barber, Jay Hebert, Julius Boros, Ken Venturi, Mike Souchak, and Don Fairfield. Tied for eighth with Boros was the 1958 Masters champion Arnold Palmer (who had draped Wall with the green jacket at Augusta earlier in the year). Just out of the top-10, six behind Wall, was 19-year-old amateur Jack Nicklaus. Bothered by a bad back, Billy Casper (fresh off his win at the United States Open three weeks earlier), played but did not contend.

Contemporaneously with the Buick Open, another event took place. With the top pros in Michigan, the most notable American in the field was 52-year-old Willie Goggin, who was the runner-up to Gene Sarazen at the 1933 PGA Championship. Only three other Americans played. None of the four made the 36-hole cut.

That "alternate" event was the Open Championship, known stateside as the British Open, played at the Muirfield Golf Links in Scotland. It was won by a 23-year-old South African, Gary Player, who pocketed £1,000, or about $2,800, approximately what Middlecoff and Barber earned for finishing third at the Buick Open.

The 1959 British Open was the last that largely would be ignored in America.

1960

January

Los Angeles Open

Pro golf in the 1960s opened in Los Angeles in early January.

On December 26, 1959, 30-year-old Don Fairfield loaded up the station wagon at his Illinois home with his golf clubs and suitcases packed with what he, his wife Iris and their infant son Jeff would need for the trip to California. Fairfield was a tall, slim man who made a decent living on the tour. Friendly, he was well-liked by his fellow pros and was a member of the tour's policy board. Before backing out the car, Fairfield shoveled the drifts from a recent snow that had accumulated against the garage door. The 1959 season had ended in Coral Gables, Florida, just 20 days before, where Fairfield finished 10th. Yet, he was eager to prepare for the new year. He needed the warmer air in Los Angeles to retool his game after the Christmas holiday.

Interstates 70 and 15 existed only on planning maps, so the Fairfields picked up old U.S. Route 66 near St. Louis. The trip would take three-and-a-half days, through Oklahoma City, Amarillo, Albuquerque, and Flagstaff until reaching the highway's terminus in Santa Monica. After they arrived, Don and Iris spent New Year's Eve with fellow pro Paul Harney and his wife Patti.

On January 1, Arnold Palmer, also 30, was interviewed at his home in Ligonier, Pennsylvania by *The Latrobe Bulletin*. He was photographed with his 16-month-old daughter, Amy, as he packed a suitcase. Palmer already had 13 wins under his belt, including three in 1959, during which his prize money totaled $33,962. He also earned several thousand dollars from exhibitions and endorsements. Palmer was not yet rich, but he was comfortable enough that he could afford to fly to Los Angeles. His wife Winnie, Amy, and his other daughter, Peggy, would stay at home for the time being.

The following day, Palmer would board a Boeing 707 at Pittsburgh Airport. He intended to arrive early to practice at the Rancho Park Golf Course. Palmer told the reporter he expected great things in 1960 from fellow pros Mike Souchak, Gene Littler, Doug Ford, Art Wall, Jr., Dow Finsterwald, Jay Hebert, and Bob Rosburg. Asked about a fellow named Palmer, he smiled and said, "I hope he's there, too." He also anticipated Mason Rudolph and Frank Wharton would make names for themselves. Rudolph would have some success, winning five times on the tour over a long career. Wharton never finished better than seventh place in any tournament and would retire with total career earnings of $21,502.

Gary Player would not be in Los Angeles. He was not then, nor would he ever become, a full-time regular on the PGA tour. He would play for extended periods in the United States, but he also competed in Africa, Europe, Australia, Asia, and any other place where golf was played. Player had just lost a five-match series in his native South Africa against American Tommy Bolt. "His behavior was appalling," one South African said of the hot-tempered Bolt. "When you play the Yanks you've got to switch off your hearing aid," quipped South African veteran Bobby Locke. Player was in the midst of a tour of his home country. He would not make the trek to the United States until April, when he would join the tour at the Masters.

Although it was a short jaunt from the ultra-exclusive Los Angeles Country Club, the Rancho Park Golf Course could not have been more different. Since its opening as a public facility in 1949, Rancho Park was open to all who wanted to play, regardless of race or religion. It was somewhat scrubby, with a small, unassuming clubhouse and limited practice areas, not atypical of other courses on the PGA tour at the time.

In 1960, top country clubs generally were averse to turning over their courses for a week to the pros, which would deprive the members of the opportunity to play and would require clean-up. Moreover, few sponsors were eager to pay the premium that would be exacted by the club. The days when golf pros were looked down upon by gentlemen members in favor of amateurs was receding but not totally over. On the other hand, public links weekenders mostly were happy to give up their home course for a week in order to watch the pros.

The Los Angeles Open always drew a strong field. In 1960, total prize money was $44,500, at a time when the typical purse was $15,000 to $25,000. The 1960 edition got underway on January 8, a cool, sunny Friday. The first-round leader, with a 66, was 41-year-old Eric Monti, the head pro at nearby Hillcrest Country Club, whose clients included stars Henry Fonda, Burt Lancaster, and Danny Kaye, and who occasionally played the tour. One stroke back in second place was Jimmy Clark, also of Los Angeles.

Yet another local pro, Charlie Sifford, was tied for eighth after shooting 69. Sifford, an African-American, played even though the PGA of America bylaws stated, "Any professional golfer of the Caucasian race and residing in North or South America is eligible to

Photo 3: *Dow Finsterwald.*
(*Historic Images.*)

become a PGA member," effectively excluding Sifford. However, in 1959, California attorney general Stanley Mosk intervened and asked the PGA to show cause why Sifford was denied membership. As a result, the tour made Sifford an approved player, and in November 1961 the PGA removed the "Caucasian race" clause.

Monti maintained his lead after the second round. Rain washed out third-round play on Sunday. On Monday, the bespectacled Monti shot 68, giving him a four-shot lead over Dow Finsterwald, winner of the 1958 PGA Championship, to move closer to an unlikely victory. However, in Tuesday's final round, Monti's luck ran out. He was 4 over after three holes on his way to an 80. Finsterwald's 71 gave him a three-shot victory and a check for $5,500. Sifford finished in a tie for 33rd to take home $153.63.

Palmer did not contend. Fairfield was forced to withdraw during the third round due to an injury. While the Los Angeles Open was being contested, Player won the Transvaal Open in Johannesburg.

Bob Goalby

Rancho Park was a public course that got more play than any course in the country. If they wanted to make it a nice country club, they could have. It's a good layout. It was never in really good shape when we played in the wintertime. They started picking up rocks and tin cans on Monday morning, getting ready for the tournament. Now, they spend four or five years (preparing a course for use in a PGA event). Then, they just said, "Okay, let's tee it up."

Don Fairfield

Rancho Park was poor. It had grass but it wasn't well-kept. Tons of divots.

Yorba Linda Open

From January 15-18, 1960, the Yorba Linda Open was held for the one and only time in Orange County, California. The small gallery was treated to a dramatic finish. Jerry Barber, a tour veteran, came to the 72nd hole—a par-5—two strokes ahead of Billy Maxwell, a short, pudgy, profane man who had won the 1951 U.S. Amateur. Barber watched helplessly as Maxwell chipped in from 40 yards off the green for an eagle. He then hit a poor chip that left him with a 12-foot putt for a birdie to avoid a playoff with Maxwell.

Barber, a diminutive 43-year-old who was the pro at Wilshire Country Club in nearby Los Angeles, had not won on tour since

1954. "I guess I'm not supposed to win a tournament on tour," he glumly said to Julius Boros, the third member of his group. "Aw, go knock it in," the genial Boros replied. Barber stepped up and sank the putt for the win to take home $2,800 from the $25,000 purse.

John Brodie, who then was the backup quarterback to Y.A. Tittle on the San Francisco 49ers, earned $112.50 after shooting even-par 288 for 72 holes, including a 67 in the second round. In 1959, during the NFL offseason, Brodie qualified for the U.S. Open at Winged Foot (he missed the 36-hole cut). Long after his successful football career ended, in 1981 he qualified for the Open a second time. Brodie holds the record for the longest gap between appearances at the U.S. Open.

March

St. Petersburg Open

George Bayer was one of the most intimidating golfers the tour has ever seen. He was 6-foot-5 and weighed about 230 pounds, sported a crewcut, and at times had an explosive temper. In the late 1940s, after service in the Navy, he played tackle at the University of Washington and was good enough to be selected to play in the 1949 East-West Shrine Game and to be drafted by the Washington Redskins. After his pro football career did not pan out, he turned to golf, though he did not become a professional until 1954, when he was 29 years old.

Photo 4: George Bayer.
(Source Unknown)

Bayer was the first pro to consistently hit 300-yard drives, a remarkable feat in the days of persimmon drivers and wound balls. His all-around game was good enough to win three times on the tour in the 1950s, including the 1957 Canadian Open. In late 1958, he beat Sam Snead in a playoff in a tournament in Havana, weeks before Fidel Castro assumed power and made golf in Cuba a thing of the past.

At the 1960 St. Petersburg Open, it was Bayer's short game that won the tournament. Tied with Jack Fleck after 72 holes, he holed a 65-foot chip from off of the green for a birdie on the first hole of the sudden-death playoff for his final tour win.

April

World Champion Golf

The first televised golf tournament was the 1947 U.S. Open at the St. Louis Country Club, which St. Louis station KSD-TV broadcast locally. In 1953, the so-called World Championship of Golf outside of Chicago was the first event to be nationally televised, by ABC. Ironically, Lew Worsham won both the 1947 Open and the 1953 WCG, where he holed a 104-yard wedge for an eagle and a walk-off victory, moments before ABC would have cut away. NBC started televising the U.S. Open in 1954, and tournaments sporadically were televised at the national and local level for the rest of the 1950s.

Game shows were the craze on television in the 1950s, and producers saw golf as a promising extension. In 1957, the show All-Star Golf premiered, a series of matches between pros that were taped, edited, and syndicated for later viewing. World Champion Golf (not to be confused with the aforementioned WCG) was a similar made-for-television event that premiered on NBC in 1959. Top pros played each other in match play at famous courses such as Colonial, Pebble Beach, Olympia Fields, and Oak Hill. The matches were edited to one hour and shown on weekends. Singer Bob Crosby (Bing's brother) was the host and commentator.

The weekend before the 1960 Masters, viewers were shown a match between Sam Snead and Mason Rudolph, taped the previous December at the picturesque Mid-Ocean Club in Bermuda, with $8,000 at stake. It was a close match. Snead was known to have failings on the green at times, but a 4-putt to lose the 16th hole was surprising. Then on 18, with the match all square, he flubbed a relatively easy pitch and then three-putted to lose to Rudolph. Even though Snead was 47 years old and past his prime, it looked a little suspicious. In fact, two weeks prior to the Masters, he won the De Soto Open in Sarasota, Florida for his 79th PGA tour victory.

Just before the Masters, Snead came clean. He threw the match but, according to him, with the best of intentions. On the 12th hole, Snead discovered he had an extra club in his bag. Under USGA and PGA rules, players can only have 14 clubs, and Snead had 15. The penalty for a violation was loss of hole—every hole in which the extra club was in the bag—meaning Snead had lost the 11 holes he already had played.

Knowing there was a sponsor who was paying a lot of money for car or razor commercials, Snead kept the rules infraction a secret. He played on the level for several more holes until he got to the 16th hole, when the time came to make sure he lost the match for the benefit of the television audience.

Whether as a result of an inquiry by a reporter as to why he suddenly played like a hacker, or whether his conscience got to him, Snead fessed up. "What could I do?" he asked a reporter, rhetorically. "I knew I was already beaten 10 and 8, under the rules, but I didn't want to spoil these people's show so I kept going, trying to make it look good." In other words, because he was honest within the rules of golf (he did not try to conceal the extra club or try to get rid of it), he decided for appearance's sake he intentionally would lose a match he knew he already had lost, if that makes sense.

"He should have disqualified himself immediately," said Harold Sargent of the PGA. "But there were very mitigating circumstances – grinding cameras, concern over the show and so forth. It would have been a great thing for golf if Sam had stopped right at the spot he recognized he had broken the rules." That, however, would not necessarily have made for good television.

Although Snead had faults, lack of honesty on the golf course was not one of them. At the 1952 Jacksonville Open, he tied with the then-unknown Doug Ford. Earlier in the tournament, he had driven his ball next to a boundary stake. His playing partner thought the ball was out-of-bounds. An official ruled it was in play. Not wanting to win under circumstances where it might appear he had been the beneficiary of a favorable ruling because of his name, Snead forfeited the playoff (though he did not disqualify himself, and he accepted the second-place money).

After a closed-door meeting with PGA brass during the Masters, Snead was let off with "a mild rebuke." The controversy blew over without any lasting damage to Snead's reputation.

Photo 5: Sam Snead at Wrigley Field, Chicago, July 1961. (Creative Commons)

The Masters

Arnold Palmer was far from unknown at the start of the decade, at least among people who followed golf, despite getting a late start on his professional career. Palmer played at Wake Forest, dropped out, and joined the Coast Guard. After finishing his stint, he got a job as a paint salesman in Cleveland and played as an amateur.

Photo 6: Arnold Palmer, 1953. (United States Coast Guard)

When he arrived at the Country Club of Detroit for the 1954 United States Amateur, he was about to turn 25 years old and was not considered a top contender. Almost all of Palmer's amateur wins were in his home state of Pennsylvania. He had not even been considered for the 1953 Walker Cup team. The field at Detroit was flush with prominent, veteran amateurs such as Frank Stranahan, William Campbell, and Billy Joe Patton. Campbell and Patton were upset in early rounds. Palmer beat Stranahan in the fifth round in an upset. In the final, he faced World War II hero Bobby Sweeny, the 1937 British Amateur champion and wealthy socialite, who was 43 years old and whose best golf was behind him. Sweeny took Palmer to the 36th hole before falling.

Palmer turned pro right after his U.S. Amateur win. In 1955, he shot a 64 in the first round of the Canadian Open. When he looked at the scoreboard, he was surprised to see he was not leading. Charlie Sifford, who had ventured to Canada because it was one the few tournaments in which he could play against White golfers, had a 63. "Who the hell is Charlie Sifford and how did he shoot a 63?" a cocky Palmer asked nobody in particular. Unbeknownst to Palmer,

Sifford was standing right behind him. "The same way you shot a 64, Mr. Palmer!" he snapped. Palmer turned around and looked at Sifford. "Nice round, Charlie," he adroitly said as he extended his hand. The two became lifelong friends.

Several days later, Palmer would win the Canadian Open for his first pro victory. For the rest of the 1950s, he established himself as a consistent winner. Years before he flew a private airplane to tournaments, Palmer and his wife Winnie made the circuit by auto, with a trailer and their daughters in tow. He cut his teeth winning outpost tournaments such as the Eastern Open in Baltimore and the Rubber City Open in Akron that merited only short wire service reports in the newspapers. In 1957, Palmer won four times, and in 1958 he was the tour's leading money winner.

At the 1958 Masters, Palmer had his first moment of national prominence. It may seem hard to believe, but at the time the Masters was struggling financially. Founders Bobby Jones and Clifford Roberts, and members at Augusta National, had to work to sell tickets. They resorted to such gimmicks as a parade in downtown Augusta, a beauty pageant, a long-drive contest, and trick-shot exhibitions to attract attention and fans. Yet, despite not affording the winner any appellation other than Masters champion, it still was the title most coveted by golfers around the world, and was one of the few tournaments that featured a truly international field.

In 1958, Palmer was a co-leader after 54 holes. In the final round, on the par-3 12th hole, his tee shot was embedded behind the green. He asked for relief, but it was denied by the official onsite, Arthur Lacey. Palmer made double bogey 5. He then announced that he would take a drop next to the embedment and play a provisional ball. Ken Venturi—his playing partner, who he led by one shot after 11 holes—told Palmer he could not do that under the rules because he had not declared his intention to do so prior to hitting the embedded ball. Palmer did so anyway and managed to get the provisional ball up and down for a 3.

Palmer played the par-5 13th hole with the assumption Lacey's ruling would stand, and that he now trailed Venturi. Thus, he went for the green in two. He hit a perfect 3-wood to within 18 feet, then made the putt for eagle. After the 15th hole, there was a rules conference that included Jones and Roberts. The result was Palmer was informed Lacey had been overruled and that he was entitled to relief on 12. The par Palmer played with his provisional ball would stand. Despite three-putting for a bogey on 18, he won by one stroke over defending champion Doug Ford and Fred Hawkins, and by two over Venturi. To his dying day, Venturi maintained he was cheated out of a victory by Palmer (though he never explained how Palmer caused Ford and Hawkins to score one better than him).

So, when he arrived at Augusta in April 1960, Palmer was established as one of the best in the game. He had won 17 times on tour, four times already in 1960. At 6-1, he was the betting favorite.

Palmer's 67 in the first round put him two shots ahead of the field. Venturi started hot with a 31 on the front nine before crashing with a 42 on the back for 73. In the second round, Palmer slipped with a 73, which still gave him a one-shot lead over four players, including 47-year-old Ben Hogan, and Dow Finsterwald.

The 31-year-old Finsterwald—who was the player of the year in 1958 after winning the PGA Championship—should have been leading but, after completing the first hole of the second round, he dropped a ball to take a practice putt. His playing partner, Billy Casper, warned him against doing so, saying it was in violation of a local rule. Finsterwald confessed to having taken a practice putt the day before. Knowing he may well be disqualified, he managed to maintain his composure for the remaining 17 holes and shot 70. After the round, he learned he would only be assessed a two-stroke penalty for Thursday's infraction instead of suffering disqualification. Venturi's 69 left him two shots back. During Saturday's rainy, windy third round, Palmer needed 33 putts to shoot 72, but he still maintained a one-shot lead over Hogan, Casper, Venturi, Finsterwald, and Julius Boros.

Sunday, April 10, 1960, was the day when Palmer introduced himself to America. The day before, the Boston Celtics wrapped up the NBA title, and it was two days before the Cincinnati Reds and the Philadelphia Phillies opened the major league baseball season. Hence, sports fans in the 45 million American households with television sets had no other option on an early Spring afternoon that was chilly throughout most of the nation than to tune to CBS to watch the final round of the Masters.

All but Venturi and Finsterwald faded. Finsterwald shot 71, which would leave him two strokes short — the margin of his first-round penalty assessment. Venturi turned in a 70 for a total of 283. He finished an hour ahead of Palmer and before the CBS telecast had begun. "Do you consider this your greatest victory?" he was asked in the clubhouse by a reporter. Remembering Palmer's 1958 win, Venturi demurred, saying it was not over.

In fact, things looked good for Venturi. The national television audience joined as Palmer faced a birdie putt on the par-5 15th hole (at the time, CBS only covered holes 15-18). His playing partner was Casper, the defending U.S. Open champion. On black-and-white TV sets, viewers saw Palmer in a stylish light-colored cardigan sweater, and Casper in a dark pullover and dark slacks. Palmer was one stroke behind Venturi, with the difficult final three holes awaiting. His best chance at catching Venturi was to make the 15-footer. Viewers watched as Palmer confidently strode around the green, looking at his putt from two angles while tugging at his sweater. Finally, he stood over the putt in his knock-kneed stance, stroked the ball, and missed. He tapped in, retraced his steps to his first putt, picked up his cigarette and took a drag.

As he walked to the par-3 16th, with late-afternoon shadows covering the tee, commentator Jim McKay summarized the situation, with Venturi finished and, "Arnold Palmer, still alive ... He needs a bird on one of these last three holes." Palmer's tee shot hit the green but was 40 feet short of the hole. Casper had an even longer birdie putt, which he left 7 feet short. After watching Casper's uphill putt, Palmer kept the flagstick in the hole. He misjudged the speed and hit his putt much too hard. Fortunately for Palmer, his ball hit the pin and stopped to within tap-in range. Casper chuckled. "Jeez, Arnie, you would've had a helluva putt out of that trap on the other side," he said.

Still one behind Venturi, Palmer hit a good drive on 17. He walked up the fairway at almost a march pace, his lips cradling a cigarette. McKay noted that Palmer and Casper were the only players left on the course, and that Palmer had only two holes on which to make a birdie to tie Venturi. Palmer left his approach about 25 feet short of the hole, to the right. Disappointed with the result, he angrily threw his cigarette on the ground and continued marching. Upon reaching the green, once again Palmer carefully surveyed the putt from multiple angles. He stroked the ball and it dropped into the hole. Palmer jumped and jigged, seemingly surprised at the result. He was tied with Venturi.

Palmer's demeanor again turned serious. He spit into his hands twice before hitting a 260-yard drive to the center of the fairway, and spit in his hands again as he prepared to hit his approach with a 6-iron. The approach was magnificent. The ball stopped 6 feet left of the hole, leaving him with a breaking putt. After marking his ball, Palmer looked at the scoreboard to confirm a birdie would win, and then sat on the ground off of the green. Casper had put his approach even closer than Palmer, below the hole, but putted first to clear the stage for Palmer. Casper missed.

Palmer replaced his ball and surveyed the putt. After standing over his ball, he stepped away, distracted by McKay's voice in the CBS tower. He reset, and stroked his ball into the middle of the cup for his second straight birdie and second Masters title. Twice on the way to the scorer's table at the back of the green, he bent over, overcome with emotion.

For almost an hour, Palmer had the national television audience almost all to himself. They saw his powerful corkscrew swing and unusual putting stance with his knees touching. They saw him smoking cigarettes between shots, stalking the greens, and placing his hands on his hips as he viewed the next shot. It was great theater, but Palmer did not look like he was showboating. It all looked natural. The difference between the handsome, brawny Palmer and the pulpy Casper was as marked as what viewers would see later in the year in the nationally televised debate between the vibrant John F. Kennedy and the pale, sweating Richard Nixon. Palmer would be golf's brightest star for the rest of the 1960s.

Photo 7: Arnold and Winnie Palmer walking to the Augusta National clubhouse after the 1960 Masters. (Getty Images)

Frank Beard

When Palmer won his second Masters in 1960, it just perked up every antenna and it was like, "Whoa, what do we have here?" All of a sudden, you got Arnold Palmer. You knew who he was going to be. You could just tell it. He had that swagger, and he had the gallery. They loved him. We loved him. Television thought, "This is it. This is our ticket into big-time golf and big-time money." And they were right. He had that look. All the women were in love with him. They wanted to go straight to the motel room. Sex appeal sells, and he had it.

And the men loved him. They wanted to be him. "Hey, Arnie's in town." They'd grab a six-pack, and they'd never been on a golf course in their life. Just raising hell and running around. He just loved it. Most players, if they holed out--Nicklaus would do it—and if people started to run, he'd hold his hand up and tell them to stop or be quiet. Palmer never did that. He loved it. He didn't care if it bothered me or anybody. They loved it.

He was Arnie, right to his grave. He was the number-one king in the sports world, and he made the money, and he made us money. He made me money. Seventy-five cents out of every dollar I made. I guarantee that.

Nicklaus couldn't have carried that. He couldn't have created that story. Nicklaus was the best player by far. People appreciated him. They liked him. But he had this arrogance about him. I call it appropriate arrogance. He earned it, and he proved it. But he didn't shove it down your throat. He'd walk around like a king, although they called Arnie the king. Nicklaus really deserved the crown, as a player. But that didn't sell.

If we depended on golf aficionados to buy tickets, we'd be broke. It was the entertainment business. That is why TV did so good.

Chi Chi Rodriguez

Arnold Palmer came into golf at the right time. He raised the purses. Some of the pros complained that tournament officials would put the flags on the left side because Palmer drew the ball. I'd say, "He's putting more money in all of our pockets."

May

Houston Classic

Photo 8: Bill Collins, 1964.
(Getty Images)

Bill Collins is mostly forgotten, but for a time he was one of the best players on tour. Blond, 6-foot-4 and handsome, Collins was from Baltimore and won four times between 1959 and 1962, earning a spot on the 1961 Ryder Cup team. His best year was 1960, when he won twice, and twice was beaten in a playoff. Collins' most memorable victory that year was at Houston, where he rallied to beat Arnold Palmer in an 18-hole playoff.

Later, Collins suffered from that bane of many professional golfers, a bad back. His career on the tour quickly went into decline. In 1965, he accepted the head pro position at the Brae Burn Country Club in Westchester County, where he served for many years.

June

Memphis Open

Tommy Bolt showed tremendous focus at the 1960 Memphis Open, but perhaps his focus should have been elsewhere.

Bolt then was a stocky 44-year-old veteran of both the tour and the U.S. Army, which he served during World War II. He had a chin that jutted far out from an often mischievous, not very handsome face. Bolt also had a sweet, easy swing that brought him the 1958 U.S. Open championship at Southern Hills in his home state of Oklahoma. He won 15 times on the PGA tour, including twice in the 1960s.

Photo 9: *Tommy Bolt on his best behavior. (Historic Images, Golf Pride Grips)*

However, Bolt was far more famous for his temper than for his golf. An oft-told joke that will be repeated for the benefit of those who have not heard it is, one day Bolt consulted his caddie as to what club he should use. "You should hit either a 2-iron or a 9-iron," the caddie responded. "What kind of caddie are you?" Bolt replied angrily. "Sir," said the caddie, "those are the only clubs you haven't broken."

Bolt's crudeness was not limited to tossing clubs. At the 1959 Memphis Open, he loudly farted while a member of his threesome was putting. "That's disgusting," one of his playing companions said. It was reported that some members of the gallery were repulsed, while others were laughing hysterically. Don Fairfield claimed it happened on the first tee at the Canadian Open in Montreal when he and Gay Brewer were playing with Bolt. In all likelihood, it happened multiple times. At some point, Bolt was brought before Bob Rosburg, the chairman of the player's committee, who reprimanded him for "conduct unbecoming a professional golfer" and imposed a $250 fine. "You're taking all the fun out of the game," Bolt told Rosburg.

But an article published during the 1960 Memphis Open suggested Terrible Tommy was a changed man, calmer and even spiritual. It said Bolt twice daily read the Serenity Prayer: "God grant me the serenity to accept the things I cannot change, the courage to change the things I can, and the wisdom to know the difference." In addition, the article stated, "Books by Dr. Norman Vincent Peale and Bishop Fulton J. Sheen also helped transform Bolt from tantrum and club-tossing Tommy to a new man with new peace of mind."

After 36 holes at Memphis, Bolt was nine shots behind Ben Hogan, Rosburg and J.C. Goosie. Overnight, his wife, Mary Lou—who was traveling with him—became seriously ill. The next morning, he took her to St. Joseph's Hospital. One might think he would withdraw and stay with his wife, particularly given how far back he was from the leaders. Instead, Tommy dropped Mary Lou off at the hospital entrance and headed to the Colonial Country Club for the third round.

While he was on the 16th fairway, Bolt was informed that Mary Lou was suffering internal bleeding and immediately was to undergo surgery. News reports stated he was "obviously shaken" upon hearing this news, but evidently not enough to rush to the hospital. Instead, Bolt birdied 16, and then birdied 18 to complete a round of 65 to get back into contention.

In the final round, Bolt shot 67, which put him into a Monday playoff with Hogan and Gene Littler. Hogan's last victory had been the year before at the Colonial National Invitational in Fort Worth. In the Memphis playoff, he was four back of Bolt after 11 holes, but rallied with an eagle on the 13th. On 14, Bolt's second shot bounced and hit a woman in the neck. He bogeyed. On 15, Bolt's second shot hit a boy. Unlike Mary Lou Bolt, neither the woman nor the boy ended up in the hospital. After Hogan birdied 16, he and Bolt were tied. But Bolt birdied 17 and held on to beat Hogan by one and Littler by two.

Ever the gamer, after the win Bolt said he did not know how long his wife would be in the hospital but vowed that "if she gets better I may fly to Oklahoma City for the next tournament." Sure enough, the following day friends gave him a ride on a private plane. He finished 20th at the Oklahoma City Open. Mary Lou Bolt recovered and still was with Tommy when he died in 2008 at age 92.

U.S. Open

At the beginning of 1960, the Grand Slam of Golf was still considered what Bobby Jones accomplished in 1930 – winning the U.S. and British Opens and Amateurs in one year. Jack Nicklaus—who won the 1959 U.S. Amateur at age 19—was a college student at Ohio State but already was making noises that his goal was to duplicate Jones' feat instead of turning pro.

Nobody talked much about a professional Grand Slam. There were three major championships in the United States open to professionals: the Masters, U.S. Open and PGA Championship. Occasionally, the press would refer to the possibility of winning all three as "Golf's Triple Crown." Likewise, when Ben Hogan won the Open Championship at Carnoustie in 1953 after winning the Masters and U.S. Open earlier in the year, it was widely regarded as "Golf's Triple Crown." In 1953, the Open Championship and the PGA overlapped (the PGA ended while the then-required qualifying for the Open was taking place), so winning the British Open and the three U.S. majors then was impossible. Because of the Open's low purse and the necessity of expensive overseas travel, Hogan's feat was assumed to be a one-off achievement.

The landscape changed when, immediately before the start of the 1960 U.S. Open at Cherry Hills Country Club outside of Denver, Arnold Palmer published (with Will Grimsley) a piece in *The Saturday Evening Post*. Palmer stated that because he could not duplicate Jones' Grand Slam by virtue of his status as a professional, "I started thinking about a professional 'grand slam.'" He stated winning the Open Championship, along with the Masters, U.S. Open and PGA Championship, would constitute the new Grand Slam. "I am very excited about the British Open, whether or not I still have any chance for my grand slam by the time I get there," Palmer stated.

Palmer was a 4-1 favorite to win at Cherry Hills. In a poll of sportswriters, 65 picked him to win. Only one selected Ben Hogan, who was seeking his fifth U.S. Open. For the first 36 holes, Palmer was paired with former U.S. Open winners Cary Middlecoff and Jack Fleck. Teeing off late on Thursday, he took a double-bogey six on the first hole, a short par-4. From there, he managed to finish with a one-over par 72, three behind leader Mike Souchak (then an 11-time tour winner who Dan Jenkins described as "a long-hitting, highly popular pro who seldom allowed his career to get in the way of a social engagement").

Tommy Bolt arrived in Colorado fresh off of his victory at Memphis two weeks prior and poised to win his second U.S. Open in three years. Bolt's purported new-found serenity was tested in the first round on the par-5 11th hole, when he drove out of bounds. He summoned his inner peace and miraculously made a par. Bolt surely said the Serenity Prayer after the next hole, the par-3 12th, where he put his tee shot in the water and made a triple bogey.

However, on 18, Bolt was not in a spiritual frame of mind after he drove two balls into a lake that extended from the tee alongside the left fairway. Instead, after the second drive, he flung his driver into the water, oblivious to his playing partner Claude Harmon, who had to take evasive action to avoid Bolt's emotional relapse. Bolt signed for an 80 and promptly withdrew, citing altitude sickness from having to play a mile above sea level. He was fined $100 for endangering Harmon, much less than the $250 he was fined for farting in 1959, an interesting commentary on how the relative danger of the two acts was viewed.

On Friday, Souchak added a 67 for a U.S. Open 36-hole record of 135. Despite hitting 16 greens in regulation, Palmer lost ground with an even-par 71, leaving him 8 shots back of Souchak going into Saturday, and one behind Hogan—who shot 67 in the second round—and Nicklaus. Palmer complained about the slow play of partners Middlecoff and Fleck. "I figure it cost me four shots in the pairings," he said. "I could play three holes while those guys were playing one." Middlecoff's excruciating pace was a regular source of contention among his peers.

Palmer only had to play in a twosome on Saturday, with Paul Harney, on a hot sunny day. Until 1965, the U.S. Open finished on "Open Saturday" with 36 holes, and the pairings remained the same for both rounds. In the morning, Souchak managed only 73, which still left him at 5 under, two ahead of 1952 U.S. Open winner Julius Boros, Jerry Barber and Dow Finsterwald. Hogan and Nicklaus both shot 69 and were tied for fifth place, two back. Palmer shot another uninspiring round, a 72. He was 2 over for 54 holes at 215, seven shots back of Souchak, whose lead would have been bigger but for a double-bogey on 18 that ensued after a camera clicked loudly on his backswing on his drive. Fourteen players were ahead of Palmer.

While eating a cheeseburger in the locker room between rounds, Palmer casually mentioned to his friend, writer Bob Drum of the *Pittsburgh Press*, that he thought he could drive the downhill 346-yard par-4 opening hole, and that if he did he might shoot 65. Drum told Palmer he was out of it. Palmer disagreed, saying a 65 would give him 280, a score he said always won the U.S. Open. He got up to get ready for the final round.

Palmer did indeed drive onto the green on the opening hole and two-putted for a birdie. He then chipped in for a birdie on 2, and birdied 3 and 4 as well. After a par on 5, Palmer birdied 6 and 7. In a flash, he was near the top of the leaderboard, even after a bogey on 8. He made the turn in 30, putting him at the moment one stroke behind Nicklaus, who—paired with Hogan two groups ahead of Palmer—shot 32 on the front. Numerous others, including Hogan, Souchak, Finsterwald, Boros, and Barber, were still in the mix.

On the final nine, Palmer was steady but not spectacular, making one birdie and eight pars to give him a 65 and the 280 score he predicted would win. One by one, the others dropped off. Souchak shot 75. He, Finsterwald and Barber would be part of a large group tied for fifth. On 13, Nicklaus—seeking to become the first amateur to win the U.S. Open since Johnny Goodman in 1933—had a 10-foot putt for birdie, but instead three-putted to drop a shot. Nicklaus, 20 years old and precocious but unpolished on the greens, three-putted again on 14 for another bogey.

Hogan came to the par-5 17th hole tied for the lead. Nicklaus was one back. Trying to stuff his third shot—a wedge—near the hole, Hogan came up just short and his ball fell into the edge of the pond in front of the green. He took his right shoe off and extricated the ball onto the green, and then two-putted for bogey. Nicklaus could do no better than par. On 18, needing a birdie to tie, Hogan drove into the water and made triple-bogey. He tied for ninth. Nicklaus bogeyed 18.

Palmer, who was on the 17th tee while Hogan and Nicklaus were around the 17th green, only needed pars on the last two holes, and he got them, for a two-stroke victory over Nicklaus.

Photo 10: Palmer flings his visor after completing his final round
65 at the 1960 U.S. Open. (United States Golf Association)

July

Buick Open

Monday, July 4, 1960, was the final round of the Buick Open in Grand Blanc, Michigan. Prize money of $52,000, with $9,000 going to the winner plus a new automobile, attracted one of the strongest fields of the year. The PGA Tour and the sponsors took advantage of the Monday holiday by playing the first round of the 72-hole tournament on Friday instead of Thursday.

The combination of the holiday, a star-studded field with the likes of defending champion Art Wall, Jr., Sam Snead, Don January, Gene Littler, Al Geiberger and amateur Jack Nicklaus, and unseasonably cool but pleasant weather, drew a gallery of 17,953 fans on Monday. They were treated to an exciting ending. Gay Brewer was tied for the lead with Mike Souchak until he missed a 6-foot par putt on the 18th hole. Souchak then rolled in a 5-footer that gave him a one-stroke victory over Brewer and Wall.

Discounting the absence of Ben Hogan—who by then rarely played outside of the Masters and the U.S. Open—there were only two top American stars who were missing. One was Billy Casper, who was home awaiting the birth of a child.

The other was Arnold Palmer. After his win at Cherry Hills, he was halfway towards his Grand Slam. He indisputably was golf's new King. On June 20, Palmer traveled to Ireland to play in the Canada Cup international team event with Snead, which they won for the United States. Unlike Snead, who returned to America after the Canada Cup, Palmer stayed in the British Isles. On July 4, he was at St. Andrews, Scotland, for the first of two days of qualifying for the Open Championship, at the time a chore required of all who hoped to make the 100-player field. Palmer easily qualified.

The Open Championship

As at Cherry Hills, Palmer had to play catch-up at St. Andrews. After 36 holes, his score of 141 (70-71) was good for a third-place tie with Peter Thomson of Australia, but seven behind the hot pace set by Argentinian Robert De Vicenzo (a pair of 67s for 134) and five back of Kel Nagle, an affable, stocky Aussie. Defending champion Gary Player had solid rounds of 72-71 but was too far back to be a factor.

Like the U.S. Open, the British Open had a 36-hole finish, scheduled for Friday July 8. Palmer, 30-years-old, had youth on his side over Nagle (39) and De Vicenzo (37), no small advantage for the ordeal of walking 10 miles in a day. After a 70 in the third round (despite bogeys on the last two holes), Palmer had cut the margin to four strokes behind Nagle. De Vicenzo soared to 75, leaving him two back of Nagle and two ahead of Palmer.

However, a heavy rainstorm ensued just after Palmer and Nagle completed their rounds. Although the sun came out after a delay and there was enough daylight in the Scottish high summer to resume play, the Royal and Ancient officials decided to postpone the final round until Saturday. Palmer expressed his displeasure to reporters. "I agree that play was bound to be suspended for a while," he said. "But the sun came out, the weather took a turn for the better and water lying on the course should have been regarded as casual water."

Palmer came out charging on Saturday. He birdied the first two holes, and the final two, for a 68. However, a well-rested Nagle—playing right behind Palmer—sank a 10-foot birdie putt on the long par-4 17th—the famous "Road Hole"—to give him a one-stroke lead. This allowed Nagle to survive the embarrassment of missing a 2-foot birdie putt on 18 to win.

So, Palmer's bid for a Grand Slam ended, but with a flourish. In short order, the golf establishment accepted Palmer's declaration as to the four major tournaments. No longer were the amateur championships considered "major." Since 1960, only Jack Nicklaus,

Tiger Woods and Jordan Spieth have won the Masters and U.S. Open in one year to come as close as Palmer did in 1960 to achieving the modern Grand Slam.

Gary Player

I think there is always a misconception among Americans. They don't understand how many great players that the rest of the world had. I mean, you had a man like Bobby Locke, who America never even rated in the top 50 in the world, and they rate Byron Nelson in the top 10. Bobby Locke was way better than Byron Nelson. You had Peter Thomson from Australia who won five Opens. You got Roberto De Vicenzo. You had so many players from all around the world playing. The Open has never been dead. The Open is the oldest championship of them all. It's the hardest to win of all the majors because you've got to fight the elements as well as links golf courses. And there's no comparison in any of the four major championships to the Open. It is the hardest to win by a mile.

Arnold Palmer, my dear friend, who I loved and adored, yes, he came to the Open and he gave it a great shot in the arm, which was wonderful. But Arnold Palmer gave every tournament he played in a shot in the arm.

Canadian Open

The Canadian Open was a minor casualty of Arnold Palmer's declaration that the Open Championship was a grand slam event. In 1955, the Canadian Open was the site of Palmer's first tour win. It was considered by the touring pros to be a major tournament, albeit not with the stature of the U.S. Open, the Masters or the PGA.

Palmer could not play in the 1960 Canadian Open because it overlapped with the Open Championship. Many of the pros completed their final round at the Buick Open—with its Monday, July 4th finish—and immediately got in their cars for the four-hour drive to Toronto, in order to get in a practice round on Tuesday ahead of the Wednesday start. Art Wall, Jr.—the runner-up at the Buick—shot four rounds in the 60s for a six-stroke win over Bob Goalby and Jay Hebert. Wall and others (including 48-year-old Sam Snead) had played nine tournament rounds in eight days.

PGA Championship

The tree-lined South Course of the Firestone Country Club in Akron, Ohio made its debut as a much-used, if not much-loved, big-time venue, at the 1960 PGA Championship (it previously had been the site of the Rubber City Open in the 1950s).

With his hope for the Grand Slam gone, Arnold Palmer focused on becoming the first player to win all three majors held in the United States in a single year. He got off to a good start with a 67 that led Sam Snead by a shot. Only four players in the unwieldy field of 184 (laden with club professionals) broke par 70.

On a hot Friday, Palmer missed three 3-foot putts on his way to a 74. Jay Hebert played in the cool of the morning and matched Palmer's 67 from the day before, to take a one-shot lead at 139 over Don January. Palmer, Snead, and Doug Sanders were two back.

A total of 91 players made the 36-hole cut of 151. Doug Sanders' third round 69 put him one shot ahead of Hebert and 1947 PGA Championship winner Jim Ferrier of Australia, whose 66 was the low round of the tournament. Ferrier's championship career dated back to 1931, when as a 16-year-old he was the runner-up in the Australian Open. By the early 1940s he had permanently moved to the U.S., became a citizen, served in the U.S. Army in World War II, and exclusively played the PGA tour for the rest of his career.

Palmer was in the thick of it when he reached the 625-yard, par-5 16th hole, known as "the Monster." He drove into a trap. Palmer used a wood on his second shot and faded his ball into the right rough. His third shot went into a ditch and was unplayable. Palmer hit his fifth shot onto the green and then three-putted for a triple-bogey, and followed with bogeys on 17 and 18. His 75 put him six behind Sanders.

The field was cut again after 54 holes, to 60 players. One of the victims was Ben Hogan, who was playing the PGA for the first time since his win in 1948 (after his 1949 auto accident, his legs were too weak to withstand the multiple match-play rounds required until the PGA switched to a stroke play format in 1958). After a third-round 78, Hogan missed the second cut by one shot. He did not manage a single birdie in 54 holes.

On Sunday, Palmer shot a solid even-par 70, which was the second-lowest round of the day. However, all it accomplished was to give him a tie for sixth place as the leaders in front of him did not wilt. Snead, playing with Ferrier in the penultimate group, was in position to win after a birdie on 16 put him two strokes ahead of Ferrier. On 17, Snead bogeyed while Ferrier laced a 4-iron to within 2 feet for a birdie. Snead also bogeyed 18 while Ferrier parred, making the latter the leader in the clubhouse with a 2-over total of 282.

Photo 11: Jay Hebert. (Historic Images)

Junius Joseph "Jay" Hebert, age 37, was the only man left on the course with a chance to win. He had a belated entry to the PGA tour, having had more important matters to deal with. During World War II, he joined the Marine Corps Fifth Division, was commissioned as a lieutenant, and sent to Iwo Jima. He was wounded in the left leg, for which he was awarded a Purple Heart, and spent almost a year in a hospital. After recovering, Hebert attended Louisiana State University where, in 1947, when he was 24, he led the Tigers to a national championship. He then worked at a tool company in Houston until, after playing a few rounds with Houston pro

Jack Burke, Jr. (winner of the 1956 Masters and PGA Championship) was told by Burke, "You belong in golf." He debuted on the tour in 1956 at age 33 and in 1957 won the Bing Crosby Pro-Am, after which he won three more tournaments.

Hebert hit his five-iron approach on the 390-yard 17th hole to within 8 feet. He sank the putt for a birdie and a one-shot lead. While Ferrier anxiously watched the press room television, Hebert played 18 conservatively and perfectly, parring for a one-shot win over Ferrier, who sullenly skulked out of the press room.

August

Insurance City Open

A tournament has been played near Hartford, Connecticut every year since 1952. During the 1950s, it was one of the few tournaments on the PGA tour where Black pros were welcome. African-American pioneers Ted Rhodes and Bill Spiller played, and in 1958 Charlie Sifford shot 63 to take the first-round lead (he ended up tied for 18th).

Both Sifford and Rhodes showed up at the Wethersfield Country Club for the 1960 ICO. It is estimated Rhodes won over 150 times on the United Golf Association tour, a circuit played primarily (but not exclusively) by Black golfers before, and for a while after, the PGA eliminated its "Caucasian race" clause. In 1960, Rhodes was 46 and past his prime, and he missed the cut. Sifford, however, shot 70-68 and was five shots back after 36 holes, tied with Arnold Palmer. After that, Sifford faded and finished out of the money. Palmer shot 66-66 on the weekend and on Sunday overcame a five-shot deficit to tie 1955 U.S. Open champion Jack Fleck and Bill Collins. Palmer won the playoff for his sixth title of the year.

Don Fairfield

Ted Rhodes had really a good golf swing. He was so fluid, like Gene Littler. He really could hit the ball well. I played several times with Charlie, and I got to know the two of them pretty well. I was pretty impressed with the two of them.

When I started on the tour in 1955, we went from Toronto to Hartford. They didn't have a ride from Toronto to Hartford, so I gave them a ride in my car. And we get to Hartford, and I say, "Where are you guys going to stay? What motel?" And they say, "Oh, we don't stay at motels, we stay at people's houses." That's how they traveled. They'd bum rides here and there. They were the only two Blacks who were really attempting to play at that time.

They really started from scratch. Charlie had a "caddie swing." He made his own swing. But Ted Rhodes had a fast golf swing.

St. Paul Open

A much-loved summer stop on the PGA tour in the 1960s was the St. Paul Open at Keller Golf Course. The course was open to the public and had a rolling, tree-lined layout. The clubhouse was designed by Clarence W. Wigington, a prominent Black municipal architect, and had a spiral staircase and chandelier more typical of a private country club. The course was short and not difficult, which assured low scoring. Players appreciated making lots of birdies, the Midwestern hospitality, and usually comfortable temperatures in the low-key event.

After winning at Hartford, Arnold Palmer passed on St. Paul, but there were plenty of established names in the field, including Gary Player, Billy Casper, Sam Snead, and Ken Venturi, along with a diminutive (116 pounds), flamboyant young man from Puerto Rico, Juan "Chi Chi" Rodriguez, who in a very short time on the tour had become a gallery favorite.

Despite his slight frame, Rodriguez was one of the longest drivers on the tour. Three weeks earlier, at the Eastern Open in Baltimore, he tied for fourth. "If you can dance the merengue, you can play golf," he said. Rodriguez developed routines after making a birdie, like tossing his straw fedora over the cup (to prevent the ball from escaping) or sliding his putter through his fingers into an imaginary scabbard, pulling his putter out as if it were a sword, and engaging in a mock duel. Many of his fellow pros and golf traditionalists initially frowned on his antics. In time, almost all of them were won over because Rodriquez undeniably was a nice, kind man, and the fans liked him.

Don Fairfield, a 30-year-old veteran of both the tour and the Air Force, won the second of his three tour victories, shooting 66-68-65-67, four shots ahead of Casper and Lionel Hebert. It was his first win in four-and-a-half years. His wife Iris was pleased. "For four years I've been hearing them announce, 'former winner of the Pensacola Open,'" she said. "I think if I heard them say that once more, I'd scream."

Frank Boynton
They had a nice locker room for us in St. Paul. I mean, it wasn't pretty or anything, but they went out of their way to see that it was well-stocked with beverages. It was a golf course that you had to make a lot of birdies. Well, it wasn't a tough golf course, but it was fun. It was a fun week because of the people that ran it.

Gary Player
Chi Chi Rodriguez was such an asset to the tour. You've got to realize that the public are paying. They're giving you the prize money. They're making it available. And Chi Chi Rodriguez, he was not a great player or a superstar. To be a superstar, you've got to win six majors. Now, Chi Chi never won majors, but he was one of the great entertainers for the tour. He did an awful lot for the tour. An awful lot.

Don Fairfield
I won the St. Paul Open in 1960. I liked the golf course. It was an old muni course, but it was my type of golf course. I think I made like 25 or 30 birdies. I think I finished 20-, 22-under par. Don January came along a couple of years later and made more. That was an old golf course and the tournament had been going on for years and years. Snead won it. Almost every one of the old pros had won that tournament at one time or another. Dutch Harrison. I was sorry to see the tour leave that course. It was an old, short, homemade golf course, you might say. Probably no architect. But everybody played there because the weather was good. There wasn't that much money. In 1960 there wasn't any more than $3,500, maybe $4,000 for first place.

We usually stayed in motels. My wife and I traveled with our son Jeff. She would always carry an electric skillet, and I had a small barbecue. I can remember being at a motel and I was out in front of the room, and I was cooking a steak. I'm looking down the row and there's this other guy cooking a steak on the grill, too. Jack Nicklaus. You'd gather together in the motels, you know, and the girls did. A little social life.

I remember a cookout in St. Paul, at a motel. Everybody was staying near the golf course and there's a bunch of fresh corn. We made a big pan of a lot of fresh corn on the cob. And Gary Player ate a bunch of the fresh corn. He loved it. The next day he paid for it around that golf course. He had to run into every outhouse.

September

Carling Open

The Carling Brewery sponsored a tournament at various venues in the United States, Canada, and England from 1953 through 1967. The 1960 version was held at the Fircrest Golf Club in Tacoma, Washington from September 15-18. Thick fog caused delays in the first round. After the fog lifted, 31-year-old Ernie Vossler won by one stroke over Paul Harney.

Photo 12: Ernie Vossler.
(Historic Images)

One gets the sense that Vossler was not really into playing tournament golf. He was the son of a Fort Worth plumber and was more interested in tennis as a youth. As a high school senior, he was talked into joining the golf team because they needed a player. He learned he was halfway decent, but after graduation he joined his father's plumbing business and did not turn pro until he was 25. Vossler was handsome, with an athletic build and glasses; he resembled actor George Reeves in the role of Clark Kent.

In 1957, Vossler got in trouble, along with Don January, George Bayer, and Doug Higgins, for something modern pro sports fans can well relate to: tanking. The four were playing the Kentucky Derby Open, which had both a

THE AGE OF PALMER

36-hole cut and a 54-hole cut. They also were rooming together for the week. All four made the 36-hole cut of 158, with Bayer the closest to the front at 146, 10 shots back of leader Billy Casper.

After the second round, they scanned the leaderboard and saw they had no chance of winning and would have to grind it out for the last 36 holes to even have a chance to earn a token paycheck. The four, along with some other pros, asked for permission from PGA tour supervisor Harvey Raynor to withdraw so they could get an early start on driving to the next tournament, the Colonial Invitational in Fort Worth, 875 miles away. Permission was denied.

In the third round, Vossler shot a plausible 38 on the front nine before remembering he wanted to head home to Fort Worth a day early, so he came in with a 46 for an 84, safely below the 54-hole cutline. Bayer was not playing well, but when he arrived at the par-4 17th hole, he decided not to leave any margin for error. He took his 7-iron and bonked it down the fairway, taking 17 shots to get his ball in the hole, ending up with a solid 90. Vossler, Bayer, January and Higgins immediately were suspended for 30 days. Raynor called the spectacle "a disgrace" and "a smack at the integrity of golfers who try." Later, the suspensions were lifted and replaced with $250 fines.

After that, Vossler got with the program and won tournaments in 1958 and 1959 before winning the Carling. In 1961, he stepped away from the weekly tour grind and became a respected club pro in Oklahoma and a developer of golf courses, including the Oak Tree Golf Club, host of the 1988 PGA Championship. In 1995, he married former LPGA star Marlene Hagge and they settled in La Quinta, California. Vossler died in 2013.

Don Fairfield

Ernie's father was a plumber, and he was a master plumber when he started the tour. And he could play. We're playing in Tacoma, Washington, Al Balding and myself, and Ernie Vossler. We teed off early in the morning. We got fog. Heavy, heavy fog. You could hardly see. We were delayed. We finally got around – we were stopped two or three times – to the fifth or sixth hole, a par-3, and we can't see the green. We're waiting there. Ernie grabbed his clubs and said, "Come on, caddie, we're going to leave this tournament. I'm going to get out of here." Al Balding says, "Well, you have to go to the clubhouse anyway, you're walking right towards it, you might as well play in." Well, it eased up a little bit, so Ernie played in. And won. Al Balding told that story for years.

October

El Camino Pro-Am

A non-tour pro-am with a purse of $10,000 was held at the El Camino Country Club in Oceanside, California towards the end of October 1960. The 36-hole event drew several prominent pros, including Billy Maxwell (who won), George Bayer, Bob Rosburg, and Jack Fleck.

In Saturday's first round, 24-year-old rookie Bob Shave, Jr, had the first ace of his career, which would have won him a Corvette, except on Sunday 39-year-old veteran Jimmy Clark also had a hole-in-one. Under the rules of the tournament, Shave and Clark had a shoot-off, during which Clark placed his ball nearer to the designated hole. However, the two previously had decided they would sell the car and divide the proceeds.

Photo 13: *Car Salesmen Bob Shave, Jr. and Jimmy Clark.*
(Courtesy of Cindy Samartino)

Bob Shave, Jr.

I had my wife and three kids with me. I had an Airstream trailer. The Airstream was a very nice trailer, and I had a Cadillac that I pulled it with. I'd take them to every tournament until the kids started going to school. The reason I did it was because I could play and have my family with me. Every tournament I went to, the women there had activities for the wives and children, every day of the tournament. So, it was nice for them to experience that, and they made friendships that lasted.

November

Cajun Classic

November 17, 1960—the week after John F. Kennedy edged Richard Nixon in the election that ushered in the New Frontier— was the start of the Cajun Classic at the Oakburne Country Club in Lafayette, Louisiana, in the heart of the Bayou. The days were shorter and temperatures cooler as the tour season was winding down. The hosts were the Hebert brothers, who were of French-Canadian ancestry and residents of Lafayette. Jay Hebert had won the PGA Championship earlier in the year. He was 6 feet tall, slim, and was viewed as the most handsome man on tour. Lionel Hebert was not. He was several inches shorter than his brother and rotund. Unlike Jay, Lionel played the trumpet almost as well as he played golf. Like Jay, Lionel won the PGA Championship, in 1957, at the Miami Valley Golf Club in Dayton, Ohio, the last time it was contested as a match-play event.

The Hebert brothers had enough charm to convince a respectable contingent of their fellow pros to make the trip to the off-the-beaten-path tournament, including Billy Casper. The Tuesday before the start, they were feted on "Hebert Brothers Appreciation Day." On Sunday, the small crowd of 3,000 went home happy when Lionel won to take home the $2,000 first prize. Brother Jay tied Casper for fourth.

Tommy Aaron
The Cajun Classic was my first tournament, towards the end of the 1960 season. Lionel and Jay Hebert gave me an exemption. I knew nothing about the tour. I drove from Gainesville, Georgia to Lafayette. I was very excited. In the first round, I played with Al Geiberger. There

were very few people in the gallery. No ropes. The tournament had a very small feel. I finished 23rd and may have won $150. But I was excited to see my name in the paper.

Because I made the cut, I got to play in the next tournament, in Mobile. I gave Don Massengale a ride. I made the cut in Mobile, so I went on to West Palm Beach. I made the cut and went to play in Coral Gables. I made the cut there and that got me into the Los Angeles Open to start 1961.

December

Coral Gables Invitational

The 1960 season ended on December 11, 1960, at the Coral Gables Invitational on a sunny south Florida afternoon. After birdies on 16 and 17, Bob Goalby arrived at the par-4 18th hole with a two-shot lead. His second shot trickled off the back of the green and onto the apron. All Goalby had to do was get down in 3 from there and he would win his second tour title. He had won the 1958 Greater Greensboro Open by two shots over five players, all of whom who had or would win majors: Sam Snead, Dow Finsterwald, Tony Lema, Don January, and Art Wall, Jr.

Enter Walter Montgomery, Goalby's young African-American caddie. The week before at the West Palm Beach Open, Montgomery signed on with Goalby, fully aware that Goalby had a reputation for a hot temper. On the 18th hole at Coral Gables, Montgomery gave Goalby the ultimate test of his composure when, stepping backwards, he inadvertently kicked Goalby's ball off of the fringe. Arnold Palmer—who was playing in the final group but atypically had a poor round and was not in contention—told Goalby it was a two-stroke penalty. Palmer prided himself on his knowledge of the rules, and never was afraid to insert himself in rules issues concerning other competitors. Goalby walked over to PGA Tour official Harvey Raynor and was relieved to learn Palmer was wrong, that the penalty was only one stroke.

The Miami Herald captured the moment in words and photographs. Reporter Tommy Fitzgerald wrote he heard a pro in the gallery drawl in a southern accent, "You all woulda had a dead caddie if that had happened to me." Fitzgerald also overheard an elderly caddie say, "If that costs Goalby the tournament, he oughta give that [censored] a nickel." Montgomery buried his face in his right hand and appeared to be close to tears. Goalby walked over to his caddie. "Forget it, pardner," he was heard to say as he put his hand on Montgomery's shoulder. "Forget it."

Now off the apron, Goalby no longer could putt. He chipped with a 7-iron to about 5 feet. To Montgomery's everlasting relief, Goalby calmly drilled the putt into the cup for a bogey and a one-shot win over Finsterwald. "If he lost the tournament, I don't know what I would have done," Montgomery told reporters afterward. "I might have done something desperate. I know I'd never have gotten over it."

After the awards ceremony, Goalby climbed into his 1957 Chevrolet with his friend, Don Fairfield, for the drive back to southern Illinois, where both lived (Goalby in Belleville, Fairfield in Jacksonville). They looked forward to spending the Christmas holidays with their families and recharging for a few weeks before the start of the 1961 season in Los Angeles.

Bob Goalby

Walter kicked it 5 feet off the green. Arnold comes out of the bunker and says, "That's two, that's two." I also thought it was a two-stroke penalty, but it was only one because it was accidental. So, I had to get it up and down to win. I chipped it with a 7-iron to four-and-a-half, 5 feet.

Finsty had unpacked his bag and he's going swish! swish! with his driver for the playoff. I'm saying to myself, what the hell is he doing? But I made the putt. Fred Hawkins, he was there watching. He told me he said to people, "That shows you what Goalby is" when I put my arm around Walter. He said most people thought I'd blow my lid, but that I handled it calmly.

Don Fairfield

We're going back through Alligator Alley through the swamps. We got started late, it was dark, it was that time of year. Goalby is driving fast. He's going about 80, 90 miles per hour. There's water on both sides. If you go in the swamp you'll be eaten by alligators. But anyway, he hollers something like "Holy shit!" I look up and there's a horse right in the middle of the right lane. Out in the middle of this swamp. And he swerved to the left. The horse moved to the left. He swerved back to the right. And we brushed by that horse by inches. If we'd hit that horse we'd have ended in that swamp, for sure. Where that horse had come from, that was most unusual.

I traveled with Goalby. A lot of times we'd eat in cafeterias, because you'd get good food, vegetables, everything, and that would be one of our meeting places at nighttime, after golf. In the South, they were all over the place.

Fred Hawkins and Dick Mayer were partners. They'd travel together. They were good time boys. They wouldn't drink that much, but the bar would be their hangout. They didn't go to the cafeterias.

We didn't travel slow, by the way. One time, we got on the turn-pike, between Oklahoma City and Tulsa. I think it's 100 miles. We got there in just over an hour. Goalby always drove like a wild man.

Photo 14: Friends Bob Goalby and Don Fairfield survived an encounter with a horse on Alligator Alley. (Duane Howell, The Denver Post via Getty Images)

1961

January

Los Angeles Open

Of course, Arnold Palmer was favored to win the season-opening Los Angeles Open. Starting his first round on the 10th hole, he was in good shape after playing his opening nine in 33. On the front side, he struggled but came to his final hole at 1-under par. His tee shot on the 508-yard, par-5 ninth hole was long and down the middle. As Palmer took out his 3-wood, Arnie's Army was flush with anticipation that their hero would knock the ball on the green for a possible eagle. At worst, he would birdie for a 69.

Instead, Palmer's second shot flew right, over a high fence onto Rancho Park's driving range and out of bounds. He dropped a ball, and again hit it over the fence and onto the driving range. Palmer dropped another ball and decided to play toward the left side. He hit it so far left that it went over another fence and ended up on Patricia Avenue. He did the same with his eighth shot. Finally, his 10th shot landed in the vicinity of the green. Palmer took a 12 for the hole, and a 77 for the round. He improved to 72 the next day but missed the cut. Since 1963, there has been a plaque behind the tee (now the 18th hole) commemorating Palmer's septuple-bogey, as an inspiration to all duffers.

Bob Goalby won for his second straight victory.

Pea Soup Andy's

Founded by Danish immigrant Anton Andersen and his French-born wife, Juliette, Pea Soup Anderson's is located in Buellton, California between Santa Barbara and San Luis Obispo, off of U.S. 101, near Solvang. The restaurant has been in business since 1924 and has the Danish-style architecture for which Solvang is known.

Bob Goalby

I'd stop at Pea Soup Andy's when I used to drive up and down the coast. Like to the L.A. Open and from there to Pebble Beach. All the guys would stop, so we'd run into some of the other players who were driving and have a little reunion on the way up. Doug Ford, Art Wall, Don Fairfield. Paul Runyan rode up with me one year, after the L.A. Open up to Pebble. They had good food, plus pea soup. It was a big place and easy to get in. Kind of a funny name.

Lucky International Open

The Lucky International was played in San Francisco at the Harding Park Golf Course, a public facility on Lake Merced. The sponsor was the company that brewed Lacky Lager, a beer then popular in the western United States. Named after President Warren Harding, the course conditions and facilities had deteriorated somewhat when the tour added the stop for 1961.

The Lucky became popular and usually drew a strong field. For most of its run, it was scheduled the week after the Crosby Pro-Am, two hours down the coast by car. Like the Crosby, the weather was always iffy, but the two tournaments offered the pros and their wives two weeks in a beautiful part of the country.

The field at the inaugural Lucky was led by Arnold Palmer, Billy Casper, and Gary Player from South Africa. At the age of 25, Player already had amassed an impressive résumé, with 27 professional victories around the world. In addition to winning the 1959 Open Championship, he had a PGA tour victory under his belt at the 1958 Kentucky Derby Open, and he also won the 1956 Dunlop tournament in England. Player had 14 victories in his home country, nine in Australia (including the 1958 Australian Open), and one in Egypt. He also finished second to Tommy Bolt at the 1958 United States Open.

Photo 15: Gary Player in 1961.
(Creative Commons)

Player was unlike any golfer America had ever seen. His 5-foot-6 frame was taut and muscular, the product of strenuous exercise, including weightlifting. On the golf course, he usually wore a black shirt and black pants in order to stand out. He liked rock and roll. Unlike many of his colleagues, he did not drink or smoke and was hypervigilant about his diet. Player was neither afraid to express his opinions nor his emotions, and would vigorously pump his fist after making a long putt in a key situation, decades before Tiger Woods. Yet, he was friendly and liked by most of his fellow pros.

After three rounds of the Lucky, Player was tied with Palmer at 207, four back of leaders George Bayer and Ted Kroll, and one behind Casper. On Sunday, it rained heavily. On the eighth green, Kroll's 40-foot putt skidded to a stop 5 feet from the hole. His playing companion, Casper, refused to putt until a member of the grounds crew swept water from the green with a broom. Kroll beseeched tournament supervisor Harvey Raynor to postpone the tournament until Monday. Raynor ordered the twosome to either putt or be disqualified. They opted to continue, but both fell out of contention, as did Palmer.

Player managed the course better than anyone, birdieing holes 15 to 17 on his way to a 65 and a two-shot win over Don Whitt. Afterward, Player did not appear pleased, saying the weather and the course conditions were the worst he had ever experienced. But he took the opportunity to talk about proper diet. "I eat lots of honey, nuts and dried fruit," he said. "It makes me strong. I feel I can play a lot of golf with that kind of food inside of me. Trouble with most Americans, they eat too many greasy foods."

Gary Player

There's a difference between playing then and now. It's a different world. It's a different game of golf. When we used to play, there were spike marks on the green. You had to rake the bunkers with your feet. They didn't change the pin every day on the green. They had hand mowers cutting the green. The fairways, they didn't have mowers to cut it short. If you played in the morning and you had dew on the grass, you were hitting flyers. It was a different shot playing in the afternoon.

And so, golf was very, very difficult in those days. No prize money. Traveling by Greyhound bus a lot of times, traveling by car, living in cheap motels. But we wanted to be the best. It wasn't a case of the money. Money wasn't the issue. We wanted the titles. We wanted to win the majors. And when we played in the '60s, we wanted to play in two pro-ams every week, because we were meeting businessmen. We were meeting people. Now, the pros, they only want to play nine holes in a pro-am, and they don't even want to play in the pro-am. What a difference the world is today.

February

Palm Springs Golf Classic

Billy Maxwell won the 90-hole tournament by two strokes over Doug Sanders to take home $5,300. Arnold Palmer, who would win in Palm Springs five times (three when it was known as the Bob Hope Desert Classic), was third.

Don January finished 14 shots behind to earn $18 from the purse. However, January left Palm Springs the big winner. During the second round, the 31-year-old Texan aced the 148-yard 15th hole at Indian Wells Country Club, the first hole-in-one of his life. His 8-iron shot went into the hole on the fly to win $50,000 offered by the sponsors for such a feat by a pro. Sam Tobias also had an ace, at the El Dorado Country Club. Because Tobias—a tractor company executive from Bakersfield, California—was an amateur, he had to settle for an electric golf cart.

Baton Rouge Open Invitational

In the early 1960s, the American majors were valued for their prestige, but also because they had the largest bounties. In 1961, the Masters' awarded $20,000 to the winner from a purse of $109,100. For the U.S. Open, $14,000 was allotted to the victor out of $60,500. At the PGA Championship the purse was $64,800, with $11,000 to the victor. The only non-major that awarded a five-figure first prize was the Tournament of Champions, where the winner took home $10,000.

At the time, the PGA tour had far more dusty outposts than garden spots. One such event was the Baton Rouge Invitational, a way station for the tour between the California-Arizona segment and the Florida swing — the so-called winter tour. The Baton Rouge tournament was held in late February or early March, and the weather, in fact, at times was wintry.

The total purse at Baton Rouge in 1961 was $15,000, with $2,800 to the winner. In 1960, Arnold Palmer won his third of eight tournaments for the year in cold conditions, despite calling a penalty stroke on himself in the second round when his ball moved while he was in the process of clearing leaves. Palmer returned to defend his title in 1961. The potential prize was tiny, but there was no reason for Palmer not to stop in Louisiana en route to Florida. Plus, he was given $250 just for showing up in Baton Rouge, at a time when appearance fees were permitted.

Once again, the weather was cold and lousy. A rainout required a 36-hole finish on Sunday. Palmer shot 65-67-68-66 to win by seven over Wes Ellis, Jr. and by eight over Gary Player, Johnny Pott, and Buster Cupit. On top of the winner's share of $2,800 and the appearance fee, Palmer also received a $1,000 bonus for being a repeat winner.

Photo 16: Marty Furgol, for once with his mouth not moving. (Getty Images)

Sam Snead finished 13th. Tied for 22nd was Marty Furgol, who had a successful career as a pro, winning five tournaments in the 1950s. In the 1954 U.S. Open at Baltusrol, he tied for 18th. That Open was won by Ed Furgol, who was one year younger than Marty. Ed and Marty grew up in New York Mills, a town of about 3,000 near Utica. According to an online source, there are approximately 250 people throughout the world with the surname "Furgol," of which 35 live in the United States. Thus, perhaps the most remarkable part of this story is that two Furgols, both successful professional golfers born one year apart in the same small town in Central New York, were not at all related.

Furgol had a good swing but had idiosyncrasies. One was that he would talk to the ball. Not when the ball was in the air like many pros do, but before hitting a shot. When he was not talking to his ball, he talked to his playing partners or to himself, incessantly.

Bob Zimmerman

I played with Sam Snead in the Baton Rouge Open. We got rained out one day, so I played with him 36 holes. That was an experience, watching him swing the golf club. There wasn't much conversation. Sam didn't talk much. I don't know if you remember Marty Furgol. They called him "Crazy Marty" because he talked to himself all the time. So here I am, 19 years old, playing with Sam Snead – one of the greatest players of all time, who's not talking at all, and the other person is Furgol and he's talking to himself, and here I am in the middle of them for 36 holes. He was quite a character, no doubt about that. In the 36 holes Snead shot 138, I shot 148, and Marty Furgol was in between. The only time that Sam Snead spoke to me was when we had lunch in between. And Marty was talking all the way around the golf course, kind of like Lee Trevino.

Tommy Aaron

"Those people are wishing the ball out of the hole!," I heard (Marty Furgol) say (about the gallery). I told him, 'Marty, that's not true. They pay to see us put the ball in the hole."

Chi Chi Rodriguez

At Tucson, they only have one tree on the whole golf course. One time (Marty Furgol) drove it against that tree four straight days. We were all staying at the Ramada Inn. Marty opened the window of his room, and he started hollering 'Trees! Trees! Trees! They make me crazy!' He hollered that for about 15 minutes then he went back to sleep. One time he threw all his balls in the water. He said, "Lippers! Lippers! Lippers!"

Then there was Ivan Gantz. I was not on tour then, but they used to tell me stories about him. When he missed a wedge shot, he would take his knuckles and hit them with the wedge, and he'd start bleeding like mad. "That'll teach you to hold your hand under the club!" Sometimes when he missed a shot he'd go to a tree and bump his head against the tree until he bled and he'd say, "That will teach you to keep your head down!"

Sam Snead, he was a super guy. He was so good. Sam was one of us. Ben Hogan was the guy that we all love and respect. Snead would go to dinner with us. Just a regular guy. They accused him of being a hustler. He used to play 5- dollar Nassaus and beat them out of 20, but he should have charged them a hundred to play with him.

March

St. Petersburg Open

Before his win at Coral Gables in December 1960, Bob Goalby had won only the 1958 Greater Greensboro Open in a pro career that began in 1952. He opened the 1961 season with his second straight win, in Los Angeles. However, he struggled until mid-March, when he fired a final-round 65 in St. Petersburg to win by three over Ted Kroll, and five over Gary Player. During the round, using an old putter he had purchased at a Miami pawn shop for $2 three years earlier, which he named "Black Maria," he set a tour record with eight straight birdies, none of which were longer than 20 feet. The record would stand for 48 years until Mark Calcavecchia made nine in a row at the 2009 Canadian Open.

Bob Goalby
In 1961 I made eight birdies in a row. I thought I was going to be pretty good. I'm not bragging, but you have to think that way.

Don Fairfield
Bob had bought a used putter at a junk store. We went down on Highway 1 in Miami, on the ocean there. There was junk stores. There was one place we went inside. There was a little bit of everything in there. He was walking around looking for a wooden shaft. He found this putter and pulled it out of a bag. I was right there. The shaft was so weak, it looked like it might have been a curtain rod or something. It had a small mallet head, with loft on it, like a chipper. Anyway, he said, "I'm going to buy this."

He putted that week with that putter. Gary Player and I were in the final threesome with Goalby. We get to the eighth hole. Bob, Gary, and me, we all birdie that hole. That's when the birdies started. We all made more birdies coming in than you can believe. Bob gets eight in a row. We were laughing about it. We finished first, third and fourth.

April

The Masters

Arnold Palmer's second quest for the Grand Slam seemed to be off to a good start. On a drizzly Thursday, his opening round of 68 put him in a tie with Bob Rosburg (the winner of the 1959 PGA Championship), one ahead of Gary Player and two of amateur Jack Nicklaus. Byron Nelson, 50 years old and making a rare appearance on the tour, shot 71 and was in a tie for fifth place.

Photo 17: Arnold Palmer and Bob Rosburg at the 1961 Masters, either putting hexes on each other, or responding to a request to show they each shot a 4-under 68 in the first round.
(Getty Images)

After the close of play on Friday, Palmer and Player were tied atop the leaderboard at 137, four clear of Rosburg. Nelson remained tied for fifth with a 72, but went 78-77 over the final two rounds to tie fellow 50-year-old Texan Ben Hogan for 32nd place. Chi Chi Rodriguez, playing in his first major, missed the cut by one stroke.

In the third round, Player appeared to take command when his 69 put him four shots clear of Palmer, who shot 73.

On Sunday, Palmer chipped two strokes off of Player's lead after nine holes. However, a chilling rain that set off tornado warnings in the area and made the course unplayable washed out all the scores, requiring the entire field (including

10 players who had completed play) to re-start their final rounds on Monday.

At the turn on Monday, Player continued to lead Palmer by four shots. When he arrived at the short par-5 13th hole, his lead was still two. However, Player sliced his drive into twigs on the right side, hit a poor second shot into a ditch, took two more shots to get onto the green, and then three-putted for a double-bogey 7. He and Palmer (who was a group behind) were tied. Player then bogeyed the par-5 15th to give Palmer the lead. By botching the two back-nine par-5s, Player seemingly had blown the Masters. He did par in (sinking putts of 14 feet on 17, and 5 feet on 18) for a 40 on the final nine.

Palmer arrived at the 72nd hole needing a par to win and become the Masters' first repeat winner. His drive on 18 was perfect. However, he pushed a 7-iron into a semi-buried lie in a bunker to the right of the green. His blast caught too much ball and it cleared the green. He now needed to get up and down to force a playoff with Player. He chose to putt from well off the green. He stroked his ball 20 feet past the hole and missed the putt coming back. His double-bogey made Player the first international Masters champion.

Gary Player

I came to No. 13, and I drove in the trees on the right. I wanted to go up the 14th fairway. There, I had a clear shot. And if I hit it up the fairway, I would've had a little sand wedge to the green and could have made my birdie. But there were so many people there and we couldn't get them out of the way. Now, I'm a young guy from South Africa. As a visitor here, I didn't want to inconvenience people. So, I played before I was ready. If it was Nicklaus, he would've waited until everybody got out the way, but I tried to chip it out, back onto the fairway, and I chipped it into the creek and I made a 7.

And then I came to 15 and I made a 6. And yet all I heard about was how Palmer made a double -bogey. They didn't mention how I made a double-bogey chipping the ball out, when if I'd had patience, I would've probably made a birdie and won that tournament by two or three shots. But Sports Illustrated was the only magazine and the only media that said, "Gary Player won the Masters. He made a double-bogey at 13 and a bogey at 15." They understood the situation.

I won the Masters three times, I was second three times. I was in the top-10 14 times. I made the most cuts in a row. And I played in the tournament the most number of times. And I don't think I made $400,000 total. Now you win it, you get almost two-and-half million or something, but it doesn't make the tournament any more important because you got prize money. That's not the issue. It might be with young people today, but it certainly wasn't in our time.

Chi Chi Rodriguez

I was the assistant pro at Dorado Beach in Puerto Rico. Ed Dudley was the head pro. He had been the pro at Augusta. One day, there was a man with him. He was Clifford Roberts. I was hitting 2-irons on the range. I liked to hit 2-irons. I would hit them until my hands bled. Mr. Roberts asked if I would play in the Masters. I told him that I hadn't won anything to qualify. He said, "You are the Puerto Rican Open Champion." So that's how I got to play in the 1961 Masters. Roberts and I became good friends.

Jack Nicklaus was still an amateur. And he was always a good guy. I was practicing putting and he walked to me, and he said, "Would you like to play?" I said, "Yeah, we got to play for some money, I don't play for free." And he said, "No, we'll just go ahead and play a practice round." So, all the members came out to see the great Jack Nicklaus hit it. And when he hit it they all went, "Oooh! Ooooh." And then I hit it, and I put it about 20 yards by him and the members say, "Did you see that little guy hit it?"

Anyway, Jack being such a nice guy, he invited me and my wife for dinner. We went to the steakhouse they had in downtown Augusta. So, we all order steak, and then I cut off all the fat on my steak. And he said, "What are you going to do with that?" I said, "I'm going to throw it away." He said, "Oh, no, no, no, no, put it over here on my plate." And I put it there and he made a sandwich out of it, and he ate it. But then he went on a diet and made himself rather skinny. And we became very good friends and we're still friends.

Texas Open

Arnold Palmer rebounded from his crushing loss at the Masters three weeks earlier by winning the Texas Open at the Oak Hills Golf Club, a short hardscrabble course in San Antonio, by one shot over Canadian Al Balding. Ken Venturi missed out on a decent check when he was disqualified during the final round.

Don Fairfield

It had been very dry. We'd played Houston the week before and the same thing. We had big earth cracks around some places where there wasn't much grass. And you got a free drop from these earth cracks. So, we go on from Houston to San Antonio and I'm playing with Ken Venturi. We went up the fairway and he's got his ball over in a crack. I said, "You could play that. How come you picked it up and dropped it?" He said, "We get a free drop." Well, the director of the week had forgot to put that on the rule sheet. You get a free drop for earth cracks. He looked kind of funny at me when I say there's no free drop this week. He just picked up his ball, put it in his pocket and walked off of the golf course. He'd already taken free drops before. He disqualified himself.

May

Tournament of Champions

On May 5, while PGA tour winners from the previous year were in Las Vegas for the second round of the Tournament of Champions, Alan Shepard was strapped into Freedom 7 and launched into space for a 20-minute suborbital flight to become the first American in space. A little less than 10 years later, Shepard strapped a Wilson 6-iron head to a lunar scoop handle and hit two golf balls on the moon.

Sam Snead—three weeks shy of his 49th birthday—also made history. With four rounds in the 60s, he won in Las Vegas by seven shots over Tommy Bolt to become the oldest winner of a PGA tour event.

Hot Springs Open Invitational

The weekend of May 19-22 offered pros the choice of two tournaments, both played at resorts. Many top names, including Arnold Palmer and Gary Player, chose the Sam Snead Festival, an unofficial event at the Greenbrier in White Sulphur Springs, West Virginia. Host Snead won.

Others opted for the regular PGA tour stop at the Hot Springs Country Club in Arkansas, where the fishing was more appreciated than the golf course. Doug Sanders' final round of 68 was marred by a single bogey on the 13th hole when his tee shot hit an empty whiskey case and went behind a tree. He held on to win by one shot over Jerry Steelsmith and Dave Ragan, by two over Al Geiberger, and by five over Bobby Nichols. Sanders also had won the previous week at the Colonial National Invitational in Fort Worth.

Jerry Steelsmith

Dave Ragan and I tied for second, one shot back. He was a good player. Spectators said if you want to see the players after the tournament, you got to go and watch them fish, rather than hit balls.

I got married in 1961 and started on tour in 1961. We didn't have any children, so off we went. Other families were doing the same thing. I would assume today it's more professional. You didn't have a tour caddie, you hit your own range balls. They didn't supply balls. You were totally on your own.

We traveled 99 percent of the time in your own car. Most people were driving in those days. Only a few people might have been flying. We just drove from tournament to tournament. Sometimes it was a long drive, but sometimes it wasn't too far. It depends on where you're going. I can remember driving from Greensboro, North Carolina down into Texas. And you had a day to get there, a day and a half. It was just the way it was. You were on your own. You made your own hotel reservations. Nobody was doing that for you. You were just out there doing your own thing and everybody else was doing the same thing, too.

Bobby Nichols

The Hot Springs Open. We used to love to go there because we'd fish a lake. I think it was Lake Hamilton. And it was the best fishing in the world! We really had fun that week. It was only a $15,000 tournament at the most.

Don Fairfield

We played a lot of golf courses that were really bad. Hot Springs, Arkansas was the worst golf course anybody ever saw. It was a goat ranch.

Prize money slowly improved every year. At the beginning of the 1960s, you were playing for $12,500 for the whole tournament. Then it got up to $15,000 for the week. In the pro-am, you might make $100 or $200 if you played well. But there wasn't much money. I was on the tour policy board, and we were approached one time by this guy who said, "I'd like to televise this tournament this weekend." I forget where it was. But he talked us into letting him televise that weekend and he gave us $1,000 to put on the purse, and we were happy with it. It was a one-time deal. It wasn't an important tournament.

When TV came—it was very primitive in those days because of the stationary cameras—but gradually those purses were all increased because of TV. It increased the popularity tremendously, and because of Arnold—he became the darling—and TV made sports people millionaires and billionaires. I can't believe today they get one million or two million for winning a golf tournament.

June

U.S. Open

The Oakland Hills Country Club South Course outside of Detroit played very tough. Arnold Palmer never was in contention. In the second round, he double-bogeyed twice and three-putted from 6 feet for a bogey on 18. His rounds of 74-75 made the cut on the number and he was 12 shots behind leaders Bob Rosburg and Doug Sanders.

In time, Staff Sgt. Cliff Harrington would prove to be the most courageous pro in the field. He went through local and sectional qualifying. For Harrington, who was African-American, golf was a side gig; his real job was non-commissioned officer in the U.S. Army. Unlike some talented conscripted athletes, Harrington was not in Special Services. He was a paratrooper. In 1959, he won the All-Army tournament, beating future U.S. Open champions Orville Moody and Lou Graham. In his only U.S. Open, Harrington shot 79-72 at Oakland Hills to miss the cut by two strokes. On November 5, 1965, while serving with the 173rd Airborne, Harrington was killed in action in the early days of the Vietnam War.

Photo 18: Gene Littler.
(Creative Commons)

On Open Saturday, Sanders took the 54-hole lead with a 71 in the morning, one ahead of Bob Goalby, Jacky Cupit and Mike Souchak. In the afternoon, Sanders played flawlessly from tee to green, but a balky putter cost him the championship, as he three-putted five greens in 36 holes for the day. Goalby parred all nine holes on the back nine, but it was not enough. Gene Littler, a San Diego native who won the 1954 U.S. Amateur championship and would end his career with 16 tour wins, started the final round three shots back. In his first 17 holes, Littler birdied three of them and parred the rest. He came to the final hole needing only a bogey, and that is what he got to win by one over Sanders and Goalby.

Bob Goalby

I played with Littler the first two rounds. We were paired together. That's funny that we finished one-two. I finished second in the Open. I didn't putt well. I could have won the Open, but Gene Littler was a good player and beat me by one shot.

July

The Open Championship

Despite his runner-up finish at the 1960 Open, his popularity, and his undisputed position as the best player in the world, Arnold Palmer was required to go through qualifying like every other aspirant at Royal Birkdale in Southport, England seeking the Claret Jug and first-place money, which now was up to about $4,000. The Canadian Open ran opposite the Open Championship; despite it having only a marginally higher winner's take, every current American pro other than Palmer opted for Winnipeg, Manitoba over the air fare needed to travel to England.

Palmer's American rivals at Birkdale were limited to 53-year-old Paul Runyan (winner of the PGA Championship in 1934 and 1938), Frank Stranahan – the Champion Spark Plugs heir (for whom the cost of transatlantic travel was no object), 50-year-old amateur Dick Chapman (victor in the 1940 U.S. Amateur and 1951 British Amateur), 52-year-old Jack Isaacs (the longtime pro at Langley Air Force Base in Virginia), and 52-year-old Joe Ezar (known primarily as a trick-shot artist). All would miss the cut but Runyan, who would finish a respectable 18th.

Harold Henning of South Africa, Dai Rees of Wales, and defending champion Kel Nagle of Australia led with 68s after Wednesday's first round, which was affected by heavy rains. Palmer shot 70. Gary Player went out in 2-under 34, but stumbled home in 39 for a 73. It rained overnight, and gale-force winds arrived in time for second round play on Thursday. Palmer shot 73 and would have tied Australian and four-time Open champion Peter Thomson's 72 for the low round of the day but for a one-stroke penalty he called on himself when the wind blew his ball as he prepared to hit out of a trap on the 16th hole. Palmer's 36-hole score of 143 was one behind Henning and Rees. "I've played in worse conditions, but not much," Palmer said after the round. Player's 77 left him eight shots back. He later would withdraw, citing a stomach ailment.

High wind—which caused thousands of dollars in damage to the Birkdale course and clubhouse—and torrential rains washed out the scheduled 36-hole finish on Friday. The organizing committee announced that if the tournament could not be completed on Saturday, it would be canceled and declared void, which had never happened in the 101 years of the Open Championship. Intermittent rain continued through the night into Saturday. At daylight, workers were on the course with blankets and buckets to dry the greens. Major Tom Harvey, tournament chairman, announced play would resume. "We're going to play on even if the golfers have to putt with irons," he said.

On Saturday, Palmer went out with a remarkable 32 on the front nine. He followed that with 37 on the back to put him one ahead of Rees, who shot 71. In the final round, Palmer had a problem again on the par-5 16th hole, topping his second shot. He scrambled for a par and finished with an even-par 72 to give him a one stroke victory over Rees, who also had 72. Palmer's four-round score of 284 was four under par, extraordinary under the harsh conditions.

British reporters anxiously asked Palmer if he would be back in 1962 to defend his title. "I'm almost sure I'll be back," he answered. "Frankly, I feel a golfer simply must win this title if he wants to be up there with such men as Walter Hagen, Ben Hogan and Sam Snead."

Tony Jacklin

I was 16. I turned pro the following year in 1962. But I was in touch with golf in terms of what was going on and aware of Arnold and all the great players because I wanted to be one. I definitely remember the impact that Arnold's victory had and how influential it was.

When Arnold came and Nicklaus came, the rest of the Americans followed. Bob Drum, who was a Palmer disciple, he rallied all of the media at that point in time, in the early '60s. He was determined that the four majors became "it." Before Arnold came and won that Open, the majors weren't necessarily "it." Many of the great players in the world – Bobby Locke and Peter Thomson and Kel Nagle – they didn't necessarily get themselves out to play in the majors. But Bob Drum, getting back to him, had significant influence over his fellow sportswriters. It was at that point in time that the majors became more significant. Hogan didn't defend his Open (in 1953) like Snead didn't defend his Open (in 1946). The Open wasn't on their agenda. They were very happy to post a victory, but, like Snead told me, it would have cost him more to go back and defend than the first prize (which) was 300 pounds or something.

PGA Championship

Oppressive heat, and then rain, played havoc with the PGA Championship in late July at Olympia Fields Country Club in suburban Chicago. After 36 holes, favorites Arnold Palmer and Gary Player—who both complained that the fairways were too high—had played themselves out of contention, as they were nine and 10 shots back, respectively, of leader Jerry Barber.

Play was rained out on Friday, requiring a 36-hole finish on Sunday. Even without the marquee names near the top of the leaderboard, fans were treated to a good show. In the third round, Don January shot 67 to take a two-stroke lead over Barber. The two were paired in the final round. When they reached the 16th tee, January had increased his lead over Barber to four shots. On 16, Barber sank a 20-foot putt for birdie while January bogeyed. The lead was down to two.

On 17, Barber hooked his drive under a tree. After a recovery shot, he was 80 yards from the green, while January was on the fringe in two. Barber only managed to pitch to 30 feet of the hole. However, he sank the putt for a par, the same score as January, so the margin remained at two. With darkness setting in on an overcast evening, on 18 January drove into a trap and was short of the green in two. Meanwhile, Barber's approach left him with a very long putt for birdie, of between 50 and 60 feet. Believing it very unlikely that Barber would make the putt and that he would win with a bogey, January played a conservative shot to within 12 feet of the hole. Improbably, Barber drained the monster putt, his third long putt in three holes. January missed. An 18-hole playoff would be necessary.

Photo 19: Jerry Barber.
(Source unknown)

On Monday, January led by two strokes after 11 holes. Barber's putter heated up again with birdies on 12 (15 feet), 14 (23 feet) and 15 (6 feet) to wrest the lead from January. On 16, January sank a seven-foot putt to tie. After both parred 17 (with Barber uncharacteristically missing a 6-footer for birdie), the match effectively was sudden death. On 18, both drove into traps. While January's second shot flew into a bunker near the green, Barber hit a fabulous three-iron to within 18 feet of the cup. January hit a good shot out of the sand to 10 feet, but missed the par putt. Barber two-putted for par and victory. January's 68 on a tough course was exceptional, but one shot too many.

Barber had put on the greatest display of pressure putting in major championship history. At age 45, the 5-foot-5, 137-pound Barber became the oldest winner of a Grand Slam championship up to that time. It would prove to be his only major victory. Barber was selected to be the playing captain of the winning 1961 Ryder Cup team, and was named PGA Player of the Year.

In 1963, Barber won the Azalea Open (for the third time) for his final tour victory. He took advantage of the lifetime exemption afforded by his PGA Championship win (the lifetime exemption was scuttled in 1970, but Barber was grandfathered) and periodically appeared at tour events. In 1993 and 1994, when he was 77 years old, Barber played in five tournaments after he had lost his exemption on the PGA Senior Tour. At the 1994 Buick Invitational, he played for the final time. Barber missed the cut but shot 71 in his last round. He died seven months later.

August

Eastern Open, Lutherville, Maryland

The Eastern Open was a tournament played in or outside of Baltimore between 1950 and 1962 and was won by the likes of Arnold Palmer, Sam Snead, Lloyd Mangrum, Cary Middlecoff, Art Wall, Jr. and Tommy Bolt.

The 1961 edition, held the week after the PGA, was played at the Pine Ridge Golf Club, a course opened in 1958. There were numerous complaints. Lionel Hebert's was the most caustic. "It's the worst golf course I've ever played," he snapped, after shooting a 73. "You can quote me on that, brother."

On Sunday, Ken Venturi missed a 4-foot putt on the 18th green that would have tied Doug Sanders. At the ceremony held immediately after, Sanders was given the $5,300 winner's check for his fourth victory of the year, while Venturi's check was $3,400. Sanders made some wisecrack remarks, and then the microphone was turned over to Venturi, who said:

"What I would really like to do is say something that has been bothering me all week. I would like to apologize for the statements made by some of the pros here. You have to overlook this, because these guys are out here to make a living and some of them aren't doing too well. Sometimes, they say something they really don't mean, just to give themselves a boost. I hope you will overlook it."

Venturi's heartfelt statement was greeted with louder applause than Sanders' victory remarks.

October

Bakersfield Open

There is a misconception that Jack Fleck's career was defined solely by his upset victory over Ben Hogan in a playoff for the 1955 U.S. Open at the Olympic Club in San Francisco, his first win after years of toiling on the tour in obscurity.

Photo 20: Jack Fleck. (Historic Images)

That appraisal does not do justice to Fleck. After his Open win, he regularly cashed checks and had some success. In 1960, he won the Phoenix Open, beating Bill Collins in an 18-hole playoff. Also in 1960, he lost in sudden-death playoffs to George Bayer in St. Petersburg and to Arnold Palmer in Hartford, and he tied for third behind Palmer at the U.S. Open. It is fair to say that he was the greatest golfer ever to come out of Iowa until Zach Johnson arrived on the scene around 2000.

At the 1961 Bakersfield Open, Fleck won for the third and final time on the PGA tour. As with his other two victories, it was in a playoff, over Bob Rosburg. From a money standpoint, his best year was 1963, when he made the cut in 19 of the 22 tournaments he entered and earned $15,950. After that, he slowly faded from the scene, but he qualified for the 1977 U.S. Open when he was 55 years old. A health and fitness buff before Gary Player, when he died in 2014 at age 92 he was the oldest living former U.S. Open champion.

W.D. & H.O Wills Golf Classic

Next to Arnold Palmer, the most important golf figure of the 1960s was Cleveland lawyer Mark McCormack. He was a fair amateur golfer himself, good enough to qualify for the 1958 U.S. Open (he shot 78-81 and missed the cut). In the late 1950s, McCormack started booking exhibitions for pro golfers (including Palmer) in his spare time. Palmer was impressed by McCormack's business acumen and in 1959 asked him to handle his affairs.

McCormack left his law firm and in 1960 founded the International Management Group. Its first client was Palmer. Soon thereafter, Gary Player signed on. When Jack Nicklaus turned pro late in 1961, he retained IMG as well. McCormack had the Big Three in his stable.

Photo 21: Mark McCormack.
(Historic Images)

In negotiating with golf equipment companies on behalf of his clients, he insisted that bonuses be included for each victory; sometimes, the bonus exceeded the amount of the client's winnings. McCormack also got his clients non-golf endorsement contracts, including a lucrative contract for Palmer to smoke Liggett & Myers cigarettes. Within two years of joining IMG, Palmer's annual income increased from about $60,000 (his tour winnings plus small endorsement deals and money from scattered exhibitions) to $500,000. IMG soon expanded beyond golf and became the world's leading sports management company.

In October 1961, McCormack sent Palmer and Player to Australia for exhibition matches. "Mark has it all mapped out, and if things go right I will be a millionaire in five years," Player told a reporter. He told another reporter he was upset that he could not bring his collection of rock-and-roll records with him. "I bought a new stereo player recently, but it is so heavy that the air freight is frightening,"

The only tournament the two played Down Under was put on by W.D. & H.O. Wills, a British tobacco company. They were joined by Australian standouts Peter Thomson, Kel Nagle, Bruce Devlin, Bruce Crampton, and Normal von Nida. In the opening round, on a day when high winds descended upon Sydney, 8,000 spectators turned out, many who were only vaguely familiar with golf but were caught up in Palmer hysteria. They ignored the gallery ropes that generally were unnecessary in tournaments in Australia, and the course marshals were helpless trying to herd them.

Palmer had trouble with the high winds and shot 80, which he said was his worst round ever as a professional. Player also struggled, shooting 78. Conditions were better the next day and Player improved to a course-record 68, but Palmer only managed 76. In Saturday's 36-hole finish, Palmer salvaged some self-respect, with 69s in both rounds. Player went 71-69 to win by three strokes over 47-year-old Australian pro Eric Cremin, and by four over Thomson and Crampton.

November

Cajun Classic

Heading into the Cajun Classic in the latter part of November, Arnold Palmer, Gary Player and Doug Sanders had won almost one-third of the tournaments on the 1961 schedule. Player, who was done for the year in the U.S., was the leading money winner. The 28-year-old Sanders—winner of four tournaments—was about $3,000 behind Player, despite missing eight weeks with a neck injury.

Palmer skipped the Cajun Classic, and the lack of marquee names resulted in even fewer spectators than the usual paltry number who turned out in Lafayette, Louisiana. Sanders won for the fifth time in 1961 by six shots over Ken Still, a 26-year-old rookie from Tacoma, Washington, who had left his job in the rug cleaning business to join the tour.

Sanders earned $2,000 for his win, but at year's end Player maintained his position as the tour's top money winner, becoming the first international player to attain that honor.

Tommy Aaron
The Cajun Classic had an old-tour feel to it, from the 1940s or 1950s. In 1961, I played with Doug Sanders in the final round. We had 50 people following us.

December

Haig & Haig Scotch Foursomes

The final tournament of the year was the Haig & Haig Scotch Mixed Foursomes, an unofficial event in Sebring, Florida. It matched 20 teams of men and women pros. The format was that each pro would hit a drive, the team chose one and hit alternate shots to the hole. What could be a more low-key, fun occasion the week before Christmas?

Arnold Palmer, Gary Player and Billy Casper were absent, but Sam Snead was there. Snead had the sweetest swing and, when he wanted, could be a good guy. He also could be a jerk. After winning the 1955 Insurance City Open, at the awards ceremony he was asked if he would return to defend his title. "I can't say what my plans are, but I'll tell you this: I can be had," he responded (this at a time when appearance fees were not prohibited), causing spectators to cringe and deflating the sponsor's feel-good moment.

Given the format, one would expect that Snead would be on his best behavior. He was not the year before, when he partnered with Mickey Wright, as he did not even speak to her. On

Photo 22: Dave Ragan. (Daytona Beach News-Journal)

one hole, Snead hit his approach to within 3 feet. Wright missed the putt. "I guess I need to hit the goddamned thing closer the next time," Snead grumbled within earshot of Wright, who was by far the best woman golfer in the world. Wright was stung by the comment and the duo finished far back in the pack. In 1961, Wright found another partner, the handsome, impeccably mannered 26-year-old Dave Ragan.

Tommy Bolt also entered and was paired with Jo Anne Prentice. Since his supposed flirtation with emotional sobriety in 1960, Bolt definitely had fallen off the wagon. But he managed to both be kind to Prentice while not disappointing members of the gallery who were hoping to witness a blow-up. "My fault, honey," *Sports Illustrated* reported he told Prentice after they bogeyed a hole. "I hit a poor second shot." Then, after missing a short putt, Bolt forcefully threw his putter into the ground and kicked at the shaft sticking up, breaking it in two, requiring him to putt with his driver the rest of the round. "Don't let it get you, honey," he drawled after Prentice missed an 18-inch putt. "If I had a dollar for every one of those I've missed, I wouldn't have to work no more." On the 17th hole, Bolt lost his cool again and thrust his nine-iron into the ground up to the grip, so deep that his caddie could not pull it out. Bolt was fined $100 for the first tantrum, but was given a pass for the second. The Bolt-Prentice team did not contend.

Snead did show up again, probably because he was paid by Wilson Sporting Goods, with whom he had a contract. With Wright unwilling to play with Snead, his partner was 43-year-old Patty Berg who, unlike Snead, already was a member of the World Golf Hall of Fame (Snead would join Berg in 1974), and who also was under contract with Wilson. Snead knew better than to be disrespectful to Berg. They shot 65 in the final round of the 72-hole tournament to finish second, seven shots behind Ragan and Wright.

1962

January

Los Angeles Open

As recently as the previous summer, when he won his second U.S. Amateur championship, Jack Nicklaus still professed the ambition to win Bobby Jones' version of the Grand Slam while he completed his studies at Ohio State and embarked on a career in business. His outlook changed when his first child, Jack Nicklaus II, was born on September 23, 1961. Initially, Nicklaus intended to start his pro career at the Bing Crosby Pro-Am. However, he accepted a $2,500 offer to play an exhibition in Miami with Arnold Palmer, Gary Player and Sam Snead on December 31, 1961, and moved up his tournament debut a couple of weeks and traveled to Los Angeles. "I won't count it as a good year unless I win more than $30,000 my first season on the tour," he said.

On Friday, January 5, Nicklaus teed off with Rex Baxter, Jr. and Leo Biagetti in the first group at 7:30 a.m. He shot 74 and followed it with a 70 on Saturday to make the cut comfortably, then followed with 72-73. His 72-hole score of 289 was good for a tie for 48th place with Billy Maxwell and Don Massengale, 21 shots behind winner Phil Rodgers, in the last place for which money was awarded. Nicklaus earned $33.33.

Nicklaus did better the next week at San Diego, tying for 15th place and earning $550. At the Crosby, a tie for 21st netted him $450. The following week, at the Lucky Lager tournament in San Francisco, a tie for 47th earned Nicklaus $62.85. Next, at Palm Springs, he received $164.44 for finishing 32nd. He finally broke through in Phoenix, finishing tied for second to Palmer, earning $2,300. Still, Nicklaus's goal of earning $30,000 for the year seemed doubtful.

Jack Nicklaus

My first five tournaments of the year, I never had less than 34 putts in any round. Including a 65 at Indian Wells, where I hit every green and every par five (in two) and a par four (with my drive). And I shoot 65. Nothing less than 34 putts. I was putting terrible. I was using a putter I got at the Walker Cup in 1959, and the putter weighed about 13-and-a-quarter ounces, which is about three ounces less than the average putter. And I was trying to putt on a variety of greens on tour with it. George Low saw that and came to me and asked me to try one of his putters, which was his George Low Sportsman, which I won 15 majors with. The first tournament I played with it was Phoenix, where I finished second.

February

Phoenix Open

Long before the Waste Management Open near Phoenix became the site of the PGA Tour's annual bacchanal, with crowds some days in excess of 200,000, tournaments in the desert city were more subdued affairs. Phoenix is one of the oldest stops on the tour, going back to 1932 and played annually since 1944.

In 1962, after winning in Palm Springs the week before, Arnold Palmer won at the Phoenix Country Club in a cakewalk, by 12 shots over Jack Nicklaus, Billy Casper, Don Fairfield, and Bob McAllister.

Bruce Crampton, a 26-year-old from Sydney, Australia who had won in Milwaukee in 1961, finished 10th and in the process enhanced his growing reputation as the most unpleasant player on the tour. *The Arizona Republic* reported that on Friday, in the course of shooting 75, he chewed out a man who had stopped to watch the threesome of Crampton, Johnny Pott and Phil Rodgers, for jiggling coins in his pocket. Unbeknownst to Crampton, the man was one of the Phoenix Open's top benefactors.

While standing over a putt on the ninth green, Crampton ordered a man to stop walking. When he missed the putt, he threw his putter and ball on the ground and glared at the man, who actually had followed Crampton's directive and stopped. The next hole, he faced a difficult shot. Blocked out by a tree, he managed to hit an 8-iron through an opening onto the apron of the green. Despite Crampton's churlish behavior, the small gallery applauded the effort. "You made me miss the green," Crampton responded, pointing to a young man standing at least 15 yards away.

On 17, Crampton hit his approach over the green and stalked off before Pott and Rodgers hit their shots. "The guy should be barred from the tour," one of them said, disgusted by Crampton's outbursts towards the paying customers. After hitting into a trap on 18, Crampton threw his three-wood at the feet of his caddie and said, "Take this bloody thing." After blasting out of the trap past the hole, he angrily twirled his wedge. One of the spectators got in a closing salvo. "Attaboy, throw your club," he said, loud enough for Crampton to hear.

Don Fairfield

When (Nicklaus) came on tour, he started out very slowly. I remember he played the Los Angeles Open for his first tournament. He got $33, $100 split between three guys.

About three or four weeks later, I played with Arnold Palmer in the final round of the Phoenix Open. He won by 12 shots. He made everything. I finished second, tied with Nicklaus.

March

St. Petersburg Open

In a Monday finish, Bobby Nichols, a 26-year-old from Louisville, won his first PGA tournament by two strokes. Nichols was playing his second year on the tour. In 1961, he played in 15 events, made the cut in 14 of them and won a grand total of $5,001.

Photo 23: Bobby Nichols.
(Historic Images)

That he was able to play at all was a miracle. On September 4, 1952, Nichols was a 16-year-old high school junior and a promising golfer. He went on a joy ride with three other teens and was involved in a high-speed car crash. Only Nichols was seriously injured. He suffered a broken pelvis, a concussion, and internal injuries, and was bedridden for more than three months. During his convalescence, he received a long, thoughtful letter from Ben Hogan, who had recovered from similar injuries to win consecutive U.S. Opens in 1950 and 1951.

At St. Petersburg, he benefited when the first round was rained out after he shot 76, and replayed in its entirety the next day. Nichols improved to 71 on Friday and closed with a 64 to win by two shots over Frank Boynton.

Bobby Nichols

I had a little bit of money. I'd say a very small amount. So, I got by on that pretty much, and then I got married in 1961. And then I won my first tournament at the St. Petersburg Open. The winner's purse was $2,800, and it pretty well got me a little more comfortable, you might say.

Still, there wasn't a whole lot of money, no matter where. I'd say half of our tournaments back in the early 1960s were $15,000 purses, at the most. I remember Sam Snead said one time, "Goddamn! Look at the money you guys are playing for!" Talking to me and a few others about how much money we were playing for.

But it was amazing, we got to meet people and they would let us stay with them for the week. We'd have dinners with them. People were extremely nice to us, and it really helped us out as far as expenses. I got to meet some wonderful people. I think that was probably the highlight of travel on the tour back in those days.

Frank Boynton

In those days when you had a rainout, they scrubbed the scoreboard. Everybody started over. Nowadays, they go out the next day to finish the round. I started out with 66 and it was rained out. And the next day, I shot 65 and got the lead again. Nobody had broken 67 on the golf course for the week, except me. And I shot 67 with the lead going into the last round. Bobby Nichols shot 65 and beat me. His first round was 76. It got rained out.

That was my way into the first Doral Open. I got paired with Nicklaus. The first two rounds with Sam Snead and Ben Hogan, the third round with Gary Player.

Doral Open

When Paul Bondeson showed up for the inaugural Doral Open in March 1962, the blond, 6-foot-2, 200-pound former high school linebacker from St. Petersburg had intriguing potential. As a

15-year-old, he won a long driving contest with a 280-yard drive. The 22-year-old had turned pro the previous fall after a stint as an Army paratrooper. He had played only 11 previous tour events and had cashed only one check. Yet already he was being called "the new George Bayer" for his prodigious length.

Photo 24: Paul Bondeson. (Historic Images, Wilson Sporting Goods Co.)

After three rounds at the windswept, brand-new Doral Country Club near Miami, Bondeson led by one stroke over Bob Goalby and by two over Nicklaus and Billy Casper. In the final round, Bondeson was paired with Billy Casper. On the 368-yard, par-4 11th hole, Bondeson drove the green. A birdie put him four shots clear of Casper. However, he promptly gave up the lead with consecutive double-bogeys. On the long par-4 18th, Casper hit a wood to the green, while Bondeson used a wedge, which he put within 10 feet. Bondeson needed that putt to force a playoff with Casper. It lipped out. It would be the closest he would ever come to winning on tour.

Bondeson played the tour full-time through 1968. Alcoholism derailed his career. He got sober in 1985 and found work as a greens superintendent in Florida. In 2001, when he was 61, Bondeson was broadsided while driving his vehicle, leaving him paralyzed from the waist down. He died in 2011.

Jack Nicklaus

Paul Bondeson was very long. Paul was about my age, came on tour about the time I did, and, in my rookie year in 1962, he almost won the first PGA tour event held at Doral. He finished second to Billy Casper, and I finished third.

Paul was about my height, with pretty broad shoulders, if I recall. Could he outdrive me? I would say that on occasion Paul probably could. But you don't play golf courses or a play a round of golf with a purpose to outdrive somebody. That's not what we did. I always felt I was as long as I needed to be, depending on the hole and the shot. But in general, I think I was probably longer than Paul.

April

The Masters

The 1962 Masters was riveting.

In Thursday's opening round, defending champion Gary Player's 67 in the rain gave him a two-stroke lead over Julius Boros, with Arnold Palmer three back after a 70. On a cool, murky Friday, Palmer shot 66 to take the lead by two over Player. The weather improved for the third round on Saturday, when a record crowd—estimated at between 40,000 and 50,000—attended, at a time when Augusta National made no effort to limit the number of tickets sold. Most of the patrons followed Palmer. On the third hole, while Palmer was preparing to putt, one of them collapsed, and play was stopped for about 15 minutes until the patron could be taken away in an ambulance. Palmer completed the round in 69, tying the 54-hole record of 205. Dow Finsterwald's 65 left him two behind Palmer and two ahead of Player.

In Sunday's final round, Palmer and Player were in the last pairing. Palmer played terribly on the front nine, shooting a 3-over 39, and then he double-bogeyed 10. It appeared certain that, for the second straight year, Palmer would blow the Masters. He parred the next five holes, failing to take advantage of the par-5s (13 and 15).

As Palmer and Player arrived at the tee of the par-3 16th, Palmer trailed Finsterwald by three and Player by two. Palmer was strong with his 5-iron, hitting it over the green, 45 feet from the hole. He proceeded to hit one of the greatest—or luckiest—shots of his career. With his wedge, he popped his ball softly on the green and watched it trickle with pace into the cup for a birdie. Had it not hit the flagstick, it would have rolled far past the hole. Player parred 16. Finsterwald had bogeyed 17, so Palmer was one back.

At 17, Palmer hit an 8-iron to within 6 feet and made the putt for his second straight birdie to tie Finsterwald and Player. Both Palmer and Player hit long, straight drives on 18. Player's 6-iron approach flew 70 feet beyond the flag. Palmer initially pulled an 8-iron from his bag but switched to a seven. He should have stayed with his initial choice as he put his ball 30 feet past the hole. Player hit a great putt to within 3 feet, Palmer to two-and-a-half feet. Both made their testers to tie Finsterwald.

On Monday, in the first three-way playoff in Masters' history, Palmer again started poorly with a 1-over 37 on the front to fall three shots back of Player. Finsterwald shot 40 on the front and never was a factor, finishing with a 77. On the 10th hole, Palmer halved his score from Sunday, holing a 25-foot birdie putt while Player bogeyed. On the short 12th, Palmer hit an 8-iron to within 3 feet and sank the putt for a deuce, while Player three-putted from 6 feet for a bogey. Palmer also birdied 13, 14 and 16 and pulled away from Player with a back-nine 31 and a 68 to win the playoff by three strokes for his third green jacket.

Bruce Devlin

I won the Australian Open as an amateur in 1960. That was how I got my invitation to Augusta in 1961 and I turned it down. I didn't have any money to fly and spend all that money to play at the Masters. I ended up turning pro after the Masters in 1961. In those days, you had to spend 12 months in Australia without accepting any prize money, just to prove that you could make a living playing golf. Talk about archaic rules. I even had to write a requisition letter to the PGA of Australia to allow me to play in the 1962 Masters, because the Masters was about five weeks before my one-year period was up. So, a lot of strange things back in those days.

I think Ben Hogan kind of had a pretty bad rap for some of the stories that you hear about him. You would not meet a nicer person than Ben Hogan, in my opinion. I first met him at Augusta in 1962, when I was introduced to him by Norman Von Nida, an Australian player who had some success in Europe, and won a lot of golf tournaments around the world. I played my first practice round with Mr. Hogan at the Masters. That was a harrowing moment for me, but we became friends and we played just about every practice round at the tournaments that we both entered. Normally it was against two other guys, which were always a lot of fun, played for a little bit of money, not much, but a little bit just to keep everybody's interest. So that was always fun having him as a partner.

May

Colonial National Invitational

After winning at Augusta, Palmer arrived in Fort Worth for the Colonial seeking his third straight victory. He had won the two previous weeks at the Tournament of Champions and the Texas Open. After 72 holes, Palmer and Johnny Pott (a personable Mississippian) were tied, requiring an 18-hole playoff on Monday for the chance to win the garish red plaid jacket awarded to the winner of the Colonial, which never quite became as coveted as Augusta National's green jacket. Interestingly, both Palmer and Pott had won the previous week, Palmer at the TOC and Pott at the alternate event, the Waco Turner Open in Oklahoma.

Photo 25: *Johnny Pott. (Historic Images)*

On the ninth hole of the play-off, Palmer led by one stroke. He was off the green and preparing to chip. Among the gallery right next to Palmer were Shirley Maples and her 4-year-old son, John. The little boy started to laugh. Palmer stepped away, looked at the boy and chuckled, causing others in the gallery to laugh, and returned to his task at hand. The boy's embarrassed mother responded by placing her hand over John's mouth, which caused him to emit a muffled scream. Palmer stepped away again, walked over to the boy and patted him on the head. "Don't choke him," he gently admonished Mrs. Maples. "This isn't that important."

Palmer bogeyed the hole but pulled away on the back nine to win for the sixth time in 1962.

John Maples

I had to hear the story told by my mother many times. It was the ninth hole, I think. There's this tournament going on. Why we're out there, I have no clue. We're under some trees near the green. Across from there is a little pond. Apparently, the guy that was playing with Palmer that day, his ball landed in the water across the fairway on the other side. When Palmer teed off, his ball came down through the trees and hit my mother in the leg. I was going to throw the ball into the pond. My mother always said the only thing she could figure is that I had seen the guy before that hit the ball into the lake and I thought that's where the ball was supposed to go.

June

Memphis Open

At the halfway point, Gary Player led the tournament with a score of 131. However, the real drama took place with players well down the leaderboard, around the cutline for determining who would stick around for the weekend.

Photo 26: Frank Boynton.
(Historic Images)

The purse for the Memphis Open was $40,000. The next event on the calendar was the Thunderbird Classic Invitational in Clifton, New Jersey, with a $125,000 purse that was by far the richest of the year. All players who made the cut at Memphis would qualify for a chance to partake of the following week's bounty. However, because the Thunderbird was an invitational event, there was no Monday qualifying.

Don Fairfield shot a 68 in the first round but struggled the next day and was at 142, 11 behind Player. He already had qualified for the Thunderbird by virtue of his top-60 status in 1961 and decided to withdraw. Frank Boynton was at 143, one shot below the cut line, with several other players who had not qualified for the Thunderbird.

Lionel Hebert won in Memphis after a playoff with Player and Gene Littler.

Frank Boynton
Oh, yes. I loved Don (Fairfield). He did one of the nicest things. The first big tournament in the $100,000 range was in Clifton, New Jersey, and you had to make the cut at Memphis and we're all sweating the cut. About seven of us are on the cusp of missing the cut, and he withdrew and got all of us in the tournament at Clifton. He just didn't have the heart to stand there when he already was in the tournament. (After that), I never saw he and his wife at a restaurant that I didn't send over for the check. Wow, that is something. So, he just figured that, I'm not going to win the tournament, and yeah, he wasn't playing that well at Memphis, but he was just ahead of us. So, he dropped out and put all of us in. I won $1,600 the next week.

Don Fairfield
I was always against invitational tournaments, which eliminated open qualifying which gives all players a chance to play for a check. We were in Memphis and scores were low with about eight to ten players on the cut line. I had finished and was at the scoreboard when I saw the cut. I decided to withdraw and take the weekend off and allow these men a chance to play. I became a hero!

U.S. Open

Arnold Palmer again was in pursuit of the Grand Slam when he arrived for the 62nd U.S. Open. He had homecourt advantage as the Open was played at Oakmont Country Club, 48 miles northwest of his hometown of Ligonier, Pennsylvania, and even closer to his boyhood home of Latrobe. The USGA chose to pair him for the first two rounds with Jack Nicklaus, who was still searching for his first pro victory, with a high noon start time on Thursday.

Of course, Arnie's Army was in full force, making up the bulk of the record first-round gallery of 17,486 on a cool, overcast day, causing one spectator to ask, "Who's taking care of the steel mills?" Nicklaus was not intimidated, as he birdied the first three holes. He cooled off after that, but his opening round of 72 was just one behind Palmer's even-par 71, and three back of leader and defending champion Gene Littler. On Friday, the temperature was barely over 50 degrees when Palmer and Nicklaus teed off early, after a fog delay. Palmer shot 68 to take the lead with Bob Rosburg, three ahead of Nicklaus.

On Open Saturday, Palmer slipped to 73 in the morning, which still left him tied (with Bobby Nichols), one ahead of Rosburg and Phil Rodgers, and two in front of Nicklaus and Gary Player. Between rounds, Nichols had a miscommunication with his caddie. At the time, caddies were assigned to players at the U.S. Open by luck of the draw. At Nichols' scheduled tee time, his young caddie did not appear. This almost resulted in Nichols' disqualification, but the boy was found just in time. Nichols double-bogeyed the first hole, which proved costly.

Early in the final round, Nicklaus fell five shots behind Palmer. Nicklaus's birdie on the par-5 ninth narrowed the gap to three strokes. Playing right behind Nicklaus, Palmer was hole-high in two on the ninth and was poised to take command of the tournament, but he left his first chip in the rough, hit another poor chip before two-putting for a demoralizing bogey. After Nicklaus birdied 11 and Palmer three-putted for a bogey on 13, they were tied at 1 under. Rodgers stayed in the thick of it until he reached the short par-4 17th hole. He drove into a small tree on the left side of the fairway. Instead of taking an unplayable lie, Rodgers attempted to knock the ball out of the tree. It took three swings to dislodge the ball. Rodgers made a quadruple bogey 8 and finished tied for third with Nichols, two shots back.

Nicklaus and Palmer remained tied when Palmer reached 18. With Nicklaus in the clubhouse, Palmer stroked a beautiful 4-iron to the green, but left himself a 12-foot winding uphill birdie putt. He missed it high. There would be an 18-hole playoff on Sunday.

After six holes of the playoff, Nicklaus's two birdies and Palmer's two bogeys put Nicklaus up by four. Palmer charged momentarily, with birdies on 9, 11 and 12 to cut Nicklaus's lead to one shot. However, Palmer three-putted from 50 feet on 13 to fall two behind. On the par-4 18th, both took three shots to get on or near the green. After Palmer's par effort from just off the back slid 4 feet past, he backhanded the ball, missed, tapped in for a 6, picked up Nicklaus's coin near the hole and congratulated him. Because the format was stroke play, USGA officials directed Nicklaus to put his ball back and finish. His bogey gave him an even-par round of 71, three shots ahead of Palmer (who was not penalized for his clumsy act of sportsmanship). Nicklaus's first tour win was a major championship.

Photo 27: Jack Nicklaus (right) receives a firm congratulatory handshake from Arnold Palmer after the 1962 U.S. Open playoff. (United States Golf Association)

THE AGE OF PALMER

Jack Nicklaus

I never really paid much attention to (Arnie's Army) back then. I didn't notice them until later on in my career. I was a young kid with blinders on, focused on winning the U.S. Open. That was my goal and that was what I was going to get to. Little did I know that there was this fellow named Arnold Palmer who lived just down the street who had a legion of people who followed him, who were loud, boisterous, and very pro-Arnold Palmer and against anything else that existed other than him. However, as I've said many times, I may have had to fight Arnold's gallery, but I never had to fight him. Arnold always treated me fantastic.

Bobby Nichols

During that time, you played two rounds on Saturday, you didn't play on Sundays. I was playing with Gary Player, and I was tied for the lead. What we did was complete the third round, and we had lunch and then you went right back out and played the final round of the tournament. We just get a small break, maybe 45 minutes. And then I had to head back out. I couldn't find my caddie. Joe Dey was the head of the USGA at the time and he was on the first tee. He said, "Bobby, you better find you your caddie because otherwise I'll have to penalize you."

Gary heard him say that. He hit his tee shot, and he came to me and he said, "Bobby, I'll walk as slow as I can off the tee, and hopefully that will give you a little time to find your caddie." I had friends of mine looking for him and they finally found him underneath a tree, having lunch. He was a kid that didn't know any better and fortunately they found him. On the first hole in the final round at Oakmont, I double-bogeyed. But coming into No. 15, I was tied for the lead, but I bogeyed 15 and 18 and finished two shots back.

Back in those days, the caddies were young kids that probably didn't caddie a whole lot, or very little prior to major championships or any tournament. And he just didn't realize what was going on, and maybe I didn't tell him. It wasn't his fault. If Gary Player had hit a second shot, on the first hole, I would have been disqualified. But he walked slow

122

enough, and I had time to find my caddie. Gary was very kind in doing everything he could to keep me from getting disqualified.

Bob Zimmerman

I was the assistant pro at Moraine Country Club in Dayton, Ohio. They had the 1945 PGA there when Byron Nelson won it. I qualified for the 1962 Open. The members at Moraine sponsored me that week. That was Jack Nicklaus's first win on the tour. It was the first time I played on greens that fast.

I was teeing off on the first hole on Thursday. They of course had people lined up every place and hanging out the windows and whatever, and they announce your name, and my hands were shaking so bad that part of my right hand was on the steel to make sure I didn't whiff. I wound up birdieing the first two holes, so I was leading the U.S. Open in 1962. One of the neatest things that ever happened to me. That's when they carried the signs around, which I guess they still do today, with your name on there, and how many under you are or how many over you are. So, on the sign, it shows "Zimmerman minus two," going down number three, and the people clap for me all the way down the fairway. So that was pretty exciting. And then I went bogey-bogey. Then after I birdied the first two holes, Nicklaus came around and birdied one, two, and three.

I grew up with Nicklaus. Nicklaus is a year older than me. I'm from Dayton and he's from Columbus and we played in a bunch of junior tournaments together. I was a junior in high school and he, of course, won. He beat me by six shots, and I finished second. He graduated and I won the state tournament the next year, so I played a lot of golf with Jack. He was always very friendly to me. He was a little bit standoffish at that time. I think Barbara, his wife, really did a lot for his personality and really helped make him the man he is. But he was always friendly, would never forget a name. Years later, after I got off the tour, I'd go up to Columbus for the Muirfield tournament. I'd be standing on the tee, and he would see me, and he'd always come over and say, "Hi Bob, how are you doing?"

July

The Open Championship

Arnold Palmer was true to his word and returned to Great Britain to defend his Open Championship title at Troon, Scotland. This time, he brought with him American stars Jack Nicklaus, Phil Rodgers, and Gene Littler. Also, 50-year-old Sam Snead came over for the first time since he won at St. Andrews in 1946. For the final time, qualifying was required of all contestants. Starting in 1963, exemptions were given to the top players.

Despite an aching back, Palmer's first round of 71 left him only two shots back. Nicklaus struggled in his Open Championship debut, shooting 80. "This course didn't play hard today," he said. "There was hardly any wind and overnight rain had improved the greens. I reckon I just can't control the small British ball." Littler had trouble with the heather gorse and sand and had a 79. "I don't want to talk about it," he told the press.

Nicklaus improved to 72 on Thursday to make the cut on the number. Littler, along with Gary Player and 1961 runner-up Dai Rees, did not. Rounds of 74 and 79 on Open Friday gave Nicklaus a 72-hole score of 305 and a tie for 34th. Sam Snead finished tied for sixth.

Meanwhile, Palmer coasted. His 69 in the second round gave him a two-shot lead over Kel Nagle. Palmer's 67 in Friday's morning round set the stage for a coronation. A 69 in the final round gave him a 72-hole total of 276, two shots better than the previous Open record, six shots clear of Nagle and 13 ahead of Rodgers, who tied for third with Brian Huggett of Wales. On the day, Palmer had 12 birdies. "I've never played four rounds of golf like these in my whole life," he said.

After winning at Troon, Palmer had won six major championships, five in a little over two years. He was 32 years old. At the time, Walter Hagen held the record for most professional majors with 11, six of which he had won before he turned 33. The only others ahead of Palmer were Ben Hogan with nine (none before he was 33), and, with seven, Sam Snead, Gene Sarazen, Harry Vardon, and Bobby Jones (as an amateur, Jones won four U.S. Opens and three Open Championships). Palmer seemed poised to shatter Hagen's record.

PGA Championship

The week after the Open Championship, the PGA Championship was played at the Aronimink Golf Club outside of Philadelphia. The tournament originally was scheduled to be played at the Brentwood Country Club in Los Angeles. However, when California attorney general Stanley Mosk threatened to shut down the PGA in his state due to the "Caucasian race" clause, the PGA of America moved the championship to Aronimink. By the time the PGA removed the clause in November 1961, it was too late to reverse the decision.

Approximately 17,000 fans turned out for the first round. In the morning, almost all of them followed the threesome of Arnold Palmer (winner of the Masters and Open Championship), Jack Nicklaus (the U.S. Open champion) and Dave Marr (whose only credential at the time was winner of the small-purse Azalea Open earlier in the year). The course marshals had their hands full. Palmer repeatedly was disturbed by spectators' cameras. Nicklaus and Marr repeatedly were disturbed by members of Arnie's Army dashing off to the next tee after their hero was finished putting. At one point, after putting out, Palmer put up his hands and shouted, "Stand still, we have another putter." It did not work. All three shot 71.

John Barnum, age 50, shot a bogeyless round of 66, a course record, to take the first-round lead over 47-year-old Chick Harbert, whose last of five tour victories had come at the 1954 PGA Championship. Barnum was a hulking 6-foot-3, 230 pound club pro from Grand Rapids, Michigan. He would fade with subsequent rounds of 74-77-81 but would make history late in the year when he won the Cajun Classic. By then, Barnum had turned 51 and became the oldest first-time winner in tour history, and the first to win using a Ping putter.

Photo 28: John Barnum. (Historic Images, Wilson Sporting Goods Co.)

In response to numerous complaints by players, before the second round, PGA officials announced that only credentialed press photographers would be permitted to bring cameras onto the course. On Friday, 39-year-old Doug Ford—winner of the 1955 PGA Championship and 1957 Masters—shot his second straight 69 to take the lead. Another player who was a vestige from earlier days, Cary Middlecoff—the 41-year-old non-practicing dentist from Memphis who won U.S. Opens in 1949 and 1956, and the Masters in 1955—shot 66. Dr. Middlecoff was one shot back of Ford, tied with Gary Player and George Bayer. One shot further back at 140 was Bob McCallister, who also had 66 on Friday. McCallister was conspicuous for the lettering on his golf bag, "The Champagne Music of Lawrence Welk." The bandleader was McCallister's sponsor.

After three rounds, Gary Player had a two-shot edge over Bayer and McAllister. In the final round, Player and McAllister were grouped with Bob Goalby, who was four strokes back. After five holes on Sunday, Goalby had dropped to six behind Player.

Mid-round, just as it started to rain heavily, Goalby got hot with birdies at 9, 11, 14 and 16, reducing the deficit to one shot. Player held on to win after Goalby just missed a 20-footer on the 18th hole that would have given him a tie.

With the win, Player won his third major championship, to go along with his 1959 win at the Open Championship and 1961 victory at the Masters. "It was the most exciting game I ever played," said Player. "It was a friendly game, but it was tense as hell. I wanted to win real bad and now I'm closer to my goal of winning the Big Four." Player made it clear he was referring to the Grand Slam as a career goal.

Bob Goalby

I had a chance to win the 1962 PGA. I played with Gary Player in the final round. We had a good match.

During the tournament, I missed a 10-inch putt on the fifth hole. I wanted to get out of the way and didn't take my time. I took the flag out myself.

September

World Series of Golf

Nothing captured pro golf's changing landscape more than the first World Series of Golf, held the weekend of September 8 and 9, 1962 at the Firestone Country Club. It was a made-for-TV exhibition announced in April, prior to the Masters. The match would include the winners of what were now universally considered the four majors: the Masters, U.S. Open, Open Championship and PGA Championship. In the event a player won more than one major, an additional contestant would be selected. The winner would receive $50,000.

It turned out that Arnold Palmer won two majors (the Masters and Open Championship). The other two majors were won by Jack Nicklaus (U.S. Open) and Gary Player (PGA). There was talk that Sam Snead would be added as the fourth member of the foursome. This idea was quickly squelched after Player's victory. Given that Mark McCormack represented Palmer, Nicklaus and Player, there was grumbling that he exercised his influence to make the World Series of Golf a showcase for his clients, now universally known as The Big Three.

Hard feelings were engendered all around by the exhibition. Snead—who never turned down money, particularly the opportunity to win lots of it—was miffed. The promoters of the Denver Open—held the same weekend—were upset (though none of the Big Three played in the 1961 edition).

Palmer shot a course-record 65 in Saturday's first round but was only one shot ahead of Nicklaus. Sunday's round was devoid of drama. By the time the threesome came into the range of television viewers on the 13th hole, Nicklaus was comfortably ahead. He beat Palmer and Player by four shots to take the $50,000. Palmer and Player each took home $12,500, almost triple the $4,300 Bob Goalby earned for winning the Denver Open.

Seattle World's Fair Open Invitational

All of the Big Three headed to Seattle right after the World Series of Golf. Nicklaus had underestimated his ability when he pronounced upon turning pro that he would not consider his rookie year successful unless he earned at least $30,000. He had earned around $50,000, and that sum did not include the $50,000 he won in Akron the week before, which in PGA tour jargon was "unofficial money," but spent just as well as official money.

The three were close to leader Billy Casper (67-63 for 130) after 36 holes at the short 6,328-yard Broadmoor Country Club course, which was rendered defenseless by rain. Nicklaus was closest with rounds of 67 and 65. Palmer and Player were at 135. On Saturday, Nicklaus put on an exhibition demonstrating how in a short time frame the game had evolved from finesse to power. He needed only a driver and wedge to reach nearly every par-4 and finished with a 65, which gave him a two-stroke edge over Player, who shot 64. Palmer lost ground with a 68. In the final round, Nicklaus' 68 gave him a 72-hole total of 265 and a two-shot win over Tony Lema.

The Seattle's winner's check of $4,300 must have seemed like small potatoes to Nicklaus. Nevertheless, he went on to the Portland Open the following week, where he won again, earning $3,500, despite suffering a two-stroke penalty for slow play. Having won $61,842 during a very successful rookie year, Nicklaus returned home to Columbus to continue his studies at Ohio State.

October

Orange County Open

Most of the stars skipped the Orange County Open, a small-purse tournament in Costa Mesa, California held in late October towards the end of the season.

Like all Americans, at that moment in time, pro golfers were worried they might be incinerated by Soviet nuclear warheads pointed at the United States from Cuba, 90 miles south of Florida. On October 28, the Cuban Missile Crisis was averted when Soviet Union leader Nikita Khrushchev agreed to remove the missiles from Cuba.

The very same day, a star was born. Tony Lema was a 28-year-old journeyman from the Bay Area who had been playing the tour since 1957, without much success. One reason is that he was handsome, single, and liked to have a good time. In September 1962, he won the Sahara Invitational in Las Vegas for his first official tour victory. At Costa Mesa, he won again, beating fellow Bay Area resident Bob Rosburg in a sudden-death playoff.

Lema handed out bottles of champagne to the press room, following through on a promise he had made to the scribes the previous day that he would bring bubbly if he won. Lema continued this practice for his subsequent 10 tour victories during his short career, earning the moniker "Champagne Tony."

Photo 29: Tony Lema, 1964, Firestone Country Club.
(Akron Beacon Journal, USA Today Network)

Doc Giffin

I was traveling mostly by car. I had my press office in the trunk and my personal belongings in my back seat. I'd travel from tournament to tournament on Mondays. I'd get to the tournament site and coordinate with the local people and the media people there and set up the press room, and make sure everything would work. Some of them were pretty small change operations, just like some of the tournaments were small purse operations.

The one where Tony Lema won, where the "Champagne Tony" story developed, the press room was in a card room in the men's locker room at the Mesa Verde Country Club. There were only half a dozen media people covering the tournament. I was the press secretary there, and he beat Bob Rosburg in a playoff. Lema was the leader going into the final round and as he sat with the newspaper guys and myself for his interview, he was drinking a beer. When he got up to leave he said, "Well, I'll tell you, guys, if I win this thing tomorrow, we're going to have champagne in here." I recognized that as something to jump on, so I talked to the manager to make sure there was champagne handy. And that's exactly what happened when he won the playoff. So, a couple of the writers dubbed him Champagne Tony. I picked it up from there and spread the word and pushed the Champagne Tony tag.

He got a contract with a company called Moet. Their deal was that any time he was in contention their local guy was supposed to be on hand at the tournament to have champagne handy so that if he won there would be champagne in the press room. In fact, in 1965, he was leading a tournament at Pleasant Valley, Massachusetts, a larger purse tournament sponsored by Carling Black Label beer. When he won there, somebody put a Carling label on the bottle of champagne that they handed out in the press room. He got a kick out of that. He said, "I think we certainly can get together with beer and champagne on an occasion like this."

December

South Africa

Arnold Palmer had a very busy and successful 1962. He won eight times, including the Masters and the Open Championship. His earnings of $81,448 were tops on the tour, he won the Vardon Trophy for lowest scoring average for the second straight year, and he was the PGA Player of the Year.

Palmer had cut back his tournament appearances from 24 in 1961 to 21 in 1962 (in 1958, he had entered 31 PGA tour events). Mark McCormack had secured a contract with ABC television for a series of 13 matches for a program called "Challenge Golf," in which his clients Palmer and Gary Player would take on two players at prime venues, with $156,000 in prize money on the table. As examples, they played Jack Nicklaus and Phil Rodgers at the Riviera Country Club outside of Los Angeles, and Byron Nelson and Ken Venturi at Pebble Beach. The matches were played from June until the end of 1962, between tournament appearances, and aired in 1963. Palmer also found time to play himself in a movie, "Call Me Bwana," starring Bob Hope and Anita Ekberg.

Thus, thanks to McCormack, Palmer could skip the small-fry tournaments in Mobile, West Palm Beach, and Coral Gables at the end of 1962. He even passed on the richer Carling Open held in Orlando, a city with which Palmer later would be connected at the hip, through the Bay Hill club and the pediatric hospital that carries his name to this day. Instead, after spending Thanksgiving with his family in Latrobe and dubbing commentary in Los Angeles for Challenge Golf, he set off for South Africa to join Player for a series of six matches over two weeks. They split the matches (played in South Africa, and in what was then known as Rhodesia and is now

Zimbabwe), but Player won by six strokes in the 108-hole aggregate. Player also won the Transvaal Open in Johannesburg over Bob Charles, where Palmer finished sixth before heading home for a well-deserved rest.

1963

January

Bing Crosby National Pro-Am

Popularly known as the Crosby Clambake, the Bing Crosby Pro-Am was one of the tour's oldest events, dating back to 1937. Originally held in Rancho Sante Fe near San Diego, after World War II the Crosby was moved to the Monterey Peninsula. It offered pros the opportunity to play with an amateur partner on three spectacular courses with ocean vistas. Few passed up the opportunity, even though it often entailed dealing with chilly weather and long rounds.

In the 1963 rendition, in addition to entertainment stars like host Crosby, James Garner, Phil Harris, and Ray Milland, the tournament had a dream field. Gary Player already had arrived in the U.S. and had won in San Diego the week before. After 36 holes of the Crosby, Player, Arnold Palmer, Jack Nicklaus and Billy Casper all were in the top-10.

On Saturday, an atypically calm, sunny day, Nicklaus and Palmer both struggled on the back nine at the Pebble Beach Golf Links. Palmer shot 42 (he was 7 over for the last seven holes) and came in with a 77, while Nicklaus had a 41 on the back for a 76. Bob Duden, a 42-year-old club pro who putted croquet-style (a practice that would be banned in 1968) fired a 67 at the Monterey Peninsula Golf Club—the easiest of the three courses—to take the lead by one over Casper (who shot 73 at Pebble Beach) and Julius Boros (who scored 70 at the Cypress Point Club, the most difficult of the venues).

On Sunday, with the entire field at Pebble Beach, Duden, Casper, Bob Rosburg, Player, Nicklaus, Art Wall, and Dave Hill (resplendent in plus-fours like those favored by Payne Stewart a generation later) all were in the mix at the end. Despite another nice day, the course played hard, with difficult pin placements on greens that Casper called "crusty." Wall, Rosburg and Hill all finished with a 72-hole-score of 286.

On the famous par-5 18th hole, with the waters of the Pacific Ocean on the left, Casper sacrificed length for accuracy by using his 2-iron but hit into a fairway bunker, nonetheless. Two shots later, he still was 70 yards short of the green. He lofted an immaculate wedge to within 6 inches and tapped in for a par for a final round of 74 and a total of 285 to take the lead.

Duden was playing with the black-attired Player when a stray black poodle wandered across the green as they were looking over key putts on the 18th hole. Duden had a 12-foot putt for birdie that would have given him a share of the lead. The dog distracted him, and he missed, and he then missed a 2-footer coming back for bogey. He finished at 287. Player's 12-foot bid for a birdie stopped on the lip of the cup. He would finish one stroke out at 286.

Nicklaus came to 18 needing a birdie to pass Casper. After an excellent drive, he pushed his second shot well to the right. Nicklaus was partially blocked by a tree and the best he could do was hit a wedge 30 feet past the hole. His birdie putt slid 6 feet by, and he missed his par putt as well to give Casper the title. Nicklaus' 70 was the low round of the day.

Arnold Palmer had another poor round. He pulled his drive on the 18th hole onto the beach. By the time he finished, he had taken a quadruple-bogey 9 for a round of 76. To add insult to injury, Palmer learned he was disqualified for an infraction that occurred the previous day on the par-3 17th hole at Pebble Beach, when he improperly played a provisional ball after hitting his tee shot over the green into the water. The disqualification cost Palmer $525 in prize money, which did not disturb him as much as the fact that it broke a two-year, 47-tournament streak of finishing in the money (which had started after he missed the cut at the 1961 Los Angeles Open, when he had a 12 on one hole). It also moved Al Mengert, Johnny Pott, Charlie Sifford and Dean Refram up from out-of-the-money (all four left the Crosby with $55).

Like Palmer, Dale Douglass (who later would win three PGA Tour events, play on the 1969 U.S. Ryder Cup, and win 11 times on the Senior Tour) also left Pebble Beach without earning a dime. Douglass hit his drive on the par-4 10th hole onto the beach. His multiple attempts to put his ball back into play failed, and he incurred several unplayable lies in the process. He finally reached the fairway on his 14th shot. His 15th landed in a greenside bunker. It took Douglass two additional shots to get onto the green. From there, he two-putted for a 19. Only the legendary Tommy Armour—who had a 23 at the 1927 Shawnee Open—has recorded a higher score in a PGA-sanctioned event. Douglass parred the rest of the way in for a 92.

March

St. Petersburg Open

Raymond Floyd, a 20-year-old rookie from Fayetteville, North Carolina, joined the tour the previous November, but had failed to earn a cent to date. In the final round at St. Petersburg, he rallied from three shots back to win by one stroke over Dave Marr. Floyd would win 22 times in four decades, the last in 1992 when he was 49, and is enshrined in the World Golf Hall of Fame.

April

The Masters

On a hot and windy Thursday, five tour veterans whose careers stretched back to the 1950s, 1940s and even 1930s held the top spots: Mike Souchak, Bo Wininger (both with 69), Sam Snead, Ed Furgol, and Jay Hebert (70). Gene Sarazen—whose pro career dated to 1920, when he finished 30th at the U.S. Open—shot an impressive 74, the same as Jack Nicklaus and defending champion Arnold Palmer.

In the second round, temperatures were more pleasant, making for better scoring. Nicklaus fired a 66, the low round of the day, to tie Hebert at 140, one behind leader Souchak, a genial former Duke football player who won 13 times between 1955 and 1961. Wininger was two back and one ahead of Snead and Tony Lema. In a blurb that might shock anybody who has hoped to attend the Masters at any time over the last 40 years, *The Atlanta Constitution* reported on Saturday that 3,000 daily tickets would be available for sale both Saturday and Sunday.

Those who arrived early on Saturday were treated to a pairing of the 61-year-old Sarazen and Palmer, who had shot 73 on Friday to fall well behind the leaders (Sarazen faded with 81-80 the last two days). They also had to deal with a drenching, miserable all-day rain that sent scores soaring. Souchak fell far down the leaderboard with a 79. Only three players broke par (Julius Boros, Billy Casper, and Chen Ching-Po of Taiwan all shot 1-under 71). The rain was so intense that when Lema and Gary Player arrived on the 10th green, they discovered that the base of the cup was warped and that the pin could not be removed. This resulted in a 30-minute delay until the problem could be resolved. At the end of the day, Nicklaus' 74 gave him a one-shot lead over Furgol, the 1954 U.S. Open champion who at 46 was twice his age and who also shot 74.

Sunshine returned on Sunday, which lowered scores but not by much. The leaderboard at the top was cluttered for most of the day. Playing four groups ahead of Nicklaus, 50-year-old Snead birdied 14 and 15 to move a shot in front. However, he three-putted from 30 feet to bogey 16, then bogeyed 18. Snead finished third. Lema capped a splendid round of 70 with a birdie on 18 to finish at 1 under, making him the leader in the clubhouse.

On the 18th tee, Nicklaus needed a par to beat Lema. He slightly hooked his drive into the edge of the rough, into a footprint. Nicklaus was given relief, and he hit a good approach shot, but it went 35 feet past the hole, leaving him with a tough two-putt. His first went 3 feet past. Nicklaus then calmly steered his ball to the left edge, and it dropped in, giving him his second major win. He was the youngest Masters victor at that time.

May

Oklahoma City Open

In 1963, the PGA tour offered events for 42 weeks from early January through late November. No player could, or even wanted to, play every week. In the early and mid-1960s, all of the marquee names marked the Masters, the U.S. Open and the PGA Championship on their calendars, as well as certain non-majors that presented big payouts including the Tournament of Champions, the Thunderbird Classic, and the Cleveland Open. Another such tournament was the Colonial National Invitational in Fort Worth, which offered a decent purse and a challenging, well-manicured layout.

For the lesser events on the circuit, the sponsors knew they could not expect Palmer, Nicklaus, and Player to appear every year. In 1963, to the misfortune of its promoters, the Oklahoma City Open fell the week after the Colonial. Julius Boros won at Colonial by one stroke over Player and by two over Nicklaus. Palmer had a terrible weekend at the Colonial, opening with a 74, followed by three consecutive 75s for a 299 total. After the final round, he announced he needed a rest and would take some time off. Nicklaus and Player also skipped Oklahoma City.

Like Palmer, veteran Don Fairfield had a bad time at the Colonial. He went 84-74-71-77 for 306 in the no-cut event and took home the minimum $150 given to all contestants who finished 72 holes. Fairfield, too, looked forward to a break, but was cajoled into coming to the Oklahoma City Open by his friend, Ernie Vossler, who was one of the promoters. It was played at the Quail Creek Golf & Country Club, a brand new course that turned out not to be ready for a PGA event. In fact, the conditions may have been the worst seen of any course used for a tour event in the 1960s.

However, Fairfield was happy he played. He beat Boros by one stroke for his final tour win. In 1964, his last year as a full-time player, Fairfield had five top-10s (including a fourth-place finish at the Tournament of Champions), and 13 top-25s, earning $22,839, the most he would ever make on the tour. At the Bob Hope Desert Classic, Fairfield met a board member of the Eldorado Country Club in Indian Wells, California. They were looking for a head professional. Later, he was offered the job. Fairfield accepted and stayed there until retiring in 1997, only occasionally playing in tournaments for the rest of the 1960s.

Don Fairfield

A pro named Ernie Vossler was an old friend of ours. He was developing this golf course, Quail Creek, and they were putting on this tournament as a promotion with this development. This course was almost brand new. I think it was in its second year. Bermuda grass, but I don't think it had really taken hold yet. There was a lot of red clay, bare spots. I played the week before in the Colonial in Fort Worth. I was on my way home to take a week off. My wife was with me.

I get this call from Ernie. He says, "We haven't got anybody in this tournament. All the guys seem to be taking off. I got to have some guys here for this tournament." So, he says, "I can get you a free motel room," so I said OK. It was in terrible shape, the golf course. I remember Johnny Pott walked off the golf course with red mud all over his shoes. Anyway, we had an unusual week. We had a lot of wind, a tornado warning on Saturday night after we got through.

In the final round, the winds were blowing like the devil but I'm in good shape and had a halfway decent round, but nobody could have a good round. It was difficult conditions. The wind would shift in every direction, so the golf course was altogether different. The 18th hole went from a driver and a three wood to a driver and a six iron. Anyway, I had a good putting week and I beat Julius Boros by one stroke.

I had played nine years. I had a boy who was 5 years old. He'd been traveling with me and my wife most of the time. I was kind of tired of motels. When I left the tour, I really didn't play that much afterwards. You lose the sharpness. That's all there is to it. When I was playing, I was thinking about playing most of the time, even at nighttime. That was my job.

Chuck Courtney

Quail Creek was a brand new golf course, and it just wasn't ready. It was just a mess. It was in the spring in Oklahoma. It was a mudhole. Ernie Vossler and Joe Walser, they got into the development business early on. Here is this awful golf course. It's one of those things you don't forget. It was a really nice layout. It just wasn't ready. You needed about two summers of growth in Oklahoma for it to be any good. They should have put an "under repair" circle around the whole golf course.

June

Thunderbird Classic, Harrison, N.Y.

On June 13, 1963, 50-year-old Ben Hogan teed off with Don Fairfield and Dan Sikes in the first round of the Thunderbird Classic at the Westchester Country Club. It was his first tournament appearance in 13 months. He had been recuperating after undergoing orthopedic surgery to correct an issue with his shoulder, a vestige of his 1949 car accident.

Hogan appeared uncharacteristically cheerful, with a soft smile, and he occasionally exchanged pleasantries with the gallery. On one hole, he came up short with his approach. "Wrong club, Ben," a gallery member said to him. "No," Hogan replied. "I'm getting old."

The Thunderbird offered a total purse of $100,000 and an opportunity for the pros to tune up for the U.S. Open the following week near Boston, a short jaunt away, which enticed all of the Big Three to show up. All contended at one time or another at the Thunderbird. In the final round, Arnold Palmer missed a 4-foot birdie putt on the 18th hole that would have won the tournament outright, but he beat Paul Harney on the first hole of the sudden-death playoff.

Don Fairfield

We started on the 10th tee that day. It was a par-3, about 180 yards, and I was up first. I was nervous as hell. I stuck it right by the hole. (Hogan) looked over at me and said, "Nice shot." And that is all he said that day.

Anyway, I'll tell you why I can remember so well. He hit all 18 greens. And two par-5s in two. And he shoots 71. I think it was something like that. He couldn't putt at all from 2 feet away. He would freeze over the ball, maybe for one or two minutes. He couldn't get (the putter) back. It was pathetic. But he could still play at that age.

U.S. Open

The USGA staged the Open in New England for the first time in 38 years, at the Country Club in Brookline, Massachusetts. The purpose was to commemorate the 50th anniversary of the historic 1913 victory by 20-year-old American amateur Francis Ouimet over British icons Harry Vardon and Ted Ray in a playoff at Brookline. As in 1913, the 1963 U.S. Open would end in a three-way playoff.

With high winds and rain, only two players broke par 71 in the first round. The leader was Bob Gajda, an obscure 46-year-old club pro from suburban Detroit with rose-tinted glasses, who managed a 69. Gajda teed off early and completed his round before winds gusting up to 30 mph sent scores soaring. One stroke behind was Jacky Cupit, a 5-foot-9, 170-pound 25-year-old from Longview, Texan whose only two tour wins came in prestigious events, the 1961 Canadian Open and the 1962 Western Open. Julius Boros was in a group of four at even-par 71, along with 1957 PGA champion Lionel Hebert, Tony Lema, and Davis Love, Jr. (father of future star Davis Love III).

Arnold Palmer started with 73, one ahead of Gary Player. Defending champion Jack Nicklaus had a difficult start, bogeying the first three holes and double-bogeying the sixth on his way to a 76.

The high winds continued on Friday. Predictably, Gajda came back to earth with an 80 for a 36-hole score of 149, which still put him comfortably above the 152 cut line. Nicklaus was the most prominent casualty, missing the cut by one shot after shooting 77. He would not be absent from another U.S. Open weekend until 1985. Palmer and Dow Finsterwald had the low rounds of the day with 69s, to tie Cupit (who shot 72) for first at 142. Walter Burkemo, who won the 1953 PGA Championship but was now primarily a club pro in Michigan, and Dean Refram were at 143. Burkemo, 44, all but counted himself out, with 36 holes ahead on Saturday. "This is a hard walking course for me," he said. "Even now my legs are tired.

You really have to be in shape." Boros, Lema and Love were at 145.

As bad as the winds were over the first two rounds, it was worse on Saturday, with regular 40-mph gusts. "The worst conditions I ever played in," said Cupit after shooting 76 in the morning. Late on Saturday, Lema tossed grass into the air on the 16th tee and laughed when some of the strands blew left and others right, giving him no clue of the wind's direction. Over the first two rounds, only 13 players matched or bettered the course's par of 71. Nobody even touched par during the third and fourth rounds. Tommy Aaron shot a 91 in the morning. Bobby Nichols' low round for the tournament was 74 and he finished with a 72-hole total of 302, which still tied him for 15th.

Boros struggled to a 76 in the morning. He was a son of New England, born in Connecticut in 1920 to Hungarian immigrants. During World War II, Boros served in the U.S. Army Air Corps. He then attended junior college in Connecticut and worked for an accounting firm while he played the amateur circuit. He did not turn pro until he was 29. His first tour win was the 1952 U.S. Open at the Northwood Club in Dallas during the Hogan Age, and he won seven more times in the 1950s.

After winning the Colonial in 1960, Boros was winless over the next three years. After turning 43 in March, he had a renaissance, winning at the Colonial (five of his 18 tour victories were in Texas) and two weeks before the U.S. Open at the Buick Open. Boros had an effortless swing. Players and spectators unfamiliar with him were taken aback by how he would amble up to his ball and quickly hit it without taking a practice swing.

Coming to the 16th hole in the final round at Brookline, Boros was 11-over par for the championship, seemingly out of contention. However, he birdied 16 and 17, and parred 18 for a 72, which was the low round of the day (matched by Player and Gene Littler, who were not near the top), to finish at 293.

Palmer went 28 holes without a birdie, during which he triple-bo-geyed the long par-4 seventh in the third round after dumping a 2-iron approach into a pond, and then on the same hole in the afternoon hit his drive into the woods but miraculously escaped with a bogey. After a third-round 77, in the afternoon Palmer fought through the wind and, on the 16th hole, knocked in a 30-foot birdie to come within one stroke of leader Cupit. On 17, Palmer hit a good approach, 25 feet below the hole. His birdie putt just missed, going 2 feet past the hole. Shockingly, Palmer's short par putt lipped out.

Meanwhile, Cupit – playing right behind Palmer – appeared to have taken command of the tournament. With the cheers of Arnie's Army still ringing in his ears from Palmer's birdie on 16, Cupit answered with a 25-foot chip-in for a birdie from the rough off of the green on 15. After Palmer's bogey on 17, Cupit led by two.

On 17, in an effort to stay in the fairway, Cupit drove with his 3-wood, but he pulled his ball left, to the edge of a trap in deep rough. Again, playing conservatively, Cupit hit his second shot short of the green, leaving him with a manageable chip. However, he chipped too hard, his ball coming to rest on the fringe beyond the hole. His 25-foot downhill putt went 5 feet past the hole. His putt for bogey did not come close. With the double-bogey, Cupit's lead had vanished.

After a good drive on 18, Palmer's approach barely cleared a trap in front of the green, leaving him with a 40-foot putt for birdie. He hit a very poor putt, 6 feet short of the hole. As he was surveying his putt for par, loud cheers from the partisan gallery alerted him that Cupit's double-bogey on 17 had been posted on the scoreboard next to the green. Now, if Palmer could make his par putt, he would join Boros in the clubhouse at 293. Palmer appeared to take nervous breaths. After assuming his putting stance, he stepped away and picked up a leaf that had blown from an elm tree next to the green and looked at the line again. He retook his stance and drilled the putt into the center of the cup.

Now, Cupit needed a par on 18 to join Palmer and Boros. He pushed his drive into the right rough, but hit an excellent approach, leaving him with a 15-foot birdie putt to win. Cupit just missed on the low side and joined Palmer and Boros at 293, 9-over par, the highest 72-hole score at a U.S. Open in 28 years. There would be an 18-hole playoff on Sunday.

Photo 30: *Jacky Cupit, Julius Boros and Arnold Palmer talk with a USGA official before the 1963 U.S. Open playoff. (United States Golf Association)*

The wind diminished significantly during the playoff. Cupit briefly held the lead after two holes, but double-bogeyed the third, where Palmer bogeyed. Boros then held a one-shot lead, which he would never relinquish. Palmer took himself out of the running when he triple-bogeyed 11 to fall seven back. Boros double-bogeyed 13, but that only cut his lead over Cupit to three shots, his final margin of victory. Boros scored 70 for his second U.S. Open victory, over Cupit (73) and Palmer (76), who suffered his second straight Open playoff loss. Boros was the second oldest Open winner ever up to that time, a month younger than Ted Ray when he won in 1920.

Bobby Nichols

At Brookline, it was a high-scoring Open because of the weather and the course itself, which wasn't easy. I can remember when you missed the green, around the edges the rough was extremely high. So, it was really tough chipping if you missed the green. And the greens were relatively little. It was quite a tournament. It was a high-scoring Open because of the weather, and the course itself wasn't easy. The rough was really brutal.

Tony Lema and I were in the locker room, which looks down on the 18th hole. We got through playing, and Jacky Cupit was coming up the 18th. I couldn't remember if we were looking out the window or had stepped out on a terrace. He had double-bogeyed 17 and was still tied for the lead. On 18 he hit, I think, a 5-iron to the green, I think, 15 feet short of the hole. He hit a putt. We looked right at it and we could see it very good. That putt was going straight in the hole. We thought he made it. Somehow, it leaked out on the right side. Of course, he lost in the playoff. I can still see that putt. I don't see how it stayed out of the hole, but it did. I think it really affected Jacky Cupit's career from then on.

Tommy Aaron

It was a very difficult course and difficult conditions. In the third round, I started very badly, and I started making bogeys and I couldn't stop that no matter what kind of shot I hit. If I missed a green, I might get it on and take three putts to get it in to make a double bogey, and then next time I might hit a pretty good second shot and then three-putt, so I couldn't stop the bleeding.

I never thought about withdrawing. My dad always said, "You've got to have some dignity. You have to finish the round." That's what you sign up for. You don't withdraw just because you're having a bad day.

July

Western Open

On Monday, July 3, the Beverly Country Club in Chicago played host to a marquee match featuring Arnold Palmer and the winners of 1963's two majors to date: Masters champion Jack Nicklaus, and U.S. Open champion Julius Boros. They happened to tie for first place at the Western Open. That threesome would have commanded a substantial fee for an exhibition.

After the completion of Sunday's round, Nicklaus, Boros and Palmer gathered to pose for press photographs in advance of Monday's 18-hole playoff. One unfortunate photographer, who clearly was not in his element, looked at Palmer and asked, "And what is your name?," to the delight of Nicklaus and Boros.

Palmer won the playoff. All three contributed their share of the playoff gate to the Chick Evans Scholarship Fund.

Canadian Open

Heading into the Canadian Open at the Scarboro Golf and Country Club in Toronto, Ed Moehling had won only $250 for the year. After the first round, the 6-foot-3, 22-year-old blond from Illinois may have been dreaming of stardom. He shot 66 to take a three-stroke lead over Doug Ford, Tommy Aaron, and Fred Hawkins. "That's the best I've shot since joining the pro tour in January," he told the press. "In fact, my average score for the opening round is 77 so I now consider myself 11 strokes under par." Even in 1963, starting a tournament with an average score of 77 was not going to win one much money.

In the second round, Moehling had a personal par of 77, and finished with 78-86 for a 72-hole total of 306, 27 strokes out of first place to take home $10 from the $50,000 purse. He would end his career with total earnings of $7,358.

Photo 31: Doug Ford. (Source unknown)

In the second round, the 40-year-old Ford shot 67 to take a two-stroke lead over 48-year-old Herman Keiser, the winner of the 1946 Masters who rarely played the tour any more.

Born Douglas Fortunato in West Haven, Connecticut, his Italian-American father—a teaching pro—shortened his surname to Ford to stem possible prejudice. Ford was raised in Upper Manhattan, and then in Yonkers. He sharpened his game hustling at the Van Cortlandt Park public course in the Bronx and did not turn pro until 1949, when he was 27.

After Ben Hogan started his long, graceful departure from the regular scene following his Triple Slam in 1953, no American golfer was better than Ford for the remainder of the 1950s. He won 14 times during the decade, including the 1955 PGA Championship and the 1957 Masters. The PGA win was at match play. In the final, he faced Cary Middlecoff. Ford may have been the fastest player in history, and Middlecoff the slowest. On a hot day outside of Detroit, Ford had his 10-year-old son carry a portable chair for his father's use during Middlecoff's interminable pauses while lining up putts.

Although Ford was masterful with the wedge and putter, he was a short hitter. As Arnold Palmer, Jack Nicklaus and others made the power game fashionable in the 1960s, Ford continued to have success, winning four times between 1960 and 1962, including a play-off victory over Palmer at Indianapolis in 1961. Palmer and Nicklaus skipped the Canadian Open to prepare for the Open Championship.

In the third round, Ford maintained his two-shot advantage. Moe Norman, the quirky straight-hitting Canadian pro, was three shots back. In the final round, Ford held off a challenge from Al Geiberger to win by one stroke. It would be the last of Ford's 19 tour victories.

Don Fairfield

Doug was a very smart player, positioning the ball on the good side of the fairway and the good side of the hole. He made mistakes, of course, but he scrambled around the golf course. A great wedge player. He was smart, like a street fighter. Most people don't realize that Doug Ford won more tournaments and more money between 1950 and 1960 than any other pro.

He was steady and he could adapt. Doug became a good friend of mine. We traveled together part of the time. He could adapt to any green. He'd go from a Bermuda green, slow and sticky, to a fast green, like the Masters. He could adapt very quickly to conditions, water, wind, whatever it was. He could create something out of nothing.

The Open Championship

Photo 32: Phil Rodgers.
(Royal & Ancient Photographs)

Long before he became known as a short-game guru, whose disciples included Jack Nicklaus, Phil Rodgers was an excellent player. The one-time Marine from San Diego was brash and loud. Physically, he resembled Nicklaus, blond and chunky, and at times was his equal on the course.

In 1962, Rodgers was a distant third to Arnold Palmer in his Open Championship debut, which whetted his appetite to return in 1963 with a still-small U.S. contingent at the Royal Lytham & St. Annes Golf Club in England. Most American pros opted to play at the Hot Springs Invitational or rest before the PGA Championship the following week. Those who showed up were required to become accustomed to the sight and sound of steam engines pulling passenger railcars along the course, to and from the nearby resort city of Blackpool.

The reserved British gallery—small by Open standards (only 20,000 came for the entire week)—did not know what to make of the emotive Rodgers, who wisecracked his way around the course for a 67, but at least some were amused. At the end of a day that started with heavy rain and ended in brilliant sunshine, Rodgers was tied with four-time Open winner Peter Thomson, one shot ahead of the left-handed Bob Charles of New Zealand and 48-year-old Tom Haliburton of England. Nicklaus shot a 1-over-par 71. Palmer, who oddsmakers made a 2-1 favorite to win for the third year in a row, struggled with his driver, shooting 76, with 41 on the back nine.

Warm sunshine on England's Irish Sea coast provided for good scoring conditions for the second round and allowed Rodgers (with 68) and Thomson (69) to keep the first two positions atop the leaderboard. Nicklaus shot 67 to move within three. Charles followed his first round 68 with a 72 and was five back. Palmer was unable to take advantage of the sublime conditions, managing only a 71 for a 36-hole total of 147, 12 shots behind Rodgers and out of contention. Tony Jacklin of England, who had just turned 19 years old and was playing in his first Open, was at 145. He would finish 30th.

On Open Friday, Charles shot 66 in the morning (the low round of the tournament) to take a one-stroke lead over Thomson. Nicklaus and Rodgers were tied, two strokes back. In the afternoon, Nicklaus was 2 under for the day and 4 under for the tournament, and in prime position to win after he sank a 17-foot birdie putt on the 16th hole. However, his 2-iron approach on the par-4 17th flew over the green into deep rough. As he was preparing to hit his shot, a train blew its whistle. Nicklaus stepped away, and when he returned to his ball he fluffed the chip and made bogey. On 18, Nicklaus drove into one of the 205 bunkers on the course, resulting in another bogey. His 72-hole score of 278, 2-under par, would leave him one stroke back, in third place.

Photo 33: Bob Charles. (Historic Images)

Playing together two groups behind Nicklaus, Rodgers and Charles were neck-and-neck throughout the day and were tied coming to the last hole. Both were on the green in two. Charles' 30-foot putt slid 30 inches past the hole. Rodgers had a 15-foor-putt to win but left it two feet short. He immediately stepped up to knock it in and almost missed, his ball wobbling momentarily before falling in. Charles calmly stroked his ball in to force a 36-hole playoff then required under R&A rules (it would be the last).

Saturday was sunny and breezy. Charles' one-putted 12 of the first 20 holes to take a commanding five-shot lead. He hooked his ball out-of-bounds on the 21st hole, and Rodgers took advantage, narrowing the gap to one shot through 24 holes. However, Rodgers double-bogeyed the next hole. On the 26th hole, Rodgers rammed in a 50-footer from the back of the green for a birdie and happily pranced about. Charles immediately followed with a 30-foot birdie of his own and stoically walked to the next tee. Rodgers was done. Charles pulled away for an eight-shot victory (140-148) to become the first left-hander to win a Grand Slam title.

PGA Championship

The 1963 PGA Championship was played in oppressive heat on the Blue Course of the Dallas Athletic Club in Texas. In the first round, aided by a hole-in-one, unknown Dick Hart—who had never finished higher than 30th in a tour event—shot 66 to take a three-shot lead. Among the five in second place with 69s were Masters champion Jack Nicklaus, U.S. Open champion Julius Boros, and Open Championship winner Bob Charles. The day could not have started any better for Arnold Palmer, who eagled the par-5 first hole. After that, Palmer required 36 putts to complete his round of 74.

On Friday, Hart was unbothered by the 100-degree heat, the wind, the fact that his wife was home in Illinois expecting to give birth any moment, or his unfamiliar position in contention. He shot 71 to maintain his three-stroke lead over Boros, Tony Lema and Shelley Mayfield, a 39-year-old club pro who had some success on the tour in the 1950s, winning three times. Nicklaus was one shot further back with a 73; he played flawlessly from tee to green but required 39 putts.

Don Fairfield and Jack Fleck played nine holes before deciding it was too hot and that a better option was to take the rest of the tournament off. Jim Ferree (not to be confused with Jim Ferrier), shot a decent 74 in the first round but was overcome by the heat after 12 holes of the second round and was escorted off the course.

Palmer struggled again, managing a 73 that left him nine shots back of Hart. He played with Bruce Crampton, the 27-year-old Australian with the unusually unpleasant disposition, who also shot 73 after a first round 70. "Those people were around there munching sandwiches and making a lot of noise," he complained about Arnie's Army. "I had three near unplayable lies before I ever got to the green. It burned me up."

Crampton was the ultimate grinder. In 1962, he played 38 tournaments in a row and the PGA marked his 28th consecutive start in 1963. In the third round, with temperatures as high as 105 degrees and no wind, but without having to contend with Arnie's Army, Crampton fired a 65 to take a two-shot lead over Dow Finsterwald, who shot 66. Nicklaus was three back after a 69. Gary Player was poised to go even lower than Crampton until 15. While preparing to hit a 6-foot putt for par, he was disturbed by a camera. After snapping at the photographer, he missed the putt. On 16, he three-putted for another bogey, including a miss from 1 foot. Player settled for a 67, which was eight shots back.

A 67 by Floridian Dave Ragan, who won twice in 1962, put him in the mix, four behind Crampton. Hart ran out of steam with a 76 to fall six back. A noteworthy competitor on the weekend was Bill Ezinicki, a 38-year-old club pro from Massachusetts. He was far better known in his native Canada as a gritty winger who helped the Toronto Maple Leafs win three consecutive Stanley Cup titles from 1947 to 1949. Ezinicki shot 74-71 in the first two rounds. However, on the second hole of the third round he put four balls into a pond on his way to a 12. He shot 83.

In Sunday's final round, Crampton hung around for most of the day but was done in by a three-putt bogey on 16. Finsterwald faded with a 72. Ragan played well until a poor drive on 17 went behind a television tower. His second shot went over the green and he bogeyed. Meanwhile, Nicklaus's putter was hot. He started with an 18-footer for eagle on the first hole and picked up another stroke with a 12-foot putt for birdie on 8. A 30-footer for birdie on 15 put him in the driver's seat. After pars on 16 and 17, he drove into the rough on 18 and was required to play short of a pond fronting the green. From there, Nicklaus pitched to within three feet. He made that putt for 68 and a 72-hole total of 279, two strokes ahead of Ragan. It gave Nicklaus his second major of the year, and third overall (one each in the American Grand Slam events).

August

American Golf Classic

At the Firestone Country Club, Johnny Pott won by four strokes over Arnold Palmer, who for the first time in the 1960s had failed to win any of the majors. However, Palmer's $4,600 in winnings at the AGC gave him $101,555 for the year, making him the first tour player in PGA history to go over the $100,000 mark.

September

Denver Open

Dave Hill's undeniable skill as a golfer often was overshadowed by his tempestuous personality. He was a hard-drinking, chain-smoking roughneck from Jackson, Michigan. Hill's "brain and mouth were connected by a superhighway," *Golfweek* scribe James Achenbach wrote after Hill's death in 2011 from emphysema.

Photo 34: Young Dave Hill, before his demons surfaced. (Paul V Young)

At the 1966 Thunderbird Classic, knowing he was not going to make the cut, Hill carelessly and petulantly wrote 108 on his scorecard for the 18th hole, believing the error would result in his disqualification. It did not. Instead, he was credited with a score of 178 for the round, which did not help his scoring average for the year. In 1969, he was suspended and fined for yelling at a tour official about slow play in Jacksonville. At the 1970 U.S. Open, he criticized the layout at the Hazeltine National Golf Club (where he would finish second to Tony Jacklin) and was fined. In 1971, he was suspended for throwing his ball out of a trap at the Colonial and signing an incorrect scorecard. Hill did not mellow with age; when he was 54, he got into a fistfight with J.C. Snead on the driving range at a Senior Tour event.

But in 1963, Hill had not met most of his demons. He had won three times on tour, including the Denver Open in 1961. Hill appeared set to win at Denver again when, after rounds of 68-67-69, he led Jacky Cupit by two shots, and Jay Hebert and Chi Chi Rodriguez by three. However, in the final round, Hill struggled to a 75. On the 18th tee, he was out of it and urged playing companion Rodriguez—who was leading by two shots—to play safe. Instead, Rodriguez ripped a 325-yard drive, hit an iron to the green and two-putted for his first PGA tour win.

Photo 35: Chi Chi Rodriguez.
(Walter Iooss, Jr.)

Chi Chi Rodriguez

In the final round of the 1963 Denver Open, I was playing with Dave Hill. On the 18th tee, I was ahead by two shots, I think. Dave said, "I want to see you win. Hit a 2-iron." I said, "David, see all these people? They paid to see me hit a driver." I hit a frozen rope. Had a flip wedge, made par, and won. It was my first win. I think I got $5,300. I thought I was the richest guy in the world. My mother was living in the Bronx. I bought her a house in Puerto Rico.

October

Canada Cup/Australian Open

The annual Canada Cup (later World Cup) featured two-man teams representing golfing nations. The United States won five of the first 10 competitions since the 1953 inception of the event. In 1963, it was held in late October at Saint-Nom-la-Breteche near Paris, a fairly new course on land that once was Louis XIV's farmyard.

The United States sent its best, Arnold Palmer and Jack Nicklaus. Palmer had completed the U.S. portion of his schedule, winning first-place money of $26,000 at the Whitemarsh Open near Philadelphia in early October. With his earlier victories at the Thunderbird ($25,000) and Cleveland ($22,000), Palmer had captured the three largest PGA tour cash prizes of 1963.

Nicklaus won the week before the Canada Cup at the Sahara Invitational by one stroke over Al Geiberger to put him close to the $100,000 mark before he made the long trip from Las Vegas to Paris. After three rounds of the scheduled 72 holes, the Americans were tied with the surprising duo from Spain, Sebastian Miguel and Ramon Sota, the latter of whom was Seve Ballesteros' uncle and who in 1965 would finish sixth at the Masters. South Africa and Australia were close behind.

Thick fog resulted in postponement of Sunday's final round until Monday. The delay caused logistical problems for six contestants: Palmer, Nicklaus, Gary Player, Bruce Crampton, Bruce Devlin and Bob Charles. All were due to fly to Australia from London on Qantas airlines to compete in the Australian Open, at a time when flights from Europe to Australia were limited. When the fog did not lift on Monday, the final round was shortened to nine holes. On the sixth hole, Nicklaus blasted from a bunker into the cup 70 feet away to help the Americans secure a three-shot victory over Spain.

Nicklaus and Palmer decided to pass on the grueling trip required for them to play the Australian Open, with no guarantee that they would arrive on time. Their planned entry was part of a junket organized by their manager, Mark McCormack, who was unsuccessful in efforts to convince the Australian Open organizers to delay the tournament by one day to accommodate his clients. Palmer and Nicklaus later made the trip Down Under to keep other commitments.

Photo 36: *Bruce Devlin.*
(Historic Images)

Player, Crampton, Devlin, and Charles did make the trip after the draw was revised to give them late tee times on Thursday, though Crampton caught a bad cold en route and withdrew. Player and Devlin—who were under contract to Slazenger—flew from Paris to New York, New York to Los Angeles, Los Angeles to Honolulu, Honolulu to Fiji, Fiji to Sydney, Sydney to Melbourne, ending with a helicopter ride to the 18th fairway of the Royal Melbourne Golf Club, arriving in time for a short nap before teeing off in the first round. The entire trip took more than 40 hours.

Player proved himself to be the ultimate road warrior, winning by seven shots over Devlin, for the third of what would be seven Australian Open titles.

Bruce Devlin

They put us off last. They changed the pairings, so that Player and I could tee off. They met the plane at the Melbourne airport and put us in the helicopter and flew us down there.

I will always remember when we left Paris, Player had no money, no cash. I paid all the expenses. There was a guy by the name of (Arthur) Huxley, who was the players' representative from Slazenger. The first thing that happened when Player and I got off the helicopter was Player said to him, "Hey, you need to give Bruce X number of dollars because I didn't have any cash when we left Paris," which I thought was pretty funny.

Interestingly enough, Gary won that year and I finished second.

Gary Player

We were playing in France, and we were fogged out. Arnold and Jack said they weren't going. I took a chance. The travel agent said, "I can get you to Royal Melbourne three hours before you play." Big time change. You must remember, in those days, you didn't have the convenience of (private) jets like we do today. I arrived there three hours before, I'd never seen the golf course in my life. They gave me new clubs and a different ball. And I went out there and won the Australian Open by seven shots.

November

W.D. & H.O Wills Golf Classic

After making their way to Sydney, Australia, Arnold Palmer eked out a win over Jack Nicklaus. The ninth hole of the Lakes course, a par-4 measuring 397 yards, was key. In the final round, with the wind at his back, Nicklaus impressed the gallery by clearing a lake with a 370-yard drive. However, he hit a poor chip and could only make par.

Palmer was aided by his knowledge of a local rule on the same hole. His second shot landed against a tall tree in back of the green. However, fortuitously for Palmer, there were two small staked trees within two club lengths of his ball. He requested and was granted a free drop and salvaged a par. Palmer beat Nicklaus by two strokes.

Frank Sinatra Open Invitational

Louisville native Frank Beard won the Frank Sinatra Invitational at the Canyon Club in Palm Springs, by one shot over Jerry Steelsmith, for his first tour victory.

Not until 1965 did Bob Hope add his name to the Desert Classic held in Palm Springs every February. The Bing Crosby Pro-Am then was the only tournament hosted by a celebrity. Sinatra intended his tournament to be an annual affair. He offered a big purse ($50,000 in total) and gave copper-plated Toney Penna putters with his likeness on the head to the participants, who could hobnob with A-List celebrities such as Sinatra's fellow Rat Packers, Dean Martin and Sammy Davis, Jr. (both of whom, in time, would host their own PGA events). However, neither money, nor trinkets, nor stars could induce the Big Three to depart from their plans to play in Australia.

Beard, who was required to qualify on Monday, earned $9,000 for his win. Steelsmith birdied 18 to take second place by himself by one shot over Dow Finsterwald and Mason Rudolph.

Photo 37: Frank Sinatra, Jill St. John, and Frank Beard. (Lester Nehamkin, MPTVIMAGES.com)

Although Sinatra had called his tournament "A shakedown cruise for many years of golf tournaments to come," it turned out to be a one-off event.

Jerry Steelsmith

I had a number of seconds, no wins. Frank hadn't won a tournament either. So, when he beat me by a shot, that was his first win, and his career took off after that. I had other seconds but, you know, seconds are not firsts. I think I finished second five times. I didn't lose it. He was a stroke ahead of me at the beginning of the final round. And then he birdied the 17th hole. So, he went ahead by two with one hole to play, and then I birdied the last hole, and it didn't make any difference.

I lost in a playoff in the 1964 Almaden Open in California. It was an 18-hole playoff, with Billy Casper and Pete Brown. I didn't play good in that playoff. I think they tied after 18 holes and went on for sudden death. I think Billy Casper won that one. Most if not all of my second-place finishes were by a stroke.

Frank Beard

I had to qualify for the tournament on Monday. I shot 77. I was getting ready to go to my car to leave when a golfer named Bud Holscher asked me what I shot. When I told him 77, he said, "You better not leave." The wind picked up in the afternoon, and I ended up making the field.

Jerry Steelsmith was a good player. I don't know why he never got over the top to win. I was playing the final round with Steely and Bob Rosburg. We get to the 18th tee at the Canyon Club. It was a tight course, with out of bounds on both sides all 18 holes. I had a two-shot lead. Rosburg hadn't said anything all day. He came up to me and said, "Don't fuck it up now. Hit an iron." I had been driving the ball good, but I hit an iron into the middle of the fairway. I had a 160-yard shot to the hole, which would have been a 6-iron for me. Then, I remembered reading an article in Golf World by Doug Ford where he wrote that when you have a lot of adrenaline, hit one club less. So, I hit 7-iron 20 feet from the hole. I wasn't the type to follow advice, but I did twice there. I two-putted for par. Steely birdied, so I won by one shot. I remember after sinking the final putt, I looked down at my shirt and could see my heart beating. I think that's the only time that has happened.

At the awards ceremony, I was standing behind Jill St. John, Frank Sinatra, Sammy Davis, Jr., Joey Bishop, and Dean Martin. The whole Rat Pack was there. Jill St. John had her arm around my waist, and I remember she had a medallion the size of four silver dollars between her breasts, and that was all I could think about.

Afterwards, there was a concert. As I was sitting by myself, I realized that this whole tournament was about Frank Sinatra and his friends, not the golfers. I asked for a car and was taken to my hotel. Across the street there was a restaurant called Sambo's. I went there and for dinner I had pancakes by myself. I had won $9,000, which doubled my money for the year and made me exempt for 1964. The next morning, I checked out of my hotel, caught a plane, and went home.

Cajun Classic

As usual, most top players skipped the season-ending Cajun Classic in Lafayette, Louisiana, which offered a total purse of only $20,000. The field consisted of some players scrapping to make the top 60 on the money so they might avoid Monday qualifying in 1964. However, Jack Nicklaus, weary from his recent travels to Europe and Australia, appeared with a mission. His winnings for the year were $98,990, and he wanted to join Arnold Palmer in the $100,000 club.

During the second round, on November 22, 1963, word arrived that President John F. Kennedy had been shot in Dallas. Nicklaus learned of the assassination while on the ninth green. Play was halted. Tournament chairman Earl Flatt wanted to stop the proceedings. Lafayette was in a region atypical of the Deep South, where many area residents, including tour pros and former PGA champions Jay and Lionel Hebert—the unofficial hosts—were of French-Canadian ancestry and, like the slain president, Catholic. Playing under the circumstances was patently disrespectful. However, Flatt was overruled by tour officials. Play resumed and continued until the round was completed. "Few of the pros cared to talk about their golf scores," the Associated Press understatedly reported.

After a pause on Saturday, the tournament was completed with 36 holes on Sunday, just as the scheduled NFL games were played (to his dying day, NFL Commissioner Pete Rozelle said not postponing those games was the biggest mistake of his long career). The reason the PGA Tour felt compelled to complete the little tournament is lost to history, though the need to accommodate those players hovering around the top-60 mark must have been a consideration.

Rex Baxter Jr. won for the only time in his career. "We played unnoticed," he acknowledged. Dave Marr had a 5-foot putt on 18 that would have resulted in a three-way tie for fifth place with Nicklaus and would have left Nicklaus $10 short of $100,000. Marr missed the putt, and Nicklaus finished the year with earnings of $100,040.

Tommy Aaron

I remember leaving the course and I heard JFK had been shot in Dallas. I was shocked. It was a distraction, to say the least, for such a terrible thing to happen.

Don Fairfield

I was on the 17th hole, and it was raining like hell. (Tournament director Earl Flatt) came out and said, "President Kennedy has been shot." He said, "We're going to continue and finish the round." That was really a shock.

Jack Nicklaus

I was on the ninth fairway. We were all in shock. We didn't know if they were going to cancel the tournament or not cancel the tournament. It wasn't the favorite thing to have happen in your life, to have your president assassinated. But you got to do what you got to do.

1964

January

San Diego Open

Art Wall, Jr., age 40, won his first tournament since 1960 by two shots over Tony Lema and Bob Rosburg.

Chuck Courtney

My first event was the 1964 San Diego Open. I got a sponsor's exemption because I'm a local guy, and I made the cut. And who do I get paired with on Sunday but Arnold Palmer.

There was no Q-School. What you had to do was show the PGA of America, who ran the tour, unlike now, that you had some financial responsibility. Which was essentially a letter from some backers that you had a few bucks in the bank, and a couple of local golf professionals, members of the PGA, from your local area, San Diego in my case, La Jolla actually, to sign up that you're kind of an OK guy, and they'd let you start to play. So, you'd try Monday qualifying.

In those days, if you made the cut, no matter your status, you're automatically in the next week. After making the cut at San Diego, my second tournament was the Crosby. It was always such a thrill to play in the Crosby. It was so wonderful because we played Cypress Point. Between Cypress Point and Pebble Beach, golf doesn't get any better than that. Especially on a clear, beautiful day.

I made the cut again. In the final round, I'm playing with Bob Goalby and Julius Boros. By the way, Julius Boros was a wonderful guy and a spectacular player. So, the weather was horrible, and we got down to the 10th green, which was as close as you could get to the little town of Carmel. Julius looked at Goalby and me and said, "You know, I've had enough of this." He and his caddie clambered down the cliffs and went to their motel, which was right down about three blocks from the beach. He already was a U.S. Open champion twice, so I guess he could afford to do that.

So, I made the cut many times and the few times that I didn't I usually was successful in whatever Monday qualifying there was. You probably heard the expression—there was a whole lot of us out here—called "rabbits." If you missed the cut and you weren't exempt, you went out to play in a Monday qualifying, and there frequently were a significant number of places on Monday, 10, 15, 20, maybe 30 sometimes.

If you didn't qualify on Monday, you'd go hang out, beg to play a little golf and practice, go stay with some friends, find a cheap motel, and wait for your next Monday if you were a long ways from home. Here I am in the Southwest corner of the United States, where I'm from, and if I'm somewhere in South Carolina, well, I just got to figure it out.

Lucky International Open

In the final round, Chi Chi Rodriguez was in a pairing with Arnold Palmer. Most of the gallery followed the group and were surprised when Rodriguez—5 foot-7 and 120 pounds—outdrove Palmer on several holes. Palmer shot 70 on Sunday to finish third. On the 18th hole, Rodriguez sank a 10-foot putt for a birdie to get within one shot of Don January, the 54-hole leader who was playing in the final group. Needing only a par 4 on 18, January hit his approach to 30 feet of the hole. His birdie putt came up 4 feet short. January missed the par putt, necessitating a playoff with Rodriguez.

At the time, many of the regular tour events—including the Lucky—still had an 18-hole playoff, though sudden-death playoffs were becoming the vogue. When there was an 18-hole playoff, the participants were given a share of the playoff gate in addition to their prize winnings. Rodriguez beat January in the playoff by one shot.

Chi Chi Rodriguez

In the third round, I played with Arnold Palmer and shot 65. Then I shot 66, which tied me with Don January for first. We had an 18-hole playoff, which I won. They gave both of us $1,300 from the playoff gate, in addition to the $7,500 I won.

February

Phoenix Open

On the night of February 9, 1964, an audience of 73 million Americans tuned in to see four young men from Liverpool, England, known as the Beatles, appear on the Ed Sullivan Show for the first time. It helped salve the wounds of a nation still recovering from the trauma of the assassination of their young president less than three months earlier, and ushered in a cultural phenomenon never before seen in popular music.

Earlier in the day, Jack Nicklaus—who, like Beatles John Lennon and Ringo Starr, was born in 1940—shot 66 to rally from three strokes back in the final round to win the Phoenix Open. Bob Brue, who made the field as the last alternate, finished second. It was the ninth tour victory for the 24-year-old Nicklaus.

April

The Masters

In the cool of Thursday morning, 62-year-old Gene Sarazen was among the early leaders before finishing with a 73. By the end of the day, a quintet topped the leaderboard with 69: Arnold Palmer, Gary Player, Kel Nagle, Bob Goalby and Davis Love Jr. Defending champion Jack Nicklaus did not miss a green but, plagued by poor putting, could manage only a 71.

Love was a club pro from Charlotte, North Carolina who qualified for the Masters by virtue of his 14th place finish in the U.S. Open at Brookline. Slight and bespectacled, he was described by Jim Becker as looking "more like a baffled bookkeeper than a golfer." His wife was home waiting for the delivery of their first child, who would be born the day after the Masters concluded. The boy would be named Davis Love III and would play at Augusta many times. Davis Jr. fell back with a 75 in the second round and would finish 43rd.

After winning seven times in 1963, Palmer was winless in 1964. He had announced that he quit smoking in January, and it had been suggested his slump was a byproduct. On Friday, he showed no signs of nicotine withdrawal. Almost unrecognizable in a garish cardigan with vertical white stripes and a visor, Palmer birdied four of the final six holes, including the 18th, for a 68 and two-round total of 137. None of the other first round co-leaders could keep up with Palmer. Player managed a 72 for sole possession of second place, four shots back. Nicklaus shot 73 for a 144 total, seven shots behind.

Teeing off at 11:42 a.m. and playing immediately behind Palmer, Sarazen was visibly frustrated by the clamor created by Arnie's Army. He was 7 over on the front nine, and when he found his ball in the pond next to the 16th green, he picked up and called it a day. Later, Sarazen was furious that his withdrawal was categorized as "misconduct" on a CBS radio broadcast. "I was guilty of nothing but exhaustion," he said. He had been told by an official that he would have to return to the tee and hit his third shot from there. Sarazen also complained about his tee time and having to play behind Palmer. "I'm all for an earlier starting time for all us old masters," he said.

On Saturday, Arnie's Army came out in droves. About 40,000 patrons attended, most of whom followed Palmer. Masters' officials took the then-unusual step of closing the gates at 1 p.m., a half-hour before Palmer started his third round, only allowing those with tickets onto the premises. Palmer responded to the adulation with a 69 to increase his lead to five shots over Bruce Devlin of Australia, who shot 67. Ben Hogan, 51, also shot 67 to ascend to the first page of the leader board.

Sunday was anti-climactic. Nobody made a charge, and it became clear that Palmer would win a record fourth green jacket. The only drama was whether Palmer would shoot 67 and break Hogan's 72-hole record of 274. Palmer was excellent, but not spectacular, with five birdies and three bogeys, for a 70 and a total of 276. Nicklaus shot 67 in the final round but that only put him in a tie for second with Dave Marr, six shots back.

Palmer was only 34, but unfathomably the 1964 Masters would be the last of his seven major championships.

May

Waco Turner Open

While Jack Nicklaus was winning the Tournament of Champions in Las Vegas, history was made at the Waco Turner Open in Burneyville, Oklahoma, which had a much less select field.

The Waco Turner Open, also known as the Poor Boy's Open, was the quirkiest tour event in the 1960s. Its namesake and sponsor, Waco Franklin Turner, was an interesting, somewhat shadowy figure. He was a member of the Chickasaw Nation, a World War I veteran, and a successful oilman. Turner designed and built a golf course on land his father had purchased in 1894 in what was then known as Indian Territory. In the early 1950s, he and his wife, Opie, sponsored the Ardmore Open, a PGA tournament in the small city of Ardmore, Oklahoma, which had a big purse for the day and attracted decent fields, until Turner had a falling out with the PGA tour and pulled the plug.

The Poor Boy's Open ran from 1961 to 1964, always opposite the Tournament of Champions, which guaranteed that it never would have a very good field, and also that it never would have a repeat winner because the victor would become eligible to play in the following year's TOC. In 1962, a then-winless Jack Nicklaus played at the Waco Turner and finished third. After the 1962 rendition, Opie Turner's participation ceased when she died under mysterious circumstances. She was shot twice in the side and succumbed from complications. The local authorities concluded that the wounds were self-inflicted.

Turner did not charge admission. Still, few spectators showed up. Turner did not care, as he held the Poor Boy's Open for his own amusement. He would drive around the course in his Cadillac to follow the action, or survey from a small plane that buzzed around the course. The purse was $20,000, which Turner supplemented by paying bonuses of $100 for the low round each day, $50 for an eagle, $25 for a chip-in, $15 for a birdie, and $500 for a hole-in-one. Even with Nicklaus, Arnold Palmer, Gary Player and their ilk in Las Vegas, there still were some notable names in Burneyville in 1964. Bruce Crampton was there; he had won the Texas Open the week before, after the cut-off date for TOC eligibility. So were Raymond Floyd, Tommy Aaron, Miller Barber, and Dan Sikes.

Photo 38: Pete Brown.
(Mississippi Today)

The big winner after the first round was Bert Weaver, a 32-year-old tour veteran from Beaumont, Texas, who shot 67, for which he earned $100 for the low round, plus $85 for his three birdies and an eagle. Second round honors went to Moon Mullins, a Californian who would win only $5,830 official money for his career but earned $170 in unofficial money on Friday, splitting the low round money with Terry Dill after both shot 67, plus $120 for his eight birdies. After three rounds, Dudley Wysong, Jr. led by one stroke over two African-American players, Charlie Sifford and Pete Brown.

On Sunday, Brown shot 70 to win by one stroke over Sikes. Brown became the first Black golfer to win an official tour event. Sifford had won the Long Beach Open in 1957, but it was not sponsored by the PGA. After his win, Brown was extended, and accepted, an invitation to play in the Colonial National Invitation the following week. He was the first African-American to play in the Colonial.

Brown was not invited to play in the 1965 Masters. At the time, Augusta National did not extend automatic invitation to all PGA tour winners the previous year.

Bert Weaver

It was a different type tournament. Nobody else would do something like that. Waco Turner was that kind of individual where he had to do something different. He came on the golf scene, and it was totally unexpected that he would present a tournament like that. What he did was give money for birdies and eagles and all that. That was unheard of at that time. Guys would do anything for a little more money. Money was a little more scarce, and it really helped me out a lot. I was one of those golfers who was successful, but I wasn't highly successful. To get that extra money meant a whole lot to me.

Chuck Courtney

Waco Turner had this little old funky golf course and he put up some money and a whole bunch of guys showed up to play several times. He had a pilot and flew around in a little twin Cessna that would literally fly right down the fairway, 20 feet off the ground. I mean, it was crazy. That was hilarious.

There was nobody there. It was out in the middle of absolutely nowhere. Near the little town of Ardmore. It's right there in what's called the Arbuckle Hills. Kind of the very, very beginning of the Ozarks. Anyway, just west of there is rolling country, ranches, and oil out there. Not very many miles north of the Red River, which is the Oklahoma-Texas border.

There was a clubhouse, golf shop, little cabins. It was a real rustic resort. He had a bunch of these little lakes, stocked with bass. One of the things he did was, he had Black caddies, and he didn't like their Black kids hanging around. He actually got a gun out and started shooting in the ground with his pistol. "Get off the porch, you guys hanging out. I don't want you here." Oh, he was a nutball. He was reputed—I have no idea that it's true or not—to have murdered one of his wives. This is all rumor stuff, but my God, it was scary.

Tommy Aaron

It was pretty strange. I was glad to play in it, though. Back then, you're glad to play in any tournament, no matter where you're playing. I think the total purse may have been $20,000. He paid bonus money for birdies and eagles, and the low round of the day. The golf course, it looked like he laid out it out himself, with a few pretty good holes. Overall, the course wasn't much to talk about.

We were just glad to play anywhere. We didn't have to get a brand new Mercedes. We didn't have to get picked up at the airport. We liked to play anywhere.

Frank Beard

He used to fly his plane over the golf course. He had his pistol and would shoot it out of the airplane. He was crazy, Waco Turner. Charlie Sifford walked by mistake into the club, and Waco Turner was playing poker and he had his gun laying on the table. Charlie told me this personally. He didn't point it at Charlie, he just picked it up and said, "You're not welcome in here." Charlie said, "It didn't take me long to get out of there."

"500" Festival

The "500" Festival was a tournament played from 1960 to 1968 in Indianapolis. It was held at the Speedway Golf Course, which included several holes inside of the speedway. Needless to say, a course built inside of a flat racing oval is not going to contain topographical features one might see at Pebble Beach or Merion. Usually, the 500 Festival was conducted just before or after the Indianapolis 500.

In 1964, the organizers decided to sandwich the tournament around the Indy 500. The first three rounds were played prior to the race, with a day off on Saturday, May 30—Memorial Day—when the race was held. For Thursday's second round, the weather was awful, with temperatures topping out in the mid-50s. Moreover, those with an afternoon tee time had to contend with the ear-splitting noise of racers tuning up for the 500 in the annual carburation test. Some golfers were amused. According to *The Indianapolis Star*, George Bayer stood by a tunnel under the track after hitting his drive on the fourth hole. "You fellows mind if I watch a while?," he asked his playing companions. "There goes Jimmy Clark!," Chi Chi Rodriguez exclaimed, referring to the Scottish Grand Prix driver and not the American golfer of the same name, who was competing in the tournament. "He's going to be tough."

Others were not happy, criticizing the tournament as "a sideshow to the race." Jack Nicklaus was very displeased. "As for the race Saturday, I wouldn't cross the street to see it," he said. "I don't like to see people killed." He said he would fly back to Columbus for the off day to see his horse run in a harness race.

Bayer, whose main gift was that he regularly hit tee shots of more than 300 yards, was well-position to take advantage of a flat, open course. His 67 (which followed a 66) included a two-putt birdie on the 308-yard 17th hole after he drove the green, giving him a two-shot lead.

The golfers who chose to watch the race did, in fact, see people killed, as they witnessed a fiery crash on the race's second lap that took the lives of drivers Eddie Sachs and Dave MacDonald. After the race, the portions of the golf course used for race day parking were cleaned up, and the final round was played on Sunday. Bayer was unable to keep pace with the much smaller Gary Player, who birdied the 18th hole for a one-stroke win over Doug Sanders and Art Wall, Jr. "I don't know which is more nerve-wracking, being a race driver or a golfer," Player said. Asked if he watched the race on Saturday, Player softly answered, "Unfortunately, yes."

Jerry Steelsmith

We were there. Any golfer that wanted to go got tickets. Horrible accident. Two of the drivers were killed. Dave McDonald and Eddie Sachs. Of course, they had to stop the race for an hour, or an hour and half, to clean everything up. They announced they had died, and then the race just went on. It did seem kind of weird.

I can remember in practice rounds the cars would be going around the track making all that noise they make and we're out there playing golf.

Frank Beard

It really was an odd tournament. Half of one nine was on the infield. At least six or seven holes, maybe the whole nine was on the infield. When they did the carburation test, we could hear them all day long, firing those cars around and pumping them up, cranking them, making noise, my God almighty.

The thing that amazed me the most about the whole thing was, if they would run the race, let's say on Sunday or whatever, we come out to play the tournament the next day and it was clean as a whistle on the infield. Not a chicken bone. Not a cup. Nothing. You wouldn't have known a person was there.

June

U.S. Open

Washington, D.C., is known for hot, humid summers. However, in 1964 the U.S. Open was slated to end—like every year—the weekend before the summer solstice. For the nation's capital, the average high temperature for the final days of spring (June 18-20) is 86 degrees, a fact certainly known by the USGA when it awarded the championship to Congressional Country Club in Bethesda, Maryland, 6 miles from the D.C. border. The tournament committee may have taken solace from knowing that in 1921—the most recent time the U.S. Open was played in the Washington area, at nearby Columbia Country Club—the tournament was staged in mid-summer (July 21-22) and the temperature was as comfortable (84 degrees) as Jim Barnes' nine-shot victory.

Thus, there was no way to anticipate that intense heat would form the backdrop to the 1964 U.S. Open and provide for one of the championship's most dramatic and heroic moments. For Thursday's first round, temperatures topped out in the mid-80s, but with high humidity. Arnold Palmer, his fourth Masters title already under his belt, shot a 68 in the first round to take a two-stroke lead over Bill Collins. It was the only round under par on the 7,053-yard course (with rough thick even by U.S. Open standards) that was playing exceptionally difficult.

On Friday temperatures touched 90 with even higher humidity. Tommy Jacobs, 29, whose most recent of four wins had come earlier in the year when he beat 53-year-old Jimmy Demaret in a playoff at Palm Springs, shot 64 to tie the U.S. Open record for the lowest round. "This has to be the greatest round of golf ever played in the history of the game," said Gary Player, who struggled to a 75 for a 149 total that barely made the cut. At the halfway point, Jacobs (136) led Palmer by a stroke. Both completed their

rounds before the heat really set in. Collins was four shots further behind at 141, one ahead of Ken Venturi and Charlie Sifford (both of whom matched 72-70 for the first two rounds). Only 24 players were within 10 shots of the lead. Jack Nicklaus, who shot 72-73, never would be in serious contention.

As was the custom, on Open Saturday, pairings were set for the entire 36 holes and were not adjusted after 54 holes to account for third round scores like they are now. Palmer and Jacobs were in the final group, Sifford and Collins ahead of them, and Venturi and Raymond

Photo 39: Tommy Jacobs. (Historic Images, Wilson Sporting Goods Co.)

Floyd in the third to last pairing. As the day went on, Congressional turned into a cauldron. Although the official high at National Airport 15 miles to the southeast was 95 degrees, it was reported that in the microsystem at Congressional it was 108 degrees. Chi Chi Rodriguez withdrew during the third round, citing an injury, but actually was overcome by the heat. More than 100 spectators were treated for heat exhaustion at first-aid stations and at a Red Cross tent set up on the course. The heat also affected two volunteer marshals, who late in the day got into a fistfight arguing about their proper stations in front of the thousands of spectators who were amassed near the 18th green.

Palmer loved playing in hot weather and thus seemed well-situated to win his second U.S. Open. However, his putter failed him, and he never was a factor on Saturday as he shot 75-74 to finish tied for fifth, eight shots back. Jacobs shot 70 in the third round to break Ben Hogan's 54-hole Open record of 207 set in 1948. At 206, Jacobs was two up on Venturi after three rounds.

Venturi started the day six back and there was no reason for anybody to believe he would be a factor. In the late 1950s, he was one of the biggest names on tour, but he had not won since the 1960 Milwaukee Open. In 1962, Venturi earned only $6,046 and in 1963 just $3,858. He had failed to qualify for the previous three Opens. In order to make the field at Congressional, Venturi was required to go through both local and sectional qualifying, and he just barely made it out of the Detroit section with rounds of 77-70. However, his game had rebounded recently, as he finished third at the Thunderbird Classic two weeks prior and then sixth at the Buick Open.

In his first nine on Saturday, Venturi shot an incredible 5-under 30, with six 3s and three 4s, tying the U.S. Open record. Then, he felt the heat. On the 15th hole, he was dizzy and almost blacked out. A physician was summoned, who examined Venturi and determined that he could complete the round. Somehow, he finished the back nine in 1-over par 36 to give him a 66. During the lunch break, Dr. John Everett, a member at Congressional, checked on Venturi in the clubhouse. Dr. Everett found Venturi's pulse to be normal but that he was seriously dehydrated and warned that continuing to play might be fatal. Venturi later said he told him, "Well, it's better than the way I've been living." Venturi made his afternoon tee time.

The USGA gave Dr. Everett permission to accompany Venturi during the round, and several officials, including Executive Director Joseph Dey, did as well. At times, somebody held an umbrella over Venturi to shield him from the sun. Venturi had no recollection of the first nine, during which he parred the first five holes, bogeyed the sixth, parred seven and eight, then birdied the par-5 ninth. Meanwhile, Jacobs had double-bogeyed the second, and bogeyed four, nine and 10 to go one over.

Venturi played at an excruciatingly slow pace. Reportedly, at one point he told Dey that if he did not penalize him he would walk even more slowly. Dey did not act. Venturi sank a 12-foot birdie putt on 13, but gave it back with a bogey on 14. As the round progressed, Venturi was invigorated by the constant applause that greeted him, which told him victory was his if he could get to the clubhouse. Floyd, his 21-year-old playing partner who was playing in his first Open, was struggling to a final-round 77; he generally played quickly and later became known for petulant on-course behavior but that day, in appreciation of the moment, he indulged Venturi in every possible way. By the time the twosome arrived at the 16th tee, every group in front of them had completed play. If Palmer, Jacobs, Sifford and Collins playing behind them had any complaints, they were not reported.

After parring 15, 16 and 17, Venturi arrived at 18 with a four-shot lead. He put his second shot in a greenside bunker, blasted to 12 feet and sank the putt for a par for a closing round of even-par 70. "My God, I've won the Open!," Venturi exclaimed after the putt dropped. Floyd picked the ball out of the hole and, with tears in his eyes, handed it to Venturi. Upon seeing Floyd's reaction, Venturi lost his composure as well. He was so overwhelmed with exhaustion he could not comprehend the writing on his card. Joe Dey put his hand on Venturi's shoulder. "Sign the card, Ken, it's correct," Dey said.

Venturi's 72-hole total of 278 was the only score under par and was four shots clear of Jacobs. It was the beginning of a resurgence in his career. Venturi won at Hartford in July and at the American Golf Classic in August. He was the PGA Player of the Year, and was named "Sportsman of the Year" by Sports Illustrated. However, it was to be a brief renaissance. After 1964, Venturi would win only one more time, in his hometown of San Francisco at the Lucky International in 1966. His career was derailed by carpal tunnel syndrome, but he found a new life as a longtime golf commentator for CBS. Venturi died in 2013 at age 82.

Don Fairfield

I remember it was so hot and humid. The worst (conditions) I ever played in. The last 36 holes in one day. It was a terrible, terrible day. I played in some bad weather and bad courses, but I want to tell you what, it was really a chore that day to finish thirty-six holes.

Chi Chi Rodriguez

We have to go 36 holes and I thought I was going to die. I mean, it was so humid. And I think I played three or four holes, and I told my wife, I say you know what? I think I'm going to die if I stay in this heat. And I say I'd rather not die and not win the U.S. Open.

Walter Iooss, Jr.

That was my first (U.S. Open as a photographer for Sports Illustrated*). Thirty-six holes on the hottest day of all time. It was unbearably hot. There was no fluid out there. It was brutal. Not something you want to re-create in your life more than once. That's a pretty good picture I took of Venturi sweating there. I rank that as one of the most difficult (assignments) for weather. Well, I went to the Ice Bowl (in Green Bay, December 1967) when it was 20 below zero. So, you can go to either extreme. It was beyond miserable.*

Frank Beard

It was the hottest place I've ever been in, and the deepest rough, and I'd played in Texas. I missed the cut.

None of us had any doctors like Venturi. They treated him like a baby and the rest of us played in the same conditions.

Jack Nicklaus

It was a great win and a great effort by Ken to get that done. He may have had some challenges and he may have been given a little bit of courtesy, which I think anybody else in a similar position would have gotten, too. I was very happy for him.

Photo 40: Ken Venturi after winning 1964 U.S. Open. (Walter Iooss, Jr.)

July

The Open Championship

The Open Championship was held at the Old Course of St. Andrews. There was no PGA Tour event conflicting with the Open, but still only eight Americans went to Scotland. U.S. Open champion Ken Venturi and tour stalwarts such as Billy Casper, Gene Littler, Bob Rosburg, and Tommy Bolt, opted to play in a $25,000 (about the same purse as the Open Championship) 90-hole non-tour event at the Wykagyl Country Club in New Rochelle, New York. The chance of glory and the potential for a spot to win $50,000 at the World Series of Golf in September still was not enough of an incentive for most American pros to incur the cost of overseas air fare.

Arnold Palmer chose to skip both the Open and Wykagyl. He wanted to prepare for the PGA Championship—the one major he had not won—the following week. Jack Nicklaus was installed as the 7-2 favorite to win the only major championship that had so far eluded him in his young career. The week before, he had won the Whitemarsh Open in Philadelphia. Tony Lema and defending champion Bob Charles were next at 7-1.

Lema was a good bet, as he was red-hot. In the previous five weeks, he had played every tour event with the following results: first at the Thunderbird, first at the Buick, 18th at the U.S. Open, first in Cleveland, and sixth at Whitemarsh. The reason his odds were not lower is because he had never set foot in the British Isles before flying over after completing play in Philadelphia on Sunday, and had never played with the smaller British ball. However, he did have the use of Tip Anderson, who had carried Palmer's bag in his two Open wins.

Winds from 20 to 40 mph and gusts of up to 60 kept scores high in Wednesday's opening round. Christy O'Connor of Ireland and Jean Garaialde of France took the lead with 1-under 71s.

Garaialde remains almost completely unknown but was the greatest French golfer of his time. He finished ninth at the 1963 Open Championship and had played in the Masters earlier in 1964. In the 1970 Swedish Open, he was paired with Nicklaus during the final round and sank a 6-foot putt on the 18th hole to beat Nicklaus by a stroke. Showing how little attention was paid to golf in France, this feat merited a single sentence in L'Equipe, France's premier sports publication. Lema was the top American with a 73. Nicklaus shot 76.

High winds continued on Thursday. Lema wrested the lead with a splendid round of 68, which included only a single bogey. With the wind at his back on the 312-yard 12th hole, he drove the green and sank a 25-foot putt for an eagle. Harry Weetman of England, age 43, who would win 20 times in Europe and play on seven Ryder Cup teams before dying in a car accident in 1971, was two back at 143. Nicklaus fell nine behind Lema after a 74.

In Friday's morning round, as the winds quieted, Nicklaus fired a 66, equaling the lowest round ever shot on the 400-year-old course. He shaved two strokes off of the lead as Lema shot 68. Nicklaus finished with a 68 in the afternoon, but fell short.

The Scottish fans enthusiastically embraced Lema, just as they had Palmer, Ben Hogan and any American who took the time to make the pilgrimage to St. Andrews, surrounding him after he ran a 7-iron to within 18 inches of the cup on the 72nd hole. Lema's closing birdie put him five shots clear of runner-up Nicklaus. He credited Anderson, his Scottish caddie, for his victory. "He was at least 50 percent of the team," Lema said. "I doubt I could have won without him."

PGA Championship

For the only time in his career, Jack Nicklaus played a major championship in his hometown. The 1964 PGA Championship was held at the Columbus Country Club, relatively short at 6,851 yards, flat and with no water hazards. "A fellow should shoot 68 or 69 if he plays reasonably well," Nicklaus stated on the eve of the tournament. "There may be a 65 here or there."

As he did in 1963 as a prelude to his win in Dallas, Nicklaus won the long-drive contest on Wednesday, with a record 341-yard drive. Asked if he was going to win, he answered, "Why, sure."

Wednesday, Nicklaus was in a jocular mood. "Gary Player is my house guest, you know. I had to miss practice Tuesday to take care of his laundry. He sent my wife to the grocery three times Tuesday, and we have fruit and snacks in every room to take care of him," Nicklaus said, tongue firmly planted in cheek. "And he's always worried about being sick," he continued, alluding to Player's borderline hypochondria. "He went to two doctors this morning, and they couldn't find anything wrong with him, so he made an appointment with another one this afternoon."

In the first round, Bobby Nichols did better than Nicklaus's prediction by shooting 64, a tournament record that gave him a three-stroke lead over Nicklaus and Mike Souchak and four over Arnold Palmer and Billy Casper. Player, Ben Hogan, and Julius Boros were in a large contingent at 70. The leaderboard also included names like Joe Conrad, Bob Keller, Scotty McBeath and Sam Reynolds, part of the onslaught of club pros who annually cluttered the field at the PGA.

Nichols was using a putter he had purchased for $5 at a bargain basement. It briefly failed him on Friday as he bogeyed three consecutive holes, but he rallied for a 1-over 71 to maintain his lead at 135. After a 68, Palmer was one back. He was assisted by a fan on the long par-4 15th hole. He drove into the rough and hit his second shot only 100 yards, under a tree. Palmer's third was skulled over the green and was headed for high grass when a spectator stopped the ball. Palmer got up and down for a bogey. "The guy played Ping Pong with the ball," Joe Campbell, who was playing with Palmer, angrily said. "If he doesn't stop it Palmer would have made a 6 or 7."

Ken Venturi followed an opening-round 71 with a 65 that left him two back. Nicklaus shot 73 for a 36-hole total of 149, five behind Nichols.

On a 90-degree Saturday, Nichols maintained his one-shot lead over Palmer when both shot 69. Nichols hit several poor drives, but scrambled masterfully. On the 474-yard, par-4 eighth hole, he drove into a clump of trees, played out to an adjoining fairway, then lofted a shot over a large oak tree to within 18 inches to save par. Managing to stifle the putting yips that had afflicted him for years, Hogan shot 68 for a 54-hole total of 210, tied with Nicklaus, Venturi and Casper, six behind Nichols.

On Sunday, Nicklaus finally broke through, shooting 64 to tie Nichols' opening round tournament and course record. Nichols played in the final round with Hogan, who 11 years earlier had written Nichols an inspiring letter while Nichols recovered from serious injuries suffered in a car accident. Nichols bogeyed the seventh and eighth holes to fall back into a tie with Palmer and Mason Rudolph who, under the radar, followed his opening-round 73 with 66 and 68. However, on the 10th hole, Nichols sank a 35-foot putt for an eagle 3 to take control again. He finished strong with a 67, three better than Palmer and Nicklaus and four ahead of Rudolph, winning wire-to-wire. Hogan closed with a 72, good for a tie for ninth.

Bobby Nichols

I was paired with Ben Hogan in the final round. That didn't happen very often. The crowds were enormous. You had Jack and Arnold, and then you had Ben Hogan. Sometimes you get that feeling, I don't know what it is exactly, something like the zone, where you feel like you're focused on what you want to do, and I felt that way that week. I wasn't able to do it every week. Things kind of clicked and went my way.

The 10th hole was a par-5. There was a ditch off to the left of the green. If you pulled your second shot, you'd put it in the water. Hogan later said, "I was surprised that you went for that green in two because you were leading the tournament by a shot, but it worked out for you." He said he would not have gone for it in two if he was leading the tournament. I probably was too naïve. I wasn't thinking too much about that. I was thinking about the shot, more or less, rather than the circumstances.

Insurance City Open

On the heels of playing the PGA Championship, Arnold Palmer, Jack Nicklaus, Gary Player and Tony Lema bypassed the $50,000 Insurance City Open. The ICO still had a decent field, with newly crowned major champions Ken Venturi and Bobby Nichols, along with Billy Casper, Sam Snead, Julius Boros and Mike Souchak.

Mark McCormack booked Palmer for an exhibition at the Princeton Country Club in New Jersey for the benefit of the Mercer County Heart Association. The plan was that on Sunday, July 28 (while the final round of the ICO was being played), Palmer would give a clinic and play an exhibition with three club pros.

On Friday, while Venturi fired a 63 to share the 36-hole lead at the ICO, Palmer posed for a photograph with Mrs. Joseph Bonatti, the executive director of the heart association, next to a poster advertising the outing. Some 1,800 tickets were sold in advance, taking in about $10,000. The sale of hot dogs and soda would bring in additional money. There would be more than enough to pay the appearance fees of Palmer and the other pros, and provide the heart association with some money. It promised to be a fun afternoon for a worthy cause.

There was a rule prohibiting PGA pros from participating in an event within 200 miles of a PGA-sponsored tournament.

McCormack was well-aware of the rule and somebody on his team measured the distance between Princeton, New Jersey and Hartford, Connecticut. It was close, barely more than 200 miles.

On Saturday, Venturi shot 69 to remain tied at the ICO with veteran Al Besselink. There were 30 players within seven shots of the lead, including Casper, Snead, and Nichols. The sponsoring Jaycees undoubtedly looked forward to a big walk-up gate for an exciting Sunday finish, with a chance for the popular Venturi to follow up his dramatic victory at Congressional five weeks earlier with another win.

Somebody thought to measure the distance between the Princeton Country Club and the ICO host Wethersfield Country Club, which was in a suburb of Wethersfield, eight miles south of downtown Hartford, only 192 miles from the site of the exhibition. Palmer had played at the ICO many times, winning in 1956 and 1960. One might assume that in past consideration of Palmer's support of the tournament, and given the effort expended by a fellow benevolent organization to stage the exhibition, the Jaycees and the PGA would grant a waiver to allow it to go forward. They did not. Palmer would have faced a six-month suspension if he had played. Thus, Palmer sent his regrets, and the exhibition was canceled at the last moment.

Despite a double-bogey on the 18th hole, Venturi held on to win the ICO by one stroke. He then flew home to San Francisco be honored on Ken Venturi Day, where he received the key to the city.

Photo 41: *Arnold Palmer before one of the many exhibitions he played in the 1960s, this one in Davenport Iowa. In the back seat are Doug Sanders, Bob Fry, and Jack Rule, Jr. Next to Palmer in the sunglasses is Johnny Lujack, winner of the 1947 Heisman Trophy. (Creative Commons, Golf Daughter)*

August

Western Open

The Western Open was one of the oldest American professional events, predating the formation of the PGA Tour. Run by the Western Golf Association, the tournament was first held in 1899. It was played in a variety of locations west of the Mississippi River. After the 1961 edition, it always was held near Chicago. For most of its existence, it had the aura of a major tournament and always had a strong field. Caddies were young college men who were employed for the tournament through the Chick Evans Scholarship Fund.

In 1964, the Western Open was held at the Tam O'Shanter Golf Club in Niles, Illinois. Tam O'Shanter was opened during the Roaring Twenties. It had no pretensions about exclusivity, as the only requirement for membership was the ability to pay dues. The elite of Chicago's mafia were members. The clubhouse was a large concrete-and-glass, triple-decker building. A 100-foot-high water tower in the shape of a red tee with a giant golf ball on top over-looked the course. In its heyday, the club had as many as 13 bars, and telephones on every tee.

In the 1940s and 1950s, Tam O'Shanter hosted the All-American Open and the so-called World Championship of Golf, as well as an array of women's and amateur tournaments, as part of an extended golf festival held every summer. The sponsor of the tournaments was Chicago businessman and one-time bible salesman George S. May, who by the late 1930s owned Tam O'Shanter. The World Championship offered first-place money of up to $50,000, an amount not seen again until the late 1960s. It was a gauche spec-tacle. Players were required to wear numbers on their backs, like athletes in a track meet, so the fans could identify them from the programs they purchased. And there were lots of fans, as many as 60,000 in a single day, enticed by cheap tickets. Circus clowns wandered the course. One year, May hired a Canadian pro named Bob Gray to wear a costume and compete as the Masked Marvel. Fans were known to set up picnics on the fairway.

May discontinued the tournaments after a disagreement with the PGA in 1957. He died in 1962 and by 1964 Tam O'Shanter was on its last legs, as May's estate was looking to sell the club. It was sold to developers, who turned most of the land into an industrial park. The clubhouse burned down.

After three rounds, Arnold Palmer and Chi Chi Rodriguez were tied for the lead. On Sunday, Rodriguez fired a 67 and then waited to see if Palmer, playing in the final group behind him, could catch him. One shot back, Palmer bogeyed 17, which made his long birdie on 18 immaterial. For Rodriguez, it was his third tour win and most lucrative ($11,000).

Chi Chi Rodriguez

I had missed the cut the previous week at the Canadian Open. My caddie kept trying to give me advice. At the Western Open, I asked for a caddie who knows nothing about golf. The caddies there were all in college. I told my caddie, "All I want you to do is carry the bag and keep your mouth shut." I asked him how much he needed to finish college. When he told me, I said, "I'll pay off the rest of what you owe if I win."

On Sunday, Arnold Palmer and I were battling for first place. I was playing with Billy Casper and Ken Venturi. On the 15th hole, I needed a ruling. While we waited, I asked my caddie to get me a hot dog. The gallery thought that was funny.

On the 18th hole, I put my second shot in the trap. I told my caddie to take out the flag. I put my shot within 3 feet and made the putt. I could see Palmer on the 17th tee. We looked at each other. Palmer made a 30-foot putt for a birdie on the 18th hole, but he finished one shot behind me.

Frank Beard

Chi Chi's big peeve was players who spat on the green. I saw him call people on it. He was right to do so. Nobody wants to see a loogy on the green.

St. Paul Open

Chuck Courtney was slim, handsome, pleasant and wore glasses. With a suit, the 23-year-old could have passed for a young Madison

Avenue adman. In his rookie year, Courtney had been grinding. When he missed a cut, he would go on to the next stop and enter Monday qualifying. He usually was successful in getting into the field one way or another; in 1964 he played in 33 events, making the cut 18 times.

At the St. Paul Open, he hit paydirt, going 66-66 over the last two rounds to win his first tournament by three shots over Charlie Sifford, Rod Funseth and Jack McGowan.

Photo 42: Chuck Courtney.
(Historic Images, Golfcraft)

Chuck Courtney

I originally was from Minneapolis, and I stayed with some friends of mine. I'd been able to win enough money off and on to get me there without digging into my sponsors' pot. Anyway, I was staying with some friends in St. Louis Park, which is about a 40-minute drive from Keller, where the golf tournament was. I remember I was sick. Like they say, it's hard to beat a guy when he's sick.

It got really, really windy the last two days and I think I shot 132 on the weekend and managed to beat everybody. I was on the last green, and I had to mark my ball and I had to move it over a putter length. I think I was playing with Frank Beard and Charlie Sifford, though I'm not sure. I had a three-shot lead on the 72nd hole, so if I didn't stub my toe I was fine. I remember I bent over to put my ball back down and I forgot to move the marker back. Two or three of my buddies are sitting up in the bleachers and the wind is blowing like hell and they yell, "Hey, move your coin back before you putt!" Thank God they were there. I moved my coin back and put it in the hole and I won.

Carling World Open

In 1964, the Carling tournament was re-branded the Carling World Open and was held at the storied Oakland Hills Country Club north of Detroit. With a total purse of $200,000, by far the largest of the year, the field was the best of any tournament in the world in 1964. Just about every pro golfer of note played (including Ben Hogan, who was returning to the site of his 1951 U.S. Open win) except for Sam Snead and Art Wall, who withdrew due to injuries.

In the 155-man field were 48 international players from 14 countries. Carling paid their travel expenses. Those who did not make the 36-hole cut would receive $400. CBS televised six holes—two more than had been tried before—and expanded the weekend coverage to two hours, which was preceded by a 30-minute preview on Friday night. Thus, the Carling had all the trappings of a major event.

In the first round, unheralded rookie George Archer shot 65 to take a three-shot lead over Bruce Devlin. Chi Chi Rodriguez played with Hogan and Jerry Barber. On the 18th hole, Rodriguez missed a 3-foot par putt. His ball stopped 6 inches past the hole, and he raked it back into the cup. Barber claimed Rodriguez tapped the ball twice. "I didn't see it," said Hogan, who was keeping Rodriguez's card. "Give me a 6," Rodriguez directed Hogan, and said of the 48-year-old Barber, "I can't call the man a liar. He's been in the game a long time."

On Friday, Archer skied to a 74 but still maintained a one-stroke advantage over Peter Butler of England and PGA champion Bobby Nichols, with Arnold Palmer, Kel Nagle, and R.H. Sikes two strokes back. In the third round, Nichols fired a 66 to lead Palmer (who shot 67) by one.

In Sunday's final round, Hogan shot 68 for a 72-hole total of 282, five better than his winning score in the 1951 Open, to finish tied for fourth with Pete Brown. *Sports Illustrated* reported that during the tournament Brown excitedly told fellow pros in the grill room that the taciturn Hogan had just said, "Hi, Pete" to him. It was the first time an African-American golfer was prominently featured in a nationally televised tournament. Hogan earned $6,850, his biggest check since winning the so-called World Championship of Golf, also in 1951, and the same sum Brown received was almost three times the amount he won at the Waco Turner Open earlier in the year.

Palmer eagled the 12th hole to tie Nichols. Minutes later, Nichols—who was in the group behind Palmer—birdied 12 to retake the lead. On 18, now two strokes back, Palmer hit an approach from thick rough that appeared headed well past the hole, but his ball hit the flagstick and landed near the cup. He sank the putt for a birdie to put pressure on Nichols. However, Nichols landed on the 18th green in regulation and two-putted for a par to beat Palmer—for the second time in seven weeks, following his win at the PGA— by one stroke, earning $35,000. Gary Player, who was paired with Palmer, shot 67 for a total of 281, good for third place.

Bobby Nichols

I won the first $200,000 tournament. That was the World Open. Then it was the Dow Jones in New Jersey, which was the first $300,000 tournament we ever had on the tour, in 1970. So, I was very fortunate.

That was the first year they had international players at the tournament. They invited people from all over the world. It was quite special. I played with Arnold the third round. I had a 66 the third round at Oakland Hills, one of the greatest golf courses I've ever had the pleasure of playing. That put me in good position to win the tournament. Hogan was there. It was quite a tournament. I was fortunate enough to be able to play in something like that. I'll carry it with me for the rest of my life.

Photo 43: Bobby Nichols winning the 1964 Carling World Open. (Walter Iooss, Jr.)

Arnold on his second shot on 18 hit it out of the rough with a 6-iron or 5-iron. It was a flyer. It hit on the green. The 18th hole at Oakland Hills slopes from front to back. It goes up the hill towards the back of the green. You don't want to hit it long. Gary said, "Bob, when he hit that shot, I thought I've got second place because that ball was going to go over the green into that high rough, and I doubt he could have gotten it up and down." But anyway, the ball was hit extremely hard, hit the pin, and bounced back. And then, of course, he made that putt. Luckily, I two-putted to still have a one-shot lead.

September

Dallas Open

Most top names did not travel to Dallas on the heels of the Carling World Open. Total prize money at the Dallas Open was $40,000, or 20 percent of that offered at the Carling. The pros assembled at Oak Cliff Country Club for the Labor Day weekend tournament (Billy Casper was the biggest name) were met by scorching 100-degree heat.

Photo 44: *Charles Coody, 1965.*
(Getty Images)

Charles Coody, from nearby Abilene, was accustomed to heat. He was 27 years old and started his pro career in 1963 after graduating from Texas Christian University, and doing a stint in the Air Force. To date, he had earned just $2,843.77. Coody grabbed the 36-hole lead and held on to win by one stroke over Jerry Edwards, and by two over Casper and Fred Haas, assuring himself exempt status for 1965.

Charles Coody

My first tournament was 1963. And now that was in say early September. I had just gotten out of the Air Force about a month before, at the very end of July. It was Denver. I think I tied for 16th or something like that, and made maybe $640. And I thought I'd found a bird's nest on the ground [a Texas idiom for gaining an advantage with little or no risk]. *I drove to the next tournament, in Salt Lake City,* and went to register. At that time, if you made the cut the previous week, you were exempt from qualifying for the following week.

They didn't have my name. They said I'd have to see a PGA official. And I found a PGA official who, later on, I had an awful lot of respect for. He said, well, the reason they didn't have your name is you didn't sign the commitment sheet. And I said, well, what is a commitment sheet? I never heard of it. And anyway, he told me what that was. The starter on the first tee at Denver had neglected to tell me. He might have told the other two guys I was playing with about the commitment sheet, but he didn't tell me. I didn't know there was such an animal anyway. So, I went from the utopia of having a good tournament the week before to not even being able to play the next week. So, that was quite an experience for me.

I had really not played well in 1964 and my wife was pregnant with our son. He was due to be born about the early part of August. And I came home the latter part of June, early part of July, just to be there with her during the last two months of pregnancy. I got to play with some friends in Abilene. I went down to Dallas, played a practice round. I think I shot something in the 60s in the pro-am, which I was surprised to be in because I hadn't played very well. I then shot four straight rounds in the 60s and won the tournament. I played with Billy Casper the last round. Billy was very, very nice to me.

At that time, winning a tournament did not get you into Augusta. They had what they called the fall tour and the winter tour, and you got points for how you finished in the tournaments. And that's what got me in the Masters for 1965. The fall tour went from Labor Day until the end of the year. With the win in Dallas, I got enough points to be in good shape to get into the Masters for the next year.

We're in Lafayette, Louisiana, playing the Cajun Classic, which is the last tournament of the year. I passed one of the older professionals by the name of Ted Kroll in the hallway that goes into the locker room. He looked at me and says, "You're a lucky little shit." And of course, I tried to be as respectful and polite to all the older professionals as I possibly could. And I said, "Mr. Kroll, if I upset you in some way, I want to know why, if I need to apologize." He said, "Oh no, you haven't done a thing. You just started on this tour and you're going to play for all this money."

I went into the locker room and sat down in front of my locker. I started changing my shoes and all of a sudden he hit me. Now, here's a guy that played his whole career in tournaments that were $5,000, $10,000, $15,000, probably a maximum of $20,000, unless you got into the Tam O'Shanter up in Chicago. And you won a tournament back then, you got $2,000 or $1,500. And, here, I just won a tournament in Dallas about two months before, I think I got almost $6,000 or something like that. And, you know, I could see his point. He had played his whole career for very, very small purses and everything. And I was coming out when the purses were starting to get larger. And they were going from those smaller that I mentioned to $35,000 and $40,000 for the tournament.

So, Kroll was right. I was just starting, and I was going be playing for a lot more money than players in his era ever even thought about playing for. And that was just an example of how the tour started to change. So, it was a sobering statement that he made to me. It taught me to respect the opportunity I was being given.

November

Cajun Classic

For the second straight year, the little Cajun Classic was the scene of end-of-year drama, this time without a tragic backdrop. In 1964, there were no official world rankings, and nothing like the FedEx Cup. The closest thing the tour had to a season-crowning achievement was the money title. The companies with whom Arnold Palmer and Jack Nicklaus had endorsement contracts paid approximately $20,000 in bonuses to the money title winner. "It's a real measure of accomplishment," Nicklaus said at the time, "the next best thing to winning a major championship."

Palmer seemed to have the money title sewn up at the Sahara Invitational in Las Vegas several weeks earlier. However, in the final round he shot 76, while Nicklaus scored 67. Both had commitments abroad that prevented them from playing in two subsequent small-purse PGA fall events in California. As a result, heading into the season-ending Cajun Classic, Palmer led Nicklaus in money earnings by $318.87 ($111,703.37 to $111,384.50). When Palmer learned that Nicklaus was heading to Lafayette, he committed as well.

In the first round, Palmer shot 74 and seemed in danger of missing the cut, while Nicklaus was 4 under after eight holes. However, heavy rain materialized, and both scores were washed out. On Friday, both shot 68 in bone-chilling conditions, with wind and temperatures in the 40s. On Saturday, Palmer shot 74, Nicklaus 71 (despite a two-shot penalty incurred when he and playing partner Butch Baird discovered they had hit the other's MacGregor ball).

With the winter solstice approaching, there was limited daylight to compress a 36-hole finish on Sunday. The unseasonably cold weather continued. When Nicklaus teed off at 8:12 a.m., the wind chill temperature was in the 20s and it was raining. "Nicklaus looked more like a polar bear than the Golden Bear he uses as a trademark; he was wearing three sweaters, a knitted yellow dickey and a rain suit," *Sports Illustrated* reported. "By the time he reached the third hole—followed by a gallery of 18—the damp towel that hung from his golf bag was frozen stiff."

After the morning round, Palmer—who drew the bulk of the 3,000 paying customers who braved the miserable weather—trailed Nicklaus by one stroke. During the final 18, Nicklaus increased his lead over Palmer to four shots, but Palmer rallied with a stretch of five holes played in 4-under par. Then, on the 15th hole, Palmer missed a 2-foot putt. He finished his round ahead of Nicklaus and waited in the clubhouse.

Miller Barber, with a five-shot lead, had the tournament won, but Nicklaus and Gay Brewer, who played together, were battling for second place. On 18, Brewer faced a 16-foot putt to finish second alone. The money title came down to that one putt. According to *Sports Illustrated*, "Brewer walked over to Nicklaus, and Jack jokingly slipped a money clip into Brewer's hand." Nicklaus then turned his back, too nervous to watch. A murmur from the small gallery told him that Brewer missed the putt. Thus, Nicklaus and Brewer tied for second, and Nicklaus won the money title over Palmer by $81.13.

Two lesser known pros, Paul Bondeson and rookie George Archer, had their own battle in Lafayette. In 1964, the top 50 players on the money list were exempt from Monday qualifying for 1965. Bondeson held the 50th spot by $1.88 over Archer at the start of the tournament. Both missed the cut, so Bondeson was exempt for 1965 and Archer was not. However, Archer quickly rectified the situation, winning the Lucky International in January to assure his exempt status for 1965.

1965

January

Los Angeles Open

Paul Harney was not your typical tour pro. He hailed from Worcester, Massachusetts, which never was known as a hotbed for world-class golfers. Harney earned an academic scholarship to the College of the Holy Cross in his hometown, where he graduated in 1952 after winning medalist honors at the 1952 NCAA Championship.

Photo 45: Paul Harney.
(The Paul Harney Golf Course)

After service in the U.S. Navy during the Korean War, Harney turned pro in 1954. He had success on the tour, winning three times in the 1950s. He was slim, 5-foot-11 and 175 pounds but regularly pounded his drives 275 yards – long for his time.

By 1965—when he was 35—his thick hair was graying. Harney promised his wife Patti that when their first child started school he would take a club position and give up playing the tour full-time. That happened in 1964, not long after he won the Los Angeles Open, his first victory since 1959. He kept his promise and took the head professional position at Pleasant Valley Country Club in Sutton, Massachusetts. With things slow at the club over the winter, in January 1965 Harney headed to Los Angeles to defend his title.

After completing his final round of 69 at Rancho Park, Arnold Palmer sought out a tour official to inquire why the tees were not as far back as they could be. Obviously, he thought he would have had an advantage if the course were played from the tips. It would not have mattered. Harney defended his title going away, with rounds of 68-71-68-69, to win by three shots over Dan Sikes. Palmer finished eight back.

Don Fairfield

I stayed with Paul (Harney) that week. I picked him up at the airport on Sunday night. He played the Puerto Rico Open at the end of the season before in heavy rain. Anyway, when I pick him up at the airport he unpacks his golf bag. His white, moldy green shoes are inside the golf bag. He hadn't picked up a club for 30 days.

Well, he gets down and he starts beating balls at this old driving range out there by the golf course. He gets a stiff neck. He comes the second day. He can't even move his head, it's so bad. He passed up the pro-am because he's still in the same condition. He was going to withdraw. I said, "Paul, you got one more night and one more day, you never know what's going to happen." Well, he got through the night and went out and he decided to play the next morning. And he started the tournament. He couldn't hardly turn his head yet, but he swung for him very slow, easily and, by golly, he got through the day. For the rest of the week, he got better, and he got his feel back and, damn, if he didn't to win that tournament.

That was the amazing part about it. It's something about when you're hurt. You somehow find another way to get around that little area. A sore left elbow, an arm, a back. You can always adapt a little bit around what your problem is.

Every morning, he got up out of bed early in the morning and found a church. Every day, sometimes at night too. He was a true Catholic believer. And he smoked constantly. When we traveled, I'd wake up in the middle of the night, and he's up in bed, having a cigarette about 2 or 3 in the morning. The last time I saw Paul was when I retired. His teeth were yellow, like a yellow pad you write on. He had smoked so much, I guess. I don't know what he finally died of, but it might have been cancer.

Bing Crosby National Pro-Am

On an overcast, misty Friday, Tony Lema shot a second-round 65 at the Monterey Peninsula Country Club for a 36-hole total of 136 to take a three-shot lead over Charlie Sifford and Bill Collins at the halfway point of the Crosby Clambake. Jack Nicklaus shot 68 at Monterey and was four behind Lema. Defending PGA champion Bobby Nichols was five back at 141.

As usual at the Crosby, the draw was fixed for the benefit of the television audience so that most of the stars played at Pebble Beach for the third round on Saturday. There could not have been many more difficult days to play golf in the 1960s. Mid-day, howling winds blew in off of the Pacific Ocean, with gusts of up to 60 mph. On the 218-yard par-3 17th hole at Pebble Beach, Jack Nicklaus hit a driver into the wind and his ball only reached a bunker in front of the green. He would shoot 77. Playing the 367-yard par-4 17th hole at Cypress Point, Paul Harney hit a driver from the tee and another driver from the fairway and found himself 30 yards short of the green.

Lema double-bogeyed 16 and 17 at Pebble Beach and ended up with a 79. Yet, he was only three shots behind leader Rocky Thompson, a 25-year-old rookie from Wichita Falls, Texas. Playing in privacy at Monterey, which was more sheltered from the wind than Pebble Beach, and able to complete 11 holes before the wind really kicked in, Thompson shot 69 to take a two-shot lead. Nichols shot 90, which was better than Bo Wininger's 91 and 1953 PGA Champion Walter Burkemo's 92. Veteran Fred Hawkins ripped up his scorecard rather than turning it in.

Photo 46: Bruce Crampton.
(Source unknown)

On Sunday, at Pebble Beach with the entire remaining field, Thompson could not keep up under calmer conditions, shooting 78. Tony Lema rebounded with a 72, which was good for second place. The winner was Bruce Crampton, who was the beneficiary of a 45-minute lesson from Nicklaus on the eve of the tournament and shot 69 in the final round. On the practice tee on Wednesday, Nicklaus told Crampton he was aiming too far to the right with his setup. Nicklaus and Billy Casper finished tied for third, four shots behind Crampton.

March

Greater Jacksonville Open

A PGA event returned to Jacksonville for the first time since 1953. Being in northeast Florida, Jacksonville weather is more similar to coastal Georgia than Miami Beach, but the sponsoring Junior League hoped that by March some nice days would be in order, particularly with Arnold Palmer, Jack Nicklaus and Gary Player heading a stellar field. That was not the case in the first round, when the Selva Marina Country Club was ravaged by rain and winds that gusted to 30 mph. Bernard Hunt, an Englishman who played in Europe but had come to the United States for the Masters, was accustomed to bad weather and tied for the early lead with tour veteran Gardner Dickinson after both shot 68.

The weather was not any better on Friday, when unknown Dick Rhyan Jr. took the 36-hole lead at 136, one better than Phil Rodgers, who shot a course-record 65. Rodgers was winless since his victory at the Texas Open in April 1963, when he appeared set to join Palmer, Nicklaus, Player and Billy Casper in golf's pantheon. Rodgers still was only 26 years old but already suffered from high blood pressure and gout. He lost 30 pound while on a diet designed to remedy those conditions. After three rounds, Dan Sikes—who was from Jacksonville—led by one over Rodgers, Bruce Devlin, and Jim Ferree.

As bad as conditions had been all weekend, it was even worse for Sunday's final round. Temperatures were in the 40s, and the course was saturated from four days of rain. Sam Snead and Gordon Jones both shot 71, the only sub-par rounds of the day, but were too far back to mount a challenge.

Photo 47: Bert Weaver.
(Getty Images)

Selva Marina was unusual, if not unique, among PGA venues in that its closing hole was a par-3. It was 225 yards in length, and in the final round a cold wind blew from the north directly towards the tee, which effectively turned it into a par-4. Nicklaus started the day three behind leader Sikes. When he arrived at the 18th tee, he was one shot out of the lead. His tee shot found trees and he bogeyed when he was unable to get up and down. Bert Weaver, who started the day two behind Sikes, held the lead, but he, too, bogeyed 18, momentarily placing him in a tie with Devlin and Dave Marr, and one ahead of Sikes.

Weaver waited for the final groups to come in. Both Devlin and Marr bogeyed. Sikes, needing a birdie on 18 to tie Weaver, bogeyed as well, fading to sixth place. As a result, Weaver won for his sole tour victory. He died in May 2022 at age 90.

Bert Weaver

(The Greater Jacksonville Open) was the first and only tournament I won in the United States, though I won the Venezuela Open, the Panama Open, the Maracaibo Open. I was one of those journeymen. I stayed out there a long time. I played about 13 years on the tour. I'm the first one from Beaumont, Texas to win a tournament. After that, Bruce Lietzke was highly successful and won a lot of tournaments. Babe Zaharias, of course, was the first female from Beaumont to win.

It was cold for that area and windy. The 18th hole was a par-3 and was right into the north wind. I hit a 1-iron right into the teeth of the wind. I missed the green just barely and chipped up, and missed about a four-foot putt. That was a really tough finishing hole, and that was the reason for all the bogeys in the last round. I had to stay there and watch. Jack Nicklaus and Dave Marr and two or three other guys all bogeyed the hole, too. The papers the next day, of course, wrote it up that it's too bad Jack Nicklaus had to bogey the last hole. Not one time in the article did they say that Bert Weaver bogeyed the last hole also.

I got into the Masters. Not because I won. At that time, tournament winners didn't automatically get in the Masters. They were on a points system. When I won, I got enough points from the winter tour to get one of the two spots reserved for the winter tour to get in the Masters that year.

My wife traveled with me. My first son was born in 1959 and my second was born in 1963. During those years, the four of us would travel in a car. I ended up with a van. A lot of the guys had a van. I wouldn't say live in them, but they certainly were easier to travel in. We'd stay in motels—very few hotels—we'd always try to find the best deal because money was in short supply. A lot of golfers and their wives and kids traveled together. Not necessarily together, but we traveled the same way, and ended up in the same motels. So, the families had a good time playing with each other while the guys were playing in the tournaments.

April

The Masters

The 29th Masters began on April 8 with conditions perfect for low scoring. It was an idyllic Georgia spring day, with temperatures in the mid-80s and only slight wind, with the greens slightly moist from rains the previous week. As a result, of the 91 players in the field, 33 broke par (shattering the previous record of 17 set in 1958) and another 11 shot an even-par 72. Gary Player led with a 65.

Scores soared dramatically on Friday, the result of winds, firm greens, and difficult pin placements. Only four players broke par, including Arnold Palmer (whose 68 was the low round of the day) and Jack Nicklaus. They and Player were tied at the top of the leaderboard at 138. However, hopes for an epic showdown on the weekend for the Big Three quickly were dashed by Nicklaus, who was better able than the others to take advantage of a windless Saturday. Nicklaus tied Lloyd Mangrum's course record of 64 set in 1940, with eight birdies and no bogeys. On Sunday, Nicklaus's 69 gave him a nine-stroke victory over Palmer and Player. His 72-hole score of 271—17 under par—shattered Ben Hogan's 1953 record by three strokes. Nicklaus would hold the record for 32 years.

At the end of the traditional interview in the Butler Cabin, after talking to Nicklaus, Clifford Roberts threw a curve ball at CBS by staring at the camera and saying, "Next year, you'll be seeing the Masters in color." CBS had no such plans. Broadcasting in color was expensive and, at a time when only 3 percent of American homes owned a color television, simply not worth it. However, Roberts would get his way.

May

Colonial National Invitational

Sports Network, Inc., paid the PGA $600,000 for rights to broadcast 13 tournaments in 1965, including the Colonial. SNI syndicated its coverage to as many as 190 local stations throughout the United States.

SNI was a low-budget, no-frills operation. Jimmy Demaret and Bob Toski, whose playing days mostly were over, provided commentary. Jack Simons was the producer. Whereas Frank Chirkinian won four Emmys during his long career as the producer of golf for CBS and is a legend, Simons' name is forgotten. Perhaps for good reason. By 1965, instant replay, stop-action, and slow motion already were in use. Simons would have none of it. "We came to cover a golf tournament. There's no time for that stuff," he said at the Colonial about the new technology. "It's good gimmickry, but I think it distracts from the coverage. The time may come when we'll have to use it, but I'm going to try to avoid it." Who would want to see a hole-out from the fairway a second time?

There was no need at the 1965 Colonial. Only Sunday's final round was slated to be broadcast, and rain caused it to be postponed until Monday, which meant there would not be television coverage at all. A golf tournament was not going to bring the ratings to SNI's affiliates that would warrant departing from the scheduled soap operas. Bruce Crampton won by three strokes over Canadian George Knudson.

Photo 48: 1965 Cleveland Open. As the 1960s progressed, tournaments with six-figure purses became commonplace. (The Cleveland Press, through ClevelandMemoryOrg)

June

Buick Open

Photo 49: Bob Zimmerman.
(Courtesy of Bob Zimmerman)

For the second year in a row, Tony Lema won the Buick Open. He played with Jack Nicklaus in the final round. On the 18th tee, trailing by a shot, Nicklaus drove out of bounds on his way to a triple-bogey. On top of the $20,000 first prize, Lema's win gave him the use of a new Buick for five years. As he already had earned such a lease in 1964, Lema was all set for a car through 1974. Sadly, he was unable to take advantage of this perk.

Bob Zimmerman

I was playing with Doug Sanders in the last round, at Warwick Hills. In those days, they didn't have scoreboards every place. I'm on the 11th hole, a par-3, and I hit it into a bunker, and I had about a 10-foot putt for par. I happened to look over at the scoreboard. It had Tony Lema in first place at 6 under and Zimmerman in second place at 3 under. And it took me almost five minutes to hit that putt. I was so nervous after I saw that, and I missed the putt. I finished seventh in the tournament, which was one of my better tournaments.

U.S. Open

The U.S. Open was played at the Bellerive Country Club in the sub-urbs of St. Louis from June 17-21. As a consequence of both Ken Venturi's ordeal at Congressional in 1964 and a desire for more television money, the USGA abandoned the 36-hole Open Saturday in favor of single rounds on Saturday and Sunday.

In addition to a monstrously long course for the time (7,191 yards), on Thursday players had to deal with gusting winds. A remarkable 43 contestants failed to break 80, including three who did not break 90. Jack Nicklaus shot 78, Palmer 76. Defending champion Venturi shot 81, including 40 putts. Only three players broke par of 70: Kel Nagle (68), Mason Rudolph (69) and short-hitting amateur Deane Beman, who also fashioned a 69 while using woods on 10 different holes for his second shot. South African Gary Player was at 70.

Scoring was just as difficult on Friday. Palmer shot another 76 and missed the cut by two shots. He did not have a single birdie in 36 holes. Nicklaus rebounded with a 72 to make the cut on the number at 150, but was too far back on the rugged course to make a run for the second leg of the Grand Slam. Player's second consecu-tive even-par 70 gave him a one-shot edge over Nagle and Rudolph. Frank Beard scored 69—one of only two sub-par rounds for the day—and was three back at 143. Eldon Briggs, a 55-year-old club pro from Michigan, went 90-91 to miss the cut by 31 strokes.

The third round provided for more laborious golf. Only Doug Sanders—who barely made the cut—broke par, though his 69 did not put him anywhere near the leaders. Player remained steady, shooting 71, which gave him at two-stroke lead over Nagle (72) and Beard (70). Beard professed to disliking the course. "I don't like any course you can't have fun playing," he told the press. As in his first two rounds, Beard avoided any three-putt greens.

Nagle was not sure of his score until after the round. On the 12th hole, he was denied relief from a bad lie. He played from the lie, but also dropped a provisional ball and played that as well. Nagle scored a bogey with his first ball and a par with the provisional. Raymond Floyd was given relief from a similar lie on Friday due to a burrowing animal. When Joe Dey of the USGA learned of this, he ruled Nagle would be credited with a par.

On Sunday, the tee times were adjusted to assure that television viewers would be able to see the leaders in the allotted afternoon time slot. Thus, the bottom half of the remaining field teed off after the leaders. Paired with Player, Beard hooked his drive on the second hole into water and made double-bogey, assuring that he would not enjoy his final round any more than the first three. However, Beard gamely played the remaining 16 holes in 1 under for a 71 to finish third.

After nine holes, Player—wearing his customary black attire— had extended his lead over Nagle to three shots. Then, after Nagle had birdied the 10th, Player bogeyed to cut his lead to one stroke. On 15, Nagle put his approach into a bunker, hit a poor shot out and three-putted from 60 feet for a double-bogey that left him a seemingly insurmountable three strokes back. However, on the 218-yard par-3 16th, Player pushed his 4-wood into a buried lie in a bunker. Incredibly, he blasted his ball to within 16 feet. His putt for par was 18 inches short, but his firm putt for bogey did a 180 around the cup and came back in his direction. He tapped in for a double-bogey to cut his lead back to one stroke.

When Player could only manage a par after Nagle had birdied the par-5 17th, the two were tied. Both parred 18, necessitating a playoff on Monday and guaranteeing that the U.S. Open would have its first non-American born winner since Ted Ray of the United Kingdom won in 1920. At age 44, Australian Nagle was one year older than Ray when he won. Remarkably, over 72 holes, in recording scores of 272, both Player and Nagle hit the green in regulation 54 times, both had 128 putts, both birdied eight times and bogeyed 11 times, and both had a double-bogey.

For all intents and purposes, the Monday playoff was decided on the fifth hole. Player was leading by one when Nagle hooked his drive left into the gallery. The ball bounced once and squarely hit Alma Pearson, a spectator from Milwaukee, in the head. When Nagle arrived at his ball—which was in deep rough—he found Pearson bleeding and unconscious. Visibly upset, with his next shot Nagle hit another spectator, Dorothy Barrea of Plainfield, New Jersey, in the calf, immediately raising a welt. Nagle made double-bogey 6 to fall three behind Player.

After nine holes, Player's lead had increased to five shots. The final scores were 71 for Player and 74 for Nagle. However, it was never close as Player bogeyed 17 and 18 after the outcome was all but decided.

With the win, Player achieved the career Grand Slam, joining Ben Hogan and Gene Sarazen. Only Nicklaus and Tiger Woods have matched that feat since. Afterwards, Player announced that he was donating his winner's share of $26,000 ($25,000 first prize, $1,000 for the playoff) to charity. He gave $5,000 for cancer research and the remaining $21,000 for the development of junior golf in the United States. This fulfilled a promise he made to Joe Dey in 1962 that if he ever won the U.S. Open he would donate his winnings, and caused Bob Rosburg to quip that Player thought the USGA was four times worse than cancer.

Neither Pearson nor Barrea were seriously injured. After receiving eight stitches, Pearson returned to the course and met with Nagle outside of the clubhouse as he was getting into a car to drive to the airport. The always-gracious Nagle apologized, reached into his bag, and gave her three golf balls. "I'm sorry that is all I have to give you, but I'm so glad you are all right," he said.

Gary Player

That was always my dream (to win all four majors). Palmer, Nicklaus, and I were great friends, but it's not possible to have three better competitors wanting to beat each other. Of course, I wanted to do it before them. And the other thing is, I wanted to win the Senior Grand Slam before them, and they never won the Senior Grand Slam. So, I'm

224

the only man on the planet who won the Grand Slam on the regular tour and the Senior Tour. That is my greatest accomplishment.

Frank Beard

I played with Gary Player in the final round. I was scared to death. The very first hole I double-bogeyed, and that was about it for me. Player was very intense. He always seemed to have hard feelings because Palmer and Nicklaus got more credit in the press. He had the small man's complex. They have to prove they're as good as the big guys. He was the best bunker player I ever saw. And the best putter from 6 feet.

Player had the theory that if you were going to make a mistake, you make it as close to the green as you could. Make it where you could have a wedge or a short iron to the green. You make a mistake off the tee, and now you're still 500 yards away and up to your ass in grass. It was a pretty good theory. I don't know if anybody else espoused it. We were all trying to hit the fairway. I hit a number of 3-woods. I drove the ball pretty good most of my career. I really had to. I couldn't compete with those guys, recovering. I had a good short game, but if I was going to compete I couldn't make too many mistakes. I had to make a minimum and hope they made a maximum of some sort.

Bellerive was almost the worst kind of Open course. It was all Bermuda grass. Bermuda rough stands up like a hairbrush, and your ball of course is straight down in it. Two to four inches straight down in the stuff, and it's like a wire brush. You can't move it. Of course, it's hot as hell. I grew up in that kind of heat, so that part didn't bother me. It was set up so hard.

It was only my second Open. I played at Congressional, which actually was hotter, and the course was more difficult, but it was not so un-fun to play. You felt like you had a chance at Congressional. You got in the rough at Bellerive, it was just godawful.

We had a lot of problems with the USGA. I can't tell you the number of times I called for rulings with a USGA official. They *were nice guys, they were doctors, lawyers, whatever. Volunteers, two-year terms, and the next thing you knew they were out on the course making rulings.*

Photo 50: Walter Iooss, Gary Player during his win at the 1965
U.S. Open. (Walter Iooss, Jr.)

July

Open Championship

Photo 51: Peter Thomson. (Mercury)

Peter Thomson may have been the greatest golfer of the 1950s. The Australian certainly was the best outside of the United States. He won the Open Championship four times in the '50s, including three in succession (1954-1956), the only golfer to ever accomplish that feat in a major championship, and won dozens of tournaments in Europe, Australia, and New Zealand.

Although Thomson expressed an aversion to American courses, saying they too often were wet and not as good as those in Europe, he periodically made trips to the United States. In 1956, he finished fourth in the U.S. Open at Oak Hill. On the way to Rochester, he won the Texas International Open, which had a then-extravagant purse of $70,000, beating Cary Middlecoff and Gene Littler in a playoff for his only PGA Tour victory. In 1957, he finished fifth at the Masters.

When he arrived at Royal Birkdale in 1965, Thomson was 35 years old and seemingly a relic from golf's previous era. His last Open title had come in 1958 and his wins had tapered off in recent years. With the PGA Championship scheduled a month out in mid-August, a larger American contingent than usual ventured to England, including Arnold Palmer, Jack Nicklaus, Tony Lema, Doug Sanders, Sam Snead, and Phil Rodgers.

Defending champion Lema led after Wednesday's opening round with a course-record, 5-under 68 on the par-73 course. Palmer shot 70 and was the only other American in the top-10. On Thursday, Lema shot 72 and shared the 36-hole lead with Bruce Devlin. Palmer sank a 45-foot putt for an eagle on 17 on his way to a 71 to share third place with Welshman Brian Huggett, who equaled Lema's 68 from the day before, and was one shot back. Thomson also shot 68 and was two behind in fifth place, tied with Eric Brown of Scotland and three players from Ireland: Christy O'Connor, Sr., Hugh Boyle, and amateur Joe Carr.

For the final time at the Open Championship, there was a 36-hole finish on Friday. Rain and wind caused scores to soar. Thomson's 72 in the morning gave him a one-shot lead over Lema and Devlin, who only managed 75s. In the end, the result was a throwback to the 1950s. Thomson won his fifth Open title, two shots ahead of Huggett and O'Connor. Lema finished tied for fifth and was the only American in the top 10. Tony Jacklin, playing in his second Open, tied for 25th.

Tony Jacklin

Peter Thomson was a good friend of mine. He was like a mentor to me. He was very friendly, a great guy. When I decided to come and get my tour card in 1967, he said, "Oh you don't want to go over there. You should play internationally." He could play golf. I loved his simplicity when it came down to explaining things. He was patient. The ability to play links golf requires patience.

August

PGA Championship

For the first time since 1944, the PGA Championship was played in the month of August (except in 1959, when its dates were July 30 to August 2), although it would return to its July slot for 1966, 1967 and 1968.

The year before, Jack Nicklaus was the unofficial host of the PGA when it was held in his hometown of Columbus, Ohio. In 1965, it was Arnold Palmer's turn. The venue was the Laurel Valley Golf Club in Ligonier, Pennsylvania, near Palmer's home, measuring 7,090 yards with a par of 71. Palmer was one of the founders of Laurel Valley. Before it opened in 1959, the other club founders urged him to retire from the tour and serve as club professional. Palmer gave serious consideration to the offer before declining.

A controversy involving Palmer arose even before the tournament's start. During practice rounds, some pros were cutting the corner on the par-5 third hole by playing down an adjacent fairway. Palmer expressed displeasure with the situation, and on Wednesday a 60-foot-high fir tree was planted to prevent this from happening during the tournament. Some of Palmer's fellow pros considered this to be another example of officials stacking the deck in favor of Palmer. The resident pro and course superintendent, Paul Erath, resigned in protest.

When play opened on Thursday—two hours late due to fog— Palmer became involved in another imbroglio. After his drive on the first hole went into a bunker, he hooked a 5-iron onto and off of a small temporary bridge installed for spectators. Palmer's ball came to rest next to a railing that was part of the bridge and driven into the ground. The railing would interfere with his next shot, so he called for a ruling. While waiting for an official, two marshals took the railing down, thus removing the obstruction, and Palmer chipped onto the green without waiting for an official.

While playing the sixth hole, Palmer was approached by an official and told to add two strokes to his score. He would have been entitled to a free drop within two club lengths, but not to have the object removed. Palmer ended the round with a 1-over 71.

Tommy Aaron shot 66 to lead after the first round by one over Gardner Dickinson and Mason Rudolph, and by two over 53-year-old Sam Snead, Raymond Floyd, and Bruce Devlin (who always seemed to be in the mix in 1960s major championships). Nicklaus was three back with a 69.

Palmer's woes continued in the second round. He started on the back nine, and on the par-5 11th hit his second shot into a dry gulley. While taking a practice swing, Palmer hit a rock. His shot from the gulley only traveled 30 feet, and his next went into a sand trap. He blasted to within 4 feet and missed the putt for an apparent double-bogey 7. But, after Palmer called for an official, it was determined that Palmer's hitting the rock constituted grounding his club in a hazard, adding two more strokes to give him a quadruple-bogey 9. Palmer ended up shooting 75 and thereafter would never be in serious contention, finishing tied for 33rd.

Aaron shot 71 in the second round and maintained a two-stroke lead over Nicklaus and Dave Marr, the latter a 31-year-old pro from Houston who at one time had been an assistant at the Winged Foot Golf Club under 1948 Masters champion Claude Harmon, and whose most recent of two tour wins came in 1962. Nicklaus shot 70 and Marr 69. Billy Casper was three back, one ahead of Dickinson and Floyd. At even and five back were Mike Souchak, two-time U.S. Amateur Public Links champion R.H. Sikes, and Don Bies, a club pro from Seattle who would prove he could keep pace with the touring pros in major championships.

On a steamy Saturday, scores were higher, most likely because of some difficult pin placements that pros grumbled about. Marr shot 70. He would have had the lead to himself, but he missed a 2-foot putt on the 18th hole. As a result, he was tied with Aaron—still looking for his first tour win—who shot 72. Dickinson's 69 was the low round of the day and left him one shot back, and one ahead of Nicklaus and Casper. Both Snead and Ben Hogan (who was playing in his last PGA Championship) shot 70. Snead was just four back, Hogan eight behind.

In the final round, Aaron withered in the 93-degree heat, shooting 78. Nobody mounted a charge on the sleepy day. Marr scrambled for pars on the final two holes to win by two shots over Nicklaus and Casper, all three of whom shot 71. It would be Marr's sole major championship. When he died in 1997 at age 63, some of his ashes were scattered at the 18th hole of Laurel Valley Golf Club.

Tommy Aaron

I remember that I was leading after three there. I had a terrible last round. It started with a double-bogey at the first hole. I hit my drive in the left rough and it was kind of stymied up against a tree, unplayable. Then, I missed the green from there and it took three to get down. So that was kind the beginning of the end for me.

Exhibition, Overland Park, Kansas

For Arnold Palmer, 1965 was a disappointing year. He won only the Tournament of Champions and would finish 10th on the money list with $57,770, his lowest total since 1959. At the Carling World Open at Pleasant Valley, Massachusetts, in August, he was tied for the lead after 15 holes, but bogeyed 16 and 17 to lose by two shots to Tony Lema. The following week, he finished second again, to Al Geiberger at the American Golf Classic.

Two days later, on an off-day on his way to the Oklahoma City Open (where he was the defending champion), Palmer stopped off in Kansas City to play an exhibition for the benefit of a cystic fibrosis charity. Local pros Bill Knapp and Stan Thirsk also played.

Thirsk brought along his 15-year-old protégé, Tom Watson.

For the front nine, Watson played even with Palmer, his idol, before Palmer bested him by six shots on the back.

Tom Watson

After the exhibition was over, Arnie was wrapped in a towel. He had just finished taking a shower and we're in the locker room with him. And my dad said, "What one thing can help my son be a better golfer?" And Arnie just turned around and he said, "Have him play in as much competition as he can."

October

Sahara Invitational

The Paradise Valley Country Club in Las Vegas was the venue for the tournament sponsored by the Sahara Hotel and Del Webb. It was held in the latter part of October, after temperatures generally had cooled off. With the season winding down and the money title often on the line, and Vegas being Vegas, it always had a strong field. Jack Nicklaus won the Sahara four times in the 1960s.

In 1965, summer-like heat returned. In the final round, the high was 90 degrees. Billy Casper was leading by four strokes when he came to the ninth green. His 3-foot putt for par spun out and hung on the lip. Casper stood over the hole for more than 30 seconds, waving his putter, and the ball finally dropped in. Casper and his playing partners, Tommy Aaron and Bruce Crampton, consulted with tour official Steve Shabala, who ruled that Casper violated Rule 35.1H, which stated that a player is allowed "not more than a few seconds" to determine if a ball hanging on the lip of the cup is at rest.

After the bogey and two-stroke penalty, Casper's lead was down to one. Casper held true to his reputation as a cut-throat competitor by making birdies on the next three holes and won his fourth tournament of the year by three shots over Bill Martindale.

Australian Open

In late October, Gary Player and Jack Nicklaus ventured to Adelaide for the Australian Open. On the front nine of the opening round, Player went eagle-birdie-birdie-birdie-birdie-birdie-par-birdie-birdie for an incredible 9-under 28. He cooled to a 2-under 34 on the back for a 62 that put him four clear of Nicklaus. In the second round, Nicklaus followed his opening 66 with a career-low 63 to take a four-shot lead over Player, who scored an even-par 71.

In the third round, Player played the first seven holes in even 3s on his way to his second 62 of the tournament. Nicklaus shot 71, so for the second straight day there was an at least eight-shot swing between he and Player. In the final round, Player added a 69 to win by six over Nicklaus and Australian Frank Phillips. Player's 72-hole score of 264 has never been matched in the Australian Open.

Gary Player

Jack Nicklaus and I had a great battle in our career to see who could win the most Australian Opens. I won seven, and he won six. And also, today—today—I have the lowest score ever shot in the Australian Open with the crappy equipment we used as compared to the modern equipment today.

In those days, the Australian Open probably was the fifth most important tournament, because everybody played in it. Trevino, Tom Watson, Jack Nicklaus, Arnold Palmer, all the Americans went to play in it. And it was a very, very prestigious event.

November

Cajun Classic

After winning the Sahara, Billy Casper's earnings for the year jumped to $96,771.90, putting him in a position to join Nicklaus, Arnold Palmer and Tony Lema as the only pros to earn $100,000 in a year. However, Casper tied for 15th at the Almaden Open the following week, good for only $935, and the following week earned $2,225 for finishing seventh in the Hawaiian Open, leaving him $69 short of $100,000. The milestone was not important enough for Casper to make the trip to Lafayette, Louisiana three weeks later for the season-ending Cajun Classic, so he would have to wait until 1966 to join the $100,000 club.

Photo 52: *Babe Hiskey holds 1965 Cajun Classic winner's check, with runner-up Dudley Wysong. (Associated Press)*

Despite having locked up the money title, Nicklaus played in the Cajun Classic in an effort to satisfy the requirement for full-fledged PGA membership that a golfer play in 25 approved tournaments a year for five years. He hoped to be eligible to play in the 1967 Ryder Cup. Nicklaus tied for third at the Cajun Classic to earn $1,900 and boost his earnings for the year to a record $140,752. It was his 24th tournament, but a scheduled event in Miami Nicklaus planned to play was canceled. He obtained a waiver of the requirement in June 1966 and then started earning Ryder Cup points. However, with the late start, Nicklaus did not earn enough points to qualify for the 1967 team, and there were no captain's choice picks at the time.

Babe Hiskey, a 27-year-old from Idaho, won by one stroke over Dudley Wysong. Hiskey used a putter created by engineer Karsten Solheim. A few weeks earlier at the Piccadilly World Match Play tournament in Wentworth, England—a showcase set up by Mark McCormack for the Big Three—contestants were seen trying out Solheim's putters. Hiskey's win helped usher in a new era in club design.

Babe Hiskey

I won $7,000. You're not going to make a living off of that. I was doing more sales on the side. I sold putters for Ping. There were only 20 guys that made a living.

(Ping founder) Karsten (Solheim) and I were together ever since 1961. I met him in Scottsdale, Arizona, on a putting green. And he said, "My putters are a lot better than what you're using." He made what you call the A-1 putter, and what was called the Ping putter. It would "ping" and would drive you nuts. He always made different putters. He didn't sell too much. He was working for General Electric.

It was right after I won that Mark McCormack wanted to buy his putter business. Karsten wanted to know who this guy is. I said, "He's the manager for Palmer and Nicklaus and Gary Player. There must be some reason." And next week I'm reading Golf World. They had used a Ping putter at the Piccadilly in Europe, and the Europeans decided that they wanted Ping Putters. That's when Karsten decided he's not going to work for GE anymore.

I won at Sahara in 1970. I was broke at the time. Karsten was excited that his clubs won. Thing is, that after that tournament, Kermit Zarley and I drove to Phoenix. We're still vagabonds. That's the culture. Most of us traveled by car. Very few of us ever flew. (At Sahara), I won $20,000. Eleven tour events after that, I'm at Doral and I'm broke again. And I'm calling Karsten and I says, "Hey, I need a job." He says, "No, you don't. If I've got money, you've got money." So, he started giving me dividend checks for playing.

1966

January

Bing Crosby National Pro-Am

Photo 53: *Don Cherry (right) sang better than Arnold Palmer. (Don Cherry Facebook page)*

Few pros had more sustained lack of success than Don Cherry. From 1960 to 1969, he played in 93 tournaments and made 37 cuts, with only two top-10 finishes. One was in the 1960 U.S. Open when, as an amateur, he contended until the final round and tied for ninth with Ben Hogan. After he turned pro in 1962, Cherry's total winnings for the decade were $6,907. A chunk of that came at the 1966 Crosby, where he finished tied for 24th, 12 shots behind winner Don Massengale, and earned $730.

Cherry could afford to fail on the golf course, for he was better known as a singer. His 1955 song "Band of Gold," backed by the Ray Conniff Orchestra, made it to No. 4 on the Billboard Hot 100 and was reprised in 2007 over the opening credits of the first episode of the long-running drama series *Mad Men*. Cherry had other hits and also was the voice for Mr. Clean in animated commercials.

Throughout both his amateur and professional career, Cherry lined up gigs at nightclubs in the towns where he played tournaments. This included Augusta, Georgia, before the 1953 Masters. Clifford Roberts found out and approached Cherry, telling him "We never had anyone play in the Masters and sing at a local nightclub at the same time." According to Cherry, he replied "Mr. Roberts, I have looked at the people playing in this tournament and can't see anyone else who can sing." Nonetheless, he canceled the gig.

Bob Zimmerman

In 1966 I played in the Bing Crosby tournament. I was at Cypress Point, on the putting green at 7:30 in the morning. It was just me, Dean Martin, and Arnold Palmer. They had a bar set up on the first tee and Dean Martin already had a drink. If you made the cut, on Sunday night they had the famous clambake. All the pros who made the cut were invited, and all the celebrities. I was in the top 20 going into the last round. And I shot 77, and I was all upset, so I went back to the motel, and I said to my wife, "Pack up your clothes, we're heading out of here." It was a once-in-a-lifetime thing, and we didn't go to it.

I don't know if you remember the name, Don Cherry. He was a singer, and he was also a golf pro. In the '60s when I was out there playing he would have a gig at the site of where the golf tournament was. A bunch of us guys would go, have dinner and drinks and so forth and listen to him sing. In those days, when we got through playing, we went out. We went to the bars. Today, they go to the gym.

Chuck Courtney

At the 1966 Crosby, I played in the pro-am with a good friend of mine, in fact one of the guys who sponsored me several years earlier, a guy named John Moler. He was a member of the La Jolla Country Club where I grew up.

In the final round, it was one of those horrible, breezy, cold days, and it was almost getting dark. That was in the old days when the TV tower was rickety, and the wind was blowing like hell. Bing and Phil Harris are up there doing the commentary, along with whoever it was. And we tied in the pro-am with Billy Martindale and a guy named Bob Roos. And they had never had a playoff before. When it was tied, they always had co-champions.

Bing and Phil Harris were both totally loaded, and they scrambled down the ladder. Roos and Bing were good friends. They played together. They were members of that fancy club, Woodside, up on the peninsula near San Francisco. Roos was a rich guy from San Francisco. His family owned a department store.

Roos went over and put his arm around Bing and said, "Finally! After all these years I've won your tournament!" And Bing said, "Fuck you, Roos, we're having a playoff." And we did have a playoff, in the dark, and we won. Interestingly, the plaque behind the first tee at Pebble Beach for years just had my name and my partner's name as the champions for 1966. I was up there two or three years ago. I go hiking at Big Sur, and I went to show my girlfriend the plaque, and they changed it. They had us as co-champions with Roos and Martindale. And I know why. Roos's family was very close to Paul Spangler, who ran the Pebble Beach Company before he retired, and they talked him into changing it.

February

Panama Open

While most pros were at the Tucson Open (won by Joe Campbell in a playoff with Gene Littler), several name players—including Art Wall, Mike Souchak, Roberto De Vicenzo, Dow Finsterwald, Bob McAllister, and Al Besselink—ventured to the Panama Open, which was part of the Caribbean tour.

Also in the field was an assistant pro from Dallas and a former Marine named Lee Trevino, who was playing his first tournament against world-class players. Canadian Wilf Homenuik, who played the PGA tour sporadically for many years without much success, won. Trevino tied for fifth with De Vicenzo.

Lee Trevino

I was working at the driving range of a par-3 course in Dallas. There was a guy that was going to SMU. He was kind of a poker gambler and whatever, but he graduated, and he wasn't a kid. He was probably 27, 28 years old. He had been watching me and playing golf with me, and he said, "Man, I think you got a future in this game." His name was Bill Gray, and he said to me, "You know, they got a tournament down in Panama, we ought to go down there and play it. I'll call and see if I can get you in." And I said OK.

You've got to understand, I had never been out of Dallas with the exception of the Marine Corps. I was all over the Pacific. So, that's the only time that I've ever left Dallas. I've never been to California, Oklahoma, New York, any other place. So anyway, I said, "How far is it down there?" He said, "I looked at a map, and it doesn't look like it's that far to Panama." We take out a map, and you know how maps are, say, one inch is 500 miles or something. He says, "We can drive to Mexico City in one day. It won't take us but a couple of days to get down there."

We didn't know anything about traveling. He had a brand new '65 Oldsmobile Cutlass. We loaded up and here we go, and we take off for Panama. Little did we know that when we got to the border of Guatemala, you got to get a permit for the car. You got to prove insurance. There's a lot of stuff you got to go through. We have to go find the consulate. And so now, you got to go back into town and find the papers to get into Guatemala. So, we do that. To make a long story short, we end up doing it in El Salvador and Honduras and every country before we got to Panama. Well, by the time we get to Panama, it took us almost seven days. We were lucky that we left early enough because we were going to practice, or we would have missed the tournament.

The Oldsmobile Cutlass was completely worn out. And I ended up finishing fifth, winning $500. (Gray) lost it in a poker game. We sold the car, jumped on a flight, and came back to Dallas dead broke. We didn't have a car or a quarter. That was my first experience of touring golf. It was unbelievable.

Kimberley 4000

Photo 54: Harold Henning.
(Historic Images)

In late February, South African Harold Henning went into the final round of the Kimberley 4000 tournament in his home country with a seemingly insurmountable six-shot lead. Henning was a 12-time winner in Africa and Europe. In 1965, he and Gary Player won the World Cup for South Africa. Henning informed the sponsors that he had a plane to catch to travel to his next tournament in Asia and politely requested permission to leave after his round. He would arrange to pick up the check and trophy. Happy that a golfer of Henning's stature had graced them with his presence at their small tournament, the sponsors agreed. Henning shot a 71 and left the course.

However, 21-year-old Tony Jacklin of England got hot and sank a 9-foot putt on the 18th green for a 65 to tie Henning, who already was on his way to Johannesburg for his connecting flight.

Tony Jacklin

I played a lot of golf in South Africa in the mid-60s. I went to South Africa once for eight weeks with Christy O'Connor, Sr. and a couple of other pros. We rented a Ford Fairlane from Harold Henning. It was a massive car, a great long thing, and drove all over for eight weeks on the South African circuit.

I ended up winning a tournament in Kimberley, where the diamonds come from. I actually tied with Harold. He posted his score, and he had an arrangement with the sponsor that he could leave. I remember a lot of the South African pros, Bobby Locke included, said, "No, you go on the tee, tee it up. You're the winner." I said, "There's no way I'm going to do that. If Harold had an arrangement, he had an arrangement." So, we tied for first place. I wasn't going to do that to Harold.

March

Pensacola Open

By 1966, Doug Sanders long had established himself as one of the best and most popular players (at least among fans) on the tour, with an unusual short backswing with which weekend hackers could identify, and a wardrobe awash in pastel that made him easily stand out from the standard banded white shirts and navy blue slacks favored by his competitors.

After 36 holes of the Pensacola Open in March 1966, Sanders was poised to win the 16th tournament of his career, and in Pensacola for the third time. A month earlier, he beat Arnold Palmer in a playoff at the Bob Hope Desert Classic, and he had top-10 finishes in three other events on the winter circuit. Sanders was the hottest player on the planet. Because Palmer, Jack Nicklaus, Gary Player, and Tony Lema were all bypassing Pensacola, the local sponsors were happy to have Sanders as the marquee name in the field.

Justifying his top billing, Sanders shot 63 in the opening round and followed up with a 67, amassing 15 birdies against only one bogey for the first 36 holes. His 130 total put him four shots clear of Gay Brewer and six ahead of Tom Weiskopf. Sanders dutifully signed the card of playing partner Johnny Pott.

While Sanders was regaling the press about his round, a voice was heard over the intercom. "Where's Sanders?" It was PGA tournament supervisor Jack Tuthill. "He's right here," replied press secretary Doc Giffin. "Well, I've got some bad news for him," said Tuthill. Sanders left the press room and met with Tuthill in a clubhouse hallway. "You didn't sign your card. You're out of the tournament," Tuthill informed.

Sanders was incredulous. "What difference does it make if it hasn't been posted yet?," he asked. Tuthill pulled out the USGA rule book and recited Rule 38. "It says the competitor shall check his score for each hole, settle any doubtful points with the committee, ensure that the marker has signed the card himself and return it to the committee as soon as possible," Tuthill recited.

"Why can't I sign it now?" Sanders queried.

"It says in the rule, 'as soon as possible,'" Tuthill rejoined.

"It is the most ridiculous thing I have ever heard of," Sanders said bitterly when he returned to the press room. The terse statement issued by the tour gave him reason to be upset: "Over the past few years, players have been recalled by our officials from such areas as the locker room and putting greens to have the cards signed. The obligation under the rule rests with the competitor and, hence-forth, the officials will not search out a competitor for non-compliance." In other words, Sanders was being made an example of.

Sanders complained that he was victimized for being a nice guy. "I was surrounded by newspaper reporters and people wanting my autograph," he related. "I didn't think I should brush them off. If I can be this nice to these people, it seems that under the circumstances a little courtesy and understanding could be shown to me."

Brewer won by three strokes over Bruce Devlin. Sanders quickly got over his shocking disappointment, winning in Jacksonville and Greensboro in the next month.

Doc Giffin

Doug Sanders was leading the tournament. He was playing the back nine first, so he finished on the ninth hole. I went out in a golf cart to the ninth hole, because the ninth hole at the Pensacola Country Club wasn't right at the clubhouse. So, when he came off the ninth green, I was waiting for him and I drove him into the press facility we had there in the clubhouse, and we began the interview. Jack Tuthill came in and took him aside and said, "I'm sorry, you didn't sign your scorecard before it was turned in, and you're disqualified." Well, this created quite an uproar in the area because Doug was very popular in that part of the country. He was from Georgia. So, a lot of fans got really hot about it. That night, we had to hastily put out a press release explaining the reason why he was disqualified.

Doug was a little hot. He said I pulled him away from the ninth green, and that's why he failed to sign his card. I didn't pull him away. I was sitting there waiting for him and he came and got into the cart. I told him I was there and wanted to take him into the press room for an interview, but I didn't feel like I pulled him away. Doug and I got along great after that. No longstanding ill-will at all.

Frank Beard

I was there. That's just one of the cardinal rules, but if you get distracted it can happen. The people in the scorer's tent are supposed to make sure the players sign their cards, but what on God's earth was he thinking of?

Sanders' swing was very functional. He hit it straighter than anybody. He'd chip with his 5-wood off the green. A good putter.

He was the only man I've ever known who everything said about him was true. Alcohol, drugs, women. He was an extraordinary golfer who could not keep his personal life in line so he could reach his potential.

Bob Goalby

Sanders was a good guy. He tried to be good to everybody. A little bit of a hustler, but no big deal. Most golf pros have to hustle to make a living. He didn't get the best of reputations, but he was a hell of a player.

Chi Chi Rodriguez

That was a terrible ruling. Doug Sanders was going to run away with the tournament. He belongs in the Hall of Fame. He was different. That's why I liked him.

Walter Iooss, Jr.

Doug Sanders broke the mold. Nobody dressed cooler than Doug Sanders. Plus, he was handsome, you know, all tangerine outfits. I always loved photographing him because he was colorful. Nobody dressed like him in the history of any sport. Maybe Walt Frazier of the Knicks.

Chuck Courtney

Doug was pretty much a degenerate, to tell the truth.

Photo 55: Doug Sanders, 1966. (Walter Iooss, Jr.)

April

Greater Greensboro Open

Tom Weiskopf became a force to be reckoned with in 1966. The 23-year-old from Ohio did not take up the game until he was 15, but quickly became good enough to play on the golf team at Ohio State, where he overlapped with Jack Nicklaus for one year before dropping out. As a rookie in 1965, he did not do much, earning only $11,264 in 27 tournaments with no finishes higher than fifth. Earlier in 1966, Weiskopf finished second at San Diego and tied for third in San Francisco.

Arnold Palmer was the only one of the Big Three in Greensboro. Nicklaus and Gary Player (and Billy Casper) chose to prepare for the Masters coming up the following week. After 36 holes, Weiskopf was tied for the lead with Doug Sanders. Palmer was seven back after consecutive 71s. On Saturday, Palmer shot 68 to get within five shots of leader R.H. Sikes, who took the lead by one over Weiskopf and Sanders. Paired with Palmer was young Steve Oppermann, who struggled to a 78 while having to contend with Arnie's Army.

In the final round, both Weiskopf and Sanders shot 70 to overtake Sikes and tie for first. On the second hole of the sudden-death playoff, after Weiskopf bogeyed, Sanders rapped in a 5-footer for a par to win. It would be another two years before Weiskopf would win (at San Diego, and at the Buick Open).

Steve Oppermann
I don't think who you play with made a difference. It might be hard to play with Arnold Palmer. I played with him two or three times, and I remember Greensboro in 1966, when he had 10,000 people following him in the third round. It was hard to play that day. He was a nice guy.

It was tough. When you finished, everybody would run because they wanted to get to see his next tee shot. And a lot of people used those periscopes. That's what they used to see. It was so crowded. You could hardly see. It was amazing how many people wanted to see him play.

They'd run before I finished the hole. They'd run before he finished. If he had a 1-footer, they wouldn't wait for that. They'd take off.

The Masters

Behind his bespectacled, scholarly façade, Clifford Roberts was a badass going back to his youth in Iowa, where he was expelled from school for beating up the principal. Having made a fortune on Wall Street, he also was good with other people's money. Thus, in the year since Roberts proclaimed to a national audience that they would see the next Masters in color, he convinced CBS to make the $600,000 investment necessary to fulfill his promise. The 1966 Masters would be the first broadcast in color and would draw a record television audience.

In advance of the tournament, Arnold Palmer was installed as the 4-1 favorite, probably because it was an even-numbered year and he had won every two years since 1958. Even after his record-setting cakewalk at the 1965 Masters, Jack Nicklaus's 6-1 odds were the same as for Gary Player and Bruce Devlin.

Before Thursday's opening round, Nicklaus was awakened in the middle of the night by a phone call informing him that a close childhood friend, Bob Barton, and a young couple he knew died in the crash of the private plane they had rented. The three were on their way to Augusta to watch Nicklaus. On a windswept day that started with overcast skies and ended in bright sunshine, the visibly somber Nicklaus still appeared to be primed to repeat when he opened with a 68, which was three shots clear of Billy Casper, Mike Souchak, Don January, and two-time U.S. Amateur champion Charles Coe.

The wind intensified on Friday, and Nicklaus struggled to a 76. Peter Butler of England and Paul Harney were tied atop the leaderboard at 143. Harney shot 68, the only round of the day under 70. Nicklaus was one back, tied with Palmer, January, Bob Rosburg and Doug Sanders.

The overnight leaders faltered on Saturday, Harney with a 76, Butler 79. Tommy Jacobs, who opened with a 75 and followed with a 71, shot 70 on Saturday, the low round of the day. Normally, an even-par score of 216 for 54 holes at Augusta National would not raise many eyebrows. In 1966, it was good enough for Jacobs to tie for the lead with Nicklaus, who rebounded with a 72 on a day on which, despite diminished wind, birdies continued to be at a premium. Most of the patrons followed the twosome of Palmer and Ben Hogan. Neither disappointed. Palmer shot 74, Hogan 73, to put them and Gay Brewer at 218, just two behind the leaders. Brewer was 6 over at one point but rallied with four consecutive birdies.

On Easter Sunday, it was sunny, chilly, and windy for the final round. Playing with Palmer, Brewer went out in 33 to take the lead. Palmer's front nine of 34 included birdies at 7 and 8 that gave him a share of the lead. However, he made costly bogeys at 12 and 14, and bogeyed 18 when he needed a birdie. Palmer finished tied for fourth, two back.

On the back nine, Brewer parred holes 10 through 17. He came to the 420-yard 18th hole needing a par to win. With the wind at his back, Brewer smoked his drive, leaving him with only a nine-iron to the green. Still, he put his approach well past the hole, leaving him with a 40-foot sidehill putt. Trying to lag for a two-putt, he left his first below the hole. His 4-foot putt to win broke left at the end, singed the cup and did not drop. It was Brewer's only bogey of the round, and he finished 72 holes at even-par 288.

Jacobs fell behind until birdies on 13 and 15 put him in a tie for the lead. On 17, he drove into the trees but shaped a 4-iron onto the green and made par. On 18, Jacobs found the trees again but got a fortunate kick into the fairway, but he was so far back that he had to hit a 4-wood for his second shot. He hit it splendidly to within 21 feet. With two putts, he joined Brewer at 288.

Nicklaus, playing with Hogan (who soared to 77 and finished tied for 13th), went out in 37 to fall three back of Brewer. He rallied with birdies on 14 and 15. On 17, Nicklaus put his approach to three-and-a-half feet. His birdie putt broke below the hole, and he missed. On the 18th, Nicklaus had the last chance to win, but his 40-foot putt for a birdie swerved a fraction of an inch to the left and stayed out of the cup. He, too, finished at even-par 288, the second-highest 72-hole score by a leader in Masters' history.

In Monday's playoff, Brewer never was a factor. He went out in 38, double-bogeyed 12 and only managed garbage-time birdies on 15 and 16 on his way to a 78. Nicklaus and Jacobs were tied at the turn. Jacobs bogeyed 10 while Nicklaus parred, then Nicklaus birdied 11 while Jacobs parred. They matched scores the rest of the way. With darkness descending, Nicklaus parred 18 for a 70 to win his third green jacket in four years and become the Masters' first repeat winner.

Ron Cerrudo

I got to play in the 1966 Masters as an amateur. I roomed with Cesar Sanudo, who also was an amateur. We didn't get to stay in the Crow's Nest in the Augusta National clubhouse, but got to stay in Lewis Maytag's cabin near the first tee. I played with Clifford Roberts in the Par Three tournament. On one hole, Mr. Roberts made a par and I had a 2-foot putt for a par. My caddie said something like, "If I were you I'd miss the putt because Mr. Roberts doesn't like to lose every hole." So I missed it. Afterwards, we had drinks with Mr. Roberts, which I enjoyed.

The USGA was pretty strict about amateur rules, so we had to pay for our meals in the dining room. One dollar for breakfast, two dollars for dinner. Early in the morning of the first round I woke up and from the house was able to see Jock Hutchison and Fred McLeod tee off to start the Masters. That was cool.

June

Memphis Open

Albert Winsborough Yancey took a circuitous route to the pro tour. Growing up in Tallahassee, Florida as one of 10 children, he had a solid, though not spectacular, high school golf career. In 1957, after completing his freshman year at Florida State University, he accepted an appointment to the U.S. Military Academy. West Point was not then, nor is now, an intercollegiate golf center, and upon graduation Yancey would be required to serve in the Army for several years. Thus, he could not have been banking on a pro career.

Photo 56: Bert Yancey. (Usma.org)

As a plebe, Al Yancey (as he was then known) played on the golf team and made the dean's list. After his junior year, he was elected golf team captain. He was undefeated in match play in four years of college (three at West Point, one at Florida State). Six-feet tall, 190 pounds, blond and handsome, with a genius level IQ, Yancey was poised to make his mark in the world outside of golf.

However, when Yancey returned to West Point in 1960 for the start of his senior year, he started exhibiting strange behavior. He was unable to sleep and began to rant nonsensically. He lined plebes up against a wall and demanded to know the meaning of truth, and the meaning of love. He was taken for examination by a psychiatrist, diagnosed as having suffered a nervous breakdown, and was sent to the Army hospital at Valley Forge, Pennsylvania. After nine months at Valley Forge, during which he received electroconvulsive therapy, Yancey was given an honorable discharge on medical grounds. Soon thereafter, he decided to try to make a living as a professional golfer.

Bert Yancey (as he now preferred to be called) struggled to make ends meet in occasional appearances on the tour, so he took an assistant pro position near Philadelphia. In 1964, he started playing the tour full-time and earned some checks. In April 1966, Yancey won his first tournament, the Azalea Open in Wilmington, North Carolina, a weak-field, small-purse event run opposite the Tournament of Champions.

In June, at the Memphis Open, there was a formidable field that included Jack Nicklaus, Ben Hogan, Tony Lema, Gary Player and Julius Boros. Yancey was the 54-hole leader. On Sunday morning, he slept late and turned on the television to watch astronaut Eugene Cernan's spacewalk during the Gemini 9A mission. At 11:10 a.m., Yancey's caddie called to inform he was scheduled to tee off at 11:20 a.m. Yancey was unaware that the tee times had been moved up an hour to accommodate CBS, which was televising the tournament. "I was never so frightened," Yancey said. "I just knew I had blown the whole works." He sprinted to the Colonial Country Club and barely made his tee time, having had no chance to warm up. Nevertheless, Yancey shot 66 to win easily, beating Gene Littler by five strokes. His first-place check was for $20,000.

"His swing was a symphony, each movement majestic in its purity and simplicity," Dave Kindred of *The Washington Post* would write of Yancey in 1978. "Putting, he was a thief working in daylight, stealing birdies from 20 feet when par was his due." Never was his putting more masterfully on display than at the Portland Open in September 1966. Tied with Pete Brown after 54 holes, he sank a 60-foot eagle putt on the first hole. He needed only 24 more putts in his round of 67, good for a three-shot win over Billy Casper. For 72 holes, Yancey took 102 putts, a tour record that stood until 1977.

After his career year in 1966, Bert Yancey would win four more times between 1967 and 1972. He finished third at the Masters in 1967 and 1968, and fourth in 1970, and third in the U.S. Open in 1968 and 1974. He traveled to Britain every July and finished fifth at the 1973 Open Championship.

But during his years of success, Yancey continued to battle with mood swings off of the course. In October 1974, Yancey came in second to Gene Littler in a tournament in Japan to earn $32,500, the largest check of his career. He stayed in Japan for clinics. He was on a manic high and had a delusion that he must save Asia from Communism. At 3 a.m., he heard a song in his hotel room, "Take a Walk, Take a Walk," which he took as a command. While returning to the hotel, he met members of the Temptations singing group, who were touring Japan. Upon learning of the group's name, Yancey believed they must be evil, and he picked a fight with one of its members. Yancey was felled by a karate chop from one of the group's entourage. After he returned to the hotel, he pulled down a Christmas tree.

Yancey was flown back to America and was hospitalized in Philadelphia for two-and-a-half months in early 1975. Upon being released, he returned to the tour and finished second behind Nicklaus at Doral, and also was second at Tallahassee. But after completing 72 holes at the Westchester Classic in August 1975, he was arrested at LaGuardia Airport. Yancey had ordered a painter to get down from a ladder. He then climbed the ladder and expounded on the evils of racism, directing the Black passengers in the terminal to move to one side and the White passengers to the other. He was taken to Payne Whitney Hospital, where he was diagnosed with bipolar disorder. Lithium was prescribed. Although the treatment was successful in controlling his mental illness, it curtailed his career as a touring pro because of the tremors the drug caused.

After turning 50, with the advent of the drug Tegretol (which did not cause tremors), Yancey was able to resume playing senior pro events. He spoke often to groups about his battles with mental illness. In 1994, while on the practice tee before the Franklin Quest Championship in

Utah, Yancey suffered a heart attack and died at age 56.

Tony Jacklin

Throughout that part of the 1960s, Bert, Tom Weiskopf and I were inseparable. It was dinner every night and practice rounds the next day. We were as close as friends can be. Bert was a manic-depressive, but I never saw that side of him. He was a very deep thinker. He just wanted to play golf. He embraced links golf. He loved going to the Open Championship, as did Tom. They knew winning there would improve their legacy. We stayed together when I won at Royal Lytham. The night before the final round, I took a sleeping pill and fell asleep. Bert guided me upstairs to my bed.

Bert had a simple, three-quarters swing, good tempo. Tempo was central to all he wanted to achieve. His wife Linda's father owned Mack Truck and had a place in Kennebunkport, Maine. I would spend a week there during the summer.

Frank Beard

Bert was one of my best friends. I was with him through all of the chaos. He was a great guy. A brilliant man. He taught me to play bridge. We played bridge together. Dave Hill, Jim Colbert, Dave Eichelberger, Harold Henning. Harold would get a party room. We'd have six or seven card games going on. Our wives would be at the door and would tell us, don't you think you should go to bed? Harold had a gambling addiction. He'd miss the cut at Tucson, fly to London to play high-stakes bridge, and he's back on Wednesday for the pro-am in Phoenix.

In the 1960s, Bert's real obsession was winning the Masters. He made a plaster of Paris model of the layout at Augusta National, about the size of your kitchen table, with every hill, every roll. It was beautiful.

Back then, nobody knew anything about manic depression.

Lee Trevino

You could tell (Yancey) was military by the way he walked down the fairway. Like he was marching. He was a tall, good-looking guy, smart, very quiet. He strutted when he went down the fairway. It's too bad, because he was a hell of a player. He could really play. He had a beautiful golf swing.

U.S. Open

In mid-June, the USGA and golf's finest descended upon the city of San Francisco for the U.S. Open at the Olympic Club's Lake Course.

A year later, San Francisco would be the epicenter of youth counterculture during the Summer of Love. As a prelude, right before the Open, the San Francisco Board of Permit Appeals reversed a ban on dances at the Fillmore Auditorium that had been imposed due to repeated arrests of teens flocking to see bands such as Jefferson Airplane and Quicksilver Messenger Service. Robert Zimmerman made an appearance at the Open; not the musician known as Bob Dylan, but the pro from Dayton, Ohio, who missed the cut.

Two young amateurs whose names would become part of U.S. Open lore—Johnny Miller and Hale Irwin—played in their first Opens. Miller played the first two days with an aspiring pro and former Marine who was several years older and also was playing in his first Open, Lee Trevino. Miller would finish eighth and was the low amateur. Irwin and Trevino played the weekend, too.

Photo 57: Rives McBee (right) made history at the 1966 U.S. Open. (United States Golf Association)

The weather throughout the weekend was typical San Francisco, mostly cloudy, damp, with temperatures in the 50s and 60s. Sweater weather, and an abrupt change for the pros who had just completed the circuit through Texas and the South. After the first round, journeyman Al Mengert led with a 67. On Friday, Arnold Palmer shot 66 to tie Billy Casper atop the leaderboard. Rives McBee, an assistant club pro from Texas and former schoolteacher who went through local and sectional qualifying to make the field, tied the Open record with a 64, leaving him in a tie with Phil Rodgers for third. McBee would finish sixth.

Playing with Casper in the third round, Palmer shot 70 to Casper's 73 to take a three-stroke lead going into Sunday. In the final round, Palmer opened with birdies on the first two holes and, after a bogey on the sixth, birdied the seventh and ninth for a front-nine 33. Meanwhile, Casper shot a 1-over 36. At the turn, Palmer's lead was seven strokes. He was at 6-under par and had his sights on breaking Ben Hogan's 72-hole scoring record of 8-under par, set at Riviera in 1948. Casper was hoping to hold off Nicklaus and Tony Lema for second place.

What followed was the most famous collapse in golf history. Palmer bogeyed 10, but matched birdies with Casper on 12 to hold a six-shot lead with six to play. On the par-3 13th, Palmer bogeyed while Casper parred. Both Palmer and Casper parred 14, so Palmer was five up with four to play. Jim McKay, doing commentary for ABC television, observed that Palmer would break Hogan's record if he parred in. On 15—another par-3—Casper hit his tee shot 20 feet from the hole. With the pin placed on the extreme right side of the green, and a broad, safe expanse to the left, Palmer inexplicably went for the flag anyway. He pushed his 7-iron into a bunker, leaving him no room to get close. Casper drained his birdie putt while Palmer two-putted for bogey. The lead was down to three, but only three holes remained.

As Palmer prepared to hit his drive on the long par-5 16th, ABC's Bill Fleming commented that the hole was beautiful and fragrant, with eucalyptus and pine trees lining the fairway. Palmer got to smell the trees up close as he duck-hooked his drive left. The ball hit a tree and fell into deep rough, well over 400 yards from the green. Palmer foolishly hit a 3-iron and muffed it, leaving his ball in even thicker rough. His third shot—a 9-iron—did not quite make it to the fairway. He lay three and was 220 yards from the green.

His fourth shot—a 3-wood—went into a bunker short of the green. From there, he miraculously was able to get up and down for a bogey 6. After the round, Palmer told Fleming, "It probably was one of the greatest sixes I've ever made." Casper conventionally followed his drive with two 5-irons and sank a birdie from 13 feet. Palmer's lead was down to one.

On the par-4 17th, Palmer again drove left. Again, his ball was nestled in thick rough. His second shot went into the right rough, 60 yards short of the green. Casper's drive found the right rough. He, too, had to lay up. His second shot went left and was 20 yards short of the green. Palmer chipped to 7 feet, Casper 5. Palmer's putt for par was in the center of the cup, but 1 inch short. Casper parred. The lead was gone. Palmer and Casper were tied.

By the time he reached the 18th green, Palmer, who just two hours before was concentrating on breaking Hogan's U.S. Open scoring record, was desperately trying to salvage a par. He put his second shot on the back of the green, while Casper's was much closer, about 13 feet. Palmer lagged his birdie putt 4 feet putt short.

Under the rules at the time, a player was required to continuously putt if he was not in a fellow player's line. Palmer asked Casper if he was in his line. According to a story Casper told late in his life to his physician and friend, Rick Parkinson, Casper replied that he was not. "Go ahead, Arnold, while you're hot," he said. Palmer made the tester, for a final round of 71. Had he matched the 53-year-old Hogan's final round of 70 (Hogan finished 12th), Palmer would have won. Instead, he shook his head sadly and watched helplessly while Casper lined up his putt to win.

Like Palmer, Casper hit a poor first putt, short and left, and tapped in for a par. An 18-hole playoff on Monday would follow.

Photo 58: *Arnold Palmer and Doc Giffin after Palmer's final round collapse at the 1966 U.S. Open. (Courtesy of Doc Giffin)*

In the playoff, Palmer squandered a two-shot lead after 11 holes, going bogey-bogey-double bogey on holes 14-16 to lose to Casper by four strokes.

Casper, who could be prickly at times, admitted to Dr. Parkinson that there was a measure of sarcasm in his comment to Palmer on the 18th green in the final round, and that it had haunted him ever since. At the Champions Dinner before the 2014 Masters, Casper apologized to Palmer. Palmer remembered the comment and was aware when it was made that it was a needle from Casper, and he accepted the apology. Casper died less than a year later, Palmer two-and-a-half years later.

Casper won 51 PGA tour events, 33 in the 1960s. He won the 1959 U.S. Open and the 1970 Masters, but the 1966 U.S. Open was the only major he won in the 1960s.

Photo 59: Billy Casper during the 1966 U.S. Open.
(United States Golf Association)

Rives McBee

It was my first U.S. Open. I'd never played in an Open before. Matter of fact, I'd never played in a PGA tour event before. I was an assistant pro at Midland Country Club, and I had just turned pro the previous August and was fortunate enough to qualify for the Open.

I thought I played pretty good the first round but I shot 76. I was having dinner that night at the airport hotel where we were staying and a gentleman walked by, by the name of Jack Fleck. And he said, "Young man, what'd you shoot today?" I said, "Well, I had 76." He said, "Well, I did, too, the first round of the year I won." And he said, "You can get it back. So just hang in there." I went out the next day and shot 64 and I was even par (after 36 holes). So, it was quite a quite an honor, just to be able to do that. I had nine birdies and I had three bogeys. So, it wasn't a perfect round, but it was a good day. It put me in a pretty good position.

Well, you know, being an assistant pro, a rookie playing in the U.S. Open. First time ever in a tour event. I was very pleased with my results. Of course, it got me back in the Open the next year at Baltusrol, and it also got me into the Masters. You don't get to play the Masters very often and I was lucky enough to finish in the top 15, which at that time got you in. And that's the only time I played in the Masters.

Frank Beard

I was staying with a friend. He told me to bring plenty of sweaters. It was the coldest weather of the year.

I was paired with Ben Hogan and Ken Venturi the first two days. Venturi was from San Francisco and was more popular locally than even Palmer. I guess I was put with them to keep the gallery from getting too big. Before the first round, Hogan said, "Play well" and that was about it for two days. But after the second round, he asked me, "Do you want a beer?" So, I sat down and had a beer. He said something like "You're off to a good start" on my career.

Later that year I got a call from my agent after Tony Lema was killed in the plane crash and asked if I wanted to play with Hogan. Lema had signed to play an outing in Fort Wayne, Indiana, with Hogan. He remembered me from the Open. Before we played, there was a clinic and Hogan introduced me and said some kind things. Billy Kratzert, who was 16, caddied for me. On the 18th hole, I missed a short putt, so Hogan and I ended up tied for the match. Ten years later, when Kratzert was on the tour, he said, "I know you missed that putt on purpose, so you wouldn't beat Hogan" and disappoint the crowd. I just laughed.

If you want to know who was the best player in the 1960s, it was Billy Casper. I didn't like him, but I liked playing with him. I didn't like playing with my friends. If I were playing with Charles Coody and he made a bogey, I'd feel bad for him. I'd want to give him one of my birdies. I didn't have that problem with Casper. If he made a bogey, I didn't care.

Charles Coody

I'm going to agree with what Frank said about Casper being possibly the best player during the '60s. If you go from about 1961 or 1962 to about 1970, when he won at Augusta, he probably was the best player for sure. I liked Casper. He was a good guy. He was out there to win, but he did it the right way.

Bruce Devlin

I remember an entire week at the 1966 Open in San Francisco where we flew into San Francisco with Ben Hogan and his wife Valerie. My wife Gloria was with me. And we spent the entire week with him, stayed at the Top of the Mark Hotel, had dinner every night, traveled to the golf course with him, played practice rounds with him. It was quite a week. In particular, to hear about the horrible accident that they were both involved in. So, it was very enlightening.

When he quit playing, I worked for NBC when they did the Legends of Golf at Onion Creek, and I was asked if I would invite Mr. Hogan to come up and spend Sunday with us in the booth. And I told our *producer that probably wouldn't happen. He'd say it was nice to get the invitation, but he wouldn't do it. And that's exactly what he said. He said, "I would be taking away from what is happening." So that'll give you an idea of how he thought.*

Jack Nicklaus

Casper was a really good player. The focus in the 1960s really became the Big Three. It could have just as easily been the Big Four, except Mark McCormack was not handling Billy Casper.

Lee Trevino

(Johnny) Miller had the long blonde wavy hair, which was kind of unusual back in those days. He was pretty good. He was hell a driver. If he had a weakness, it was his putter at the time. He crouched way over the putt. His arms moved all over the place. I remember him with a Bullseye putter. He could play.

July

The Open Championship

The 1966 Open Championship at the Muirfield Golf Links on the Firth of Forth in Scotland was the first to be played over four days, from Wednesday through Saturday. Jack Nicklaus was the pre-tournament favorite at 7-2. He arrived two weeks early, playing slow rounds at Muirfield while pacing off yardages, in intense preparation for the one major championship he had not won.

Despite unusually fair weather for the first round, only two players broke par of 71, Nicklaus and Jimmy Hitchcock of England, both of whom shot 70. It was a testament to just how tough the Muirfield layout was, with narrow fairways and knee-high rough, and with the wind blowing to the east instead of its usual westerly direction. Tony Lema, Doug Sanders, Harold Henning of South Africa, and Scottish amateur Ronnie Shade were one back.

On Thursday, the weather remained fair, and the normal westerly wind returned. As a result, scores dropped dramatically. Early in the day, Phil Rodgers shot a 66 to equal the course record, only to see Englishman Peter Butler—the 36-hole co-leader at the Masters earlier in the year—better it with a 65 later in the day. Nicklaus birdied two of the final three holes for a 67, putting him one ahead of Butler at 5-under par for the tournament, three ahead of Rodgers, Henning and Kel Nagle at the halfway point.

In the third round, Nicklaus was even par for the round until he bogeyed 14, 15, 16 and 18 for a 4-over round of 75. Meanwhile, Rodgers, using a 40-inch-long putter that he anchored to his stomach in a manner that would become common two decades later until it was banned in 2016, went out in 40 to fall nine strokes behind Nicklaus. Rodgers birdied five holes on the incoming nine for a 30 while Nicklaus was making bogeys. Rodgers' 70 gave him a 54-hole score of 210, 3 under and two better than Nicklaus. Sanders was three back at even-par 213. Arnold Palmer shot 69, the same score as Dave Thomas of Wales. The two were tied at 214, four back of Rodgers.

Sunshine again greeted the players for Saturday's final round. The lack of precipitation and wind made Muirfield's difficult greens even more treacherous.

Few players loved the Open Championship more than Rodgers. He was one of the first prominent American pros to join Palmer in making the annual voyage to Britain. He finished third in 1962 and second in 1963. Playing with Nicklaus, Rodgers quickly lost his lead when he bogeyed the first hole while Nicklaus made birdie. From there, he shot a 5-over par 76 to finish tied for fourth, four shots back.

Nicklaus would go out in 3-under 33. As on the previous day, he briefly lost his edge, with bogeys on 11, 13 and 14 to fall back into a tie with Sanders, who had enhanced his chances by chipping in from 40 yards for an eagle on the ninth hole. Sanders gave the strokes back with a double-bogey on the 11th.

The 528-yard par-5 17th hole was where the Open was decided. Nicklaus used his driver only 17 times in four days. With the wind at his back, he split the fairway off the tee with a 3-iron. He needed only a 5-iron for his second shot and put his ball 15 feet from the hole. He narrowly missed his eagle putt and tapped in for birdie to give him a one-shot lead. On the par-4 18th, Nicklaus reached the green in two and two-putted for a par. His 72-hole score of 282 was 2-under par, one ahead of Sanders and Thomas.

Nicklaus joined Gene Sarazen, Ben Hogan, and Gary Player as the only players to win the professional Grand Slam. To date, only Tiger Woods has joined them. In homage to his win, Nicklaus named his signature golf course in Dublin, Ohio—where the Memorial Tournament has been played since 1976—the Muirfield Village Golf Club.

Jack Nicklaus

I never even thought about the career Grand Slam. That was never a thing we looked at or thought anything about. It was something people started talking about a few years later. In those years we were trying to win the Grand Slam in one year. Nobody could quite get it done, so the career Grand Slam became the thing people talked about.

PGA Championship

The 1966 PGA Championship was played at the Firestone Country Club South Course in Akron, Ohio. Uncharacteristically, none of golf's Big Three, nor Billy Casper, made a serious challenge, though Gary Player finished six shots back and tied for third place.

For the first two rounds, 54-year-old Sam Snead was the big story, as he shot 68-71 to take a one-stroke lead over Al Geiberger and Don January. Geiberger was a 28-year-old pro from California who already was known for munching on peanut butter sandwiches during a round to combat his problem with fatigue. He had won three tournaments, including the American Golf Classic the previous year at Firestone. Later in his career, he would become known as "Mr. 59" after being the first to shoot that score at the 1977 Danny Thomas Memphis Classic.

On Saturday, Snead inadvertently double-hit an 18-inch putt for a bogey on the 10th hole, then double-bogeyed the long par-5 16th after finding water. He skied to a 75 to fall out of contention and ended up tied for sixth. Geiberger closed with 68-72 to pull away and win by four shots over Dudley Wysong.

Geiberger's win immediately was overshadowed by the death of Tony Lema. After finishing in a tie for 34th place, Tony and his wife, Betty, boarded a twin-engine Beechcraft with another passenger and a pilot and headed to Chicago for the Lincolnshire Open, a one-day pro-am on Monday. The plane crashed and burned at a golf course in Munster, Indiana, near their destination, killing all four occupants.

Next to Arnold Palmer, Lema may have been pro golf's brightest star of his time. He was handsome, witty, charming, and charismatic. Two months before his death, the 32-year-old Lema won the 12th and last of his tour victories—all within four years—at the Oklahoma City Open. There was no reason to doubt that his best years may have been in front of him. Lema's passing was golf's most painful tragedy of the 1960s.

Photo 60: Arnold Palmer and Tony Lema before playoff at the 1964 Cleveland Open, won by Lema. (Source unknown)

Bobby Nichols

Tony Lema was a good friend of mine. We played a lot of rounds together. Tony, Gay (Brewer) and I were good friends. We were in Akron, Ohio, at Firestone of all places. Bill Richards, one of the business guys there in Akron, always had a pro-am after the American Golf Classic. He'd invite about a dozen of us to stay over and play on Monday after, and he'd give us each $1,000 to play. That was quite nice.

So, we all agree to play. Ken Venturi. There's another guy that I just loved. Ken really treated me wonderfully. We had 12 guys going to play in the in the pro-am Monday. Well, Tony says "Hey boys, I'm not going to be there. I'm going to another pro-am in Illinois." And Venturi said, "Tony, you committed to Bill Richards' tournament here. Why are you not staying over? You going to cancel that?" He said, "Yeah. They offered me $1,400." He was going to go there for $400 or $500 more. And Venturi, I forgot exactly the words, but he said something to Tony, "Tony, you'll regret the day you do that. You don't do people like that. You don't cancel the day before and go elsewhere." Anyway, the plane went down.

Doc Giffin

Tony was a great guy. He had a great sense of humor, and I liked him a lot. That was a sad day. My last tournament with the press office was the PGA at Firestone. I had seen Tony that morning at the hotel. Later that day, most of the media guys were done and we were wrapping up things at the club. The bartender took a phone call in the grill room, and that's when we found out that Tony had been killed in that plane crash.

Walter Iooss, Jr.

I think in 1964 I was sent by Sports Illustrated to shoot Tony Lema. I was standing in the middle of a fairway. I had no idea. He was pissed off. Everyone was pissed off at me. I went to his hotel room to apologize. And we became fast friends.

And then in 1966, I guess it was the PGA, when he crashed. I was bringing film back from the PGA from wherever we were, out in the Midwest. And that was the last time I saw him. I was standing at the urinal. I said, "See you at the next tournament." And that was it.

September

Carling World Open

A measure of the success that Arnold Palmer, Jack Nicklaus, and Gary Player had attained on and off the course is that not even a purse of $200,000 and an all-expenses paid trip could induce any of them to travel to the Royal Birkdale Golf Club in Southport, England, the venue selected by the Carling Brewery for its annual tournament.

Carling did achieve its goal of attracting an international field. The first-round leader was Australian Kel Nagle, whose 68 led countryman Peter Thomsen, Englishmen Hedley Muscraft and Peter Butler by one stroke, and Bob Charles of New Zealand by two. The top Americans after one round were second- or third-tier players Jacky Cupit, John Lotz, Terry Dill, and Rex Baxter, Jr., all of whom shot 71. Also at 71 were Sebastian Miguel of Spain and three South Africans: Harold Henning, Sewsunker "Pawpa" Sewgolum, and Trevor Wilkes.

Sewgolum had an interesting, ultimately tragic, story. Dark-skinned, of Indian descent, he was born into poverty in Durban, worked as a caddie and was illiterate. He was completely self-taught and swung cross-handed, and somehow developed enough game to win the Dutch Open three times and to qualify for six Open Championships, finishing 13th in 1963. Also in 1963, he won the Natal Open in South Africa. Among the players he beat were Henning and future South African standout Bobby Verwey. In ensuing years, apartheid tightened its grip and Sewgolum's opportunities to compete in tournaments with Whites in his home country vanished, and he could not afford to compete abroad. He died impoverished in 1978 at the age of 49.

In Thursday's second round, Bert Yancey shot 68 to ascend to the top of the leaderboard by one over Nagle and Bruce Devlin of Australia, Neil Coles of England, and American journeyman Mike Fetchick. On Friday, strong winds from the Irish Sea kept scores high. Nagle's 73 was good enough for a one-shot lead over pre-tournament favorite Billy Casper, who followed rounds of 73-74 with 69, the low round of the day. Yancey and Devlin were two back.

Before a disappointingly small crowd of 6,000 in Saturday's final round, Nagle ballooned to a 76 to finish in a tie for fifth. Casper managed a 71 in the windy conditions. Again, the low round of the day was 69, which was Devlin's score. He won by one stroke over Casper to take home first prize of $35,000. Sewgolum played steadily all four rounds and finished tied for eighth, seven shots back.

Bruce Devlin
(The Carling World Open) was a little bit out of character for all the golf tournaments we played. They were getting bits and pieces of players from all over the world. It was different. I don't know if it felt like a major championship so much, but it certainly was nice to win. It paid a lot of money, quite remarkable actually at the time. And in those days, you could defer your compensation over a period of time. And I think at that time, interest rates were pretty high. So, I think I took a third of my prize money and deferred the other two thirds. It was drawing interest at eight or nine percent.

Chuck Courtney
I got in at the last minute because I had a real nice finish in Philadelphia to barely slip into the Carling World, which was the very next week. It was in Southport, at Royal Birkdale. Carling paid for everything. They'd pay your air fare, it was a trip to Europe and they paid you 500 bucks or something.

October

Hawaiian Open

The headliners at the second Hawaiian Open were Billy Casper and Doug Sanders, who were in a threesome with Pete Brown early in Thursday's first round. A local pro, Ted Makalena, shot 66 to share the lead with Sanders and Miller Barber. Sanders followed with 67 for a 36-hole score of 133 to lead Barber and Ken Still by three shots. Makalena, defending champion Gay Brewer, and veteran Al Besselink were four back. Casper's second-round 66 put him at 138, five behind Sanders.

In Saturday's third round, Makalena took the lead by firing another 66, two better than Casper. Makalena was a stocky, long-hitting, easy-going 32-year-old native of Hawaii who had started as a caddie before becoming a successful local pro. He played most of his golf in Hawaii but qualified for the U.S. Open five times, finishing 23rd in 1964. When the Canada Cup was played at the Kaanapali Golf Resort on Maui in 1964, Makalena competed for Hawaii, which back then had a team notwithstanding that it had joined the United States five years earlier. In the individual competition, Makalena tied for third with Gary Player, behind Jack Nicklaus and Arnold Palmer.

On Sunday, Makalena shot 68 for a three-shot victory over Casper and received a check in the amount of $8,500. "I doubt if I have earned more than $4,500 from tournaments since I became a pro in 1964," he said.

Makalena's win made him the most popular athlete in Hawaii. He played the PGA Tour in 1967 and part of 1968, with limited success. On September 8, 1968, Makalena was on an outing in Honolulu with his family after returning from the mainland for a break from the tour. He dived into shallow water, broke his neck and died five days later, sending all of Hawaii into mourning.

Photo 61: Billy Casper, Ted Makalena and Gay Brewer after the 1966 Hawaiian Open. (Hawaii Sports Hall of Fame)

1967

January

San Diego Open

On January 16, 1967, the Green Bay Packers defeated the Kansas City Chiefs 35-10 in the first Super Bowl, at the Los Angeles Coliseum before 63,036 fans, two-thirds of its capacity. About 120 miles down the coast, one-time Illinois quarterback Bob Goalby won the San Diego Open, the opening event of the 1967 PGA tour season, by one stroke over Gay Brewer.

February

Bob Hope Desert Classic

Arnold Palmer, Jack Nicklaus, and Billy Casper headed the field for the 90-hole tournament in Palm Springs. Palmer and Nicklaus already had wins under their belts early in the year, Palmer at Los Angeles the week prior and Nicklaus at the Bing Crosby two weeks earlier.

Under the unique format, the pros would play in a foursome with three amateurs for the first four days over four different courses in the Coachella Valley. In the final round, pros making the cut would play at La Quinta Country Club. In sparkling weather in the desert, Palmer, Nicklaus, and Casper did not mount serious challenges.

Tom Nieporte was a 37-year-old club pro at the Piping Rock Club on Long Island outside of New York City. He won the 1951 NCAA individual championship while he was at Ohio State and played the tour full-time for five years, winning the 1959 Rubber City Open and 1960 Azalea Open, before taking a club pro job to provide a steady income for his large family.

In 1967, the then-father of seven was on his annual winter loop of the tour after finishing second in the PGA club pro championship near his winter home in Florida. In preparing for his trip to the West Coast, he inadvertently packed mismatching white shoes. Two weeks before, at the Crosby, in horrible conditions he shot a 19-over 55 after nine holes at Pebble Beach before the round mercifully was cancelled and replayed in its entirety the next day, when he managed 75. Nieporte barely made the 54-hole cut, earning $84, which put him in the field at Los Angeles, where he tied for 14th and allowed him to extend his trip to Palm Springs.

In the first round at the Hope, Nieporte shot 76, 10 strokes behind the leader. From there, rounds of 68-68-68 put him one stroke behind leader Doug Sanders. In the final round, he shot 69, capped by a 12-foot putt for birdie on the 90th hole to beat defending champion Sanders by one stroke.

During the awards ceremony, either Delores Hope (wife of host Bob Hope) or former First Lady Mamie Eisenhower commented on Nieporte's shoes. "I have another pair just like that at home," Nieporte responded. He then headed home to Florida. Nieporte is the last full-time club pro to win an event on the PGA tour.

Photo 62: *Former President Dwight Eisenhower, Tom Nieporte and Bob Hope after 1967 Bob Hope Desert Classic. (Golf Digest)*

Tucson Open

By 1967, 27 tournaments had purses of more than $100,000. The Tucson Open dated back to 1945 but by 1967, with total payouts of $60,000, was on the lower end in terms of money and prestige and was the last event on the California-Arizona swing. Many of the stars skipped it, so the sponsors were pleased to have Arnold Palmer in the field.

Palmer took the early lead with a six-under 66 at the 7,200 yard Tucson National Golf Club, one stroke better than Bruce Crampton, Joel Goldstrand and Chuck Courtney. In the frost-delayed second round, Palmer added a 67 to increase his lead over Courtney to three shots. On Saturday, Courtney knocked in a 3-iron on the par-5 second hole for a double-eagle on his way to a 68, but still lost ground on Palmer, who fired another 67 for a three-round total of 200, four shots ahead of Courtney and Crampton.

In the sun-splashed final round, most of the modest gallery of 12,000 followed the last threesome of Palmer, Courtney, and John Schlee in expectation of witnessing Palmer's 50th tour victory. Instead, Palmer appeared set on giving the tournament away. On the par-4 ninth hole, he drove into a bunker, was short of the green with his second shot, hit a poor chip and then three-putted for a double-bogey. Courtney's par drew him even with Palmer.

Palmer and Courtney remained tied after 17 holes. They were four shots ahead of the remainder of the field. Courtney drove first on the par-4, 465-yard 18th hole and put his ball into a lake that ran down the right side of the fairway. Instead of playing safe, Palmer launched a drive that soared 70 yards past Courtney, hit the right side of the fairway before the ball rolled off a bank, joining Courtney in the water. After a drop, Courtney hit a 3-wood into a bunker left of the green. Palmer's 2-iron sailed over the green. Thus, they both lay three and appeared to be doing their best to let the other win.

Courtney's blast from the trap was strong and went 40 feet past the hole. Putting from off the green, Palmer got his ball to within 6 feet. Courtney's putt for bogey went five-and-a-half feet past the cup, and he missed coming back to end with a triple-bogey 7. Palmer's bogey putt to win stayed on the lip, but he tapped in for double-bogey and 73. It was far from artful, but it was the 50th tour win for Palmer.

Chuck Courtney

The Tucson National Golf Club was in a development out in the middle of nowhere, out in the desert. It's probably practically downtown Tucson these days. It was flat and windy and cold. They dyed the grass because it was Bermuda grass which goes totally dormant in Arizona, especially at 2,500 feet or so. It freezes there almost every night in the winter, so it's totally brown. So, they painted the fairways and you'd hit your ball, and pretty soon your ball was green. You couldn't wipe it off, either. I think they dyed the fairways in Palm Springs, too.

It was one of those super windy days and Arnold had a five-shot lead, so it pretty much was a foregone conclusion that he was going to win. I'm playing with him and on the 18th hole we're all even. I was 5 or 6 under (for the day). Arnold was even (for the day). I was having the round of the day by far. So, there we are even on the last hole. And we both hit it in the water on the last hole. There was nobody even close to us. If we finished on our feet we were going to be first and second. I finished second.

April

The Masters

In his attempt at a three-peat, after the first round of the 1967 Masters Jack Nicklaus was part of an eclectic top-10 leaderboard.

Bert Yancey was so driven to win a green jacket that he created a topographically accurate table-top model of Augusta National to aid in his preparation. Yancey opened with a 67 to give him a three-stroke lead over Billy Casper and amateur A. Downing Gray. At 71 were 47-year-old Julius Boros and 22-year-old Englishman Tony Jacklin, who was playing in his first Masters.

Among the 11 players tied for sixth at even-par 72 were Nicklaus, 51-year-old Tommy Bolt, 19-year-old amateur Johnny Miller, Peter Butler of England (who had made a splash at the 1966 Masters and Open Championship), Canadian George Knudson, 54-year-old Sam Snead, and 44-year-old former PGA champion Jay Hebert.

In Friday's second round, played in temperatures that soared to 91 degrees—the hottest day in Masters history up to that time—only one of those who shot 72 or better the day before missed the cut. That player was twice-defending champion Nicklaus, who unfathomably shot 79. Only four players in the 80-man field had a worse score on Friday. Yancey shot 73 but his 36-hole total of 140 was one better than Boros, Jacklin, Gay Brewer, and Bobby Nichols.

Saturday again brought 90-degree heat. The day belonged to 54-year-old Ben Hogan, who shot 66, the low round of the tournament. After an even-par front nine, Hogan set a course record with a 30 on the back nine, including four consecutive birdies on holes 10-13. He just missed an eagle on 15, and capped off his round with a 20-foot birdie on 18 that earned him a standing ovation from the gallery. Hogan was tied for fourth with Brewer at 213, two shots behind leaders Yancey, Boros and Nichols.

In the final round, Hogan bogeyed three straight holes early and soared to 77, finishing tied for 10th along with Snead. It would be his last Masters, a tournament he won in 1951 and 1953. Boros hung in for a while, but was done in over a five-hole stretch between 8 and 12 where he dropped four shots, capped off by a five at the 155-yard, par-3 Golden Bell, when he hit his tee shot into thick brush behind the green. Yancey was in the thick of it until he bogeyed 16 and 17. He finished third.

Gay Brewer was paired with Nichols, his good friend and fellow Kentuckian. They both played well on the front nine, after which Nichols led Brewer by a shot. Both bogeyed 10, and Nichols bogeyed 11 as well to fall back into a tie with Brewer and, for a time, Yancey. On 13, Brewer sank a 10-foot putt for birdie, while Nichols only managed a par, to take the lead. Brewer followed with birdie putts of 18 feet on 14, and 10 feet on 15, while Nichols had birdies on 14 and 15 as well.

With Brewer still leading by one on 18, both he and Nichols reached the green in two. After Brewer watched Nichols' 25-foot birdie putt slide by, he lagged his putt to within tap-in range to win for his lone major championship among 10 tour wins.

Bobby Nichols

In 1966, Gay Brewer lost a playoff to Tommy Jacobs and Jack Nicklaus, and Jack won. Then, in 1967 Gay beat me by a shot. We finished first and second, and closest to us was about four or five shots back. We had a two-horse race going into the final seven or eight holes. I was happy for him. We weren't pulling against each other. We were both trying to play our best. But when it's all over with I was happy for him winning because he deserved it. Like I say, he could have won the year prior. I think he three-putted the 18th hole to go into a play-off.

I think I shot 70. I had a two-shot lead on Gay going to the final round. I think Julius Boros and I were tied. And I said, "If I could shoot

70 that would be 280, 281." Because I had 211. Well, that's what I shot. But Gay was two shots back and he shot a 67 final round and won by a shot. I didn't lose it. I shot exactly what I was hoping I'd shoot, but it wasn't good enough. Most of the time, 280 or 281 would win back in those days.

Gay went out on tour about 1957. He was about three or four years older than me. I played a lot of practice rounds with him, and we were good friends. Back in those days, a lot of places had a practice range and they had golf balls for you to buy. They were 25 cents for a small bucket and 50 cents for a large bucket. You had to pay for them. But the thing about the golf balls, they're all balata. We played with balata balls for a long time until they came in with two-piece. The balls we got to practice with would look like walnuts. They were just beat up, so bad, cut up and everything. And so, during those days we'd say, "Hell, we're not going to spend money to hit these things." Like I say, they'd look like walnuts.

So, we'd just go to the locker room and have a beer. Gay was always a top-notch storyteller. Sometimes off the cuff, but he was so funny. So, we just stayed in the locker room and listened to Gay tell jokes and things like that. We practiced a lot, but not like they do today. Which is understandable, why they practice so hard.

I think the reason why all the players today practice is to maintain feel. Golf is based on feel. You got to keep that feel in your hands. The kids, they'll take off two or three weeks. Back then we tried not to take off that long. It took about a week or two to get back in the swing of things. And the reason being is your hands are the life blood of golf and you got to have that feel in your hands. If you don't have that feeling in your hands you're not going to score well. I mean, you're still swinging the same basically, but you got to have that feel, especially around the greens or on the greens, scoring shots and stuff like that. People don't think much about it, but that's why guys practice, to maintain feel. And like I say, when you take off a couple, three weeks, when you come back you don't have that feel unless you practice a lot.

Rives McBee

That's the only time I played in the Masters and I never would want to play there again. Well, it is only for the elite. They don't care about any of the new names or anything. They care more about the amateurs than they do about the rookie pros. I had probably one of the worst experiences I've ever had at a golf tournament.

Well, it's a long story. I had problems with room reservations. When I got my invitation, I was in Los Angeles on the tour. And I went immediately and got a room reservation with the Holiday Inn, and they gave me a Holidex [pertaining to a nationwide computerized reservation system Holiday Inn had at the time] and everything stating that I had a room that week. Well, when I get down the manager of the hotel said, "Sir, we haven't had an opening for anybody else for the last 10 years, and I don't know when we'll ever have another opening during the Masters." So, I didn't have a room, so I went to the tournament officials and asked them at registration, did they help with rooms? They said they only took care of the amateurs. They didn't care what happened to the pros. It was up to me.

I might have had to go to Myrtle Beach and drive across Carolina every day if I hadn't had a buddy, Don Wilson, a teammate at North Texas State who was stationed in the Army at Fort Gordon. And he was out watching me play a practice round with Billy Casper and he yelled at me. I went over and talked to him, and he says, "What are you doing after you get through playing?" I said, "I got to go find a room somewhere." He said, "Well, if you want, stay with me and my wife. It's a bivouac deal for the soldiers. We'll put a bed in the in the living room and you can stay with us." Well, that's what I did. I slept on a rollaway bed in the living room of a buddy's room at Fort Gordon and it saved me from having to drive across Carolina every day.

And then the crowning glory was on Wednesday night after dinner. I'd already played in the Par Three tournament and that night I took my wife and daughter, who was 15 months old, out to the golf course. I got my putter and some balls and was headed for the putting green and the Pinkerton man stopped me. He said, "Where you going?" I said I'm going to the putting green." He said, "Where's your badge?" And I showed him my badge, my wife showed him her badge. And he says, "Where's the young lady?" And I say "You're kidding me. She doesn't have to have a badge. I was told that at registration." He said, "Everybody has to have it." I said "It's 6:30 at night. For the putting green? There's nobody on the golf course." He said, "Well, you can, but she has to stay out." In other words, my 15-month daughter wasn't going to be allowed on the premises. Well, there went my practice on the putting green. I picked her up, went to the front office and I said, "You better give me a badge before I explode." It was just a bad tournament for me. I would much rather go to Hattiesburg, Mississippi, and play in the Magnolia Classic than to play in the Masters.

Billy Casper was so nice to me. I think we played three times. I hadn't qualified at Greensboro (the week before), so I went down there early, and he was there early, and we got to play three practice rounds together. And Billy said, "I'm thrilled to death to get to play with you because you were the talk of the U.S. Open at San Francisco, and then I won the tournament in the playoff." And I said, "Well, I got to read about that. I was on my way back home. The day you got in the playoff with Arnie." I got to know Billy pretty well after that. Billy was awful nice to me. Matter of fact, there are a lot of guys out there who were nice to me, and I can't brag on them enough. I know a lot of rookies are treated a little bit rough in some spots, but I don't think I had that problem. My problem was more with hotels and reservations.

Texas Open

Chi Chi Rodriguez won the Texas Open at the Pecan Valley Golf Club in San Antonio by one shot over Bob Charles and Bob Goalby to take home $20,000.

Chi Chi Rodriguez

Lee Lynch was my caddie. He won with more players on the tour than any other caddie ever. He won with Bobby Nichols. He won with David Hill. He won with me and he won with Tony Lema.

I have the ball before a big tree on this par-5. And, I mean, it was a very, very tough shot. And I told him, I said, "I'm just going to put it where I can reach the green with my next shot and see if we can pick up a par." Lee says, "No, you see that little hole?" There was a hole in that tree about maybe two feet wide. He says, "You can put it right through the hole." I thought he was crazy. Lee said, "You were born broke, I was born broke, you are broke, and I am broke. Let's go for broke." I put it right through a little hole. I ended up with a birdie.

We get to this hole where there is a creek, and everybody laid up. Well, Lee gave me this ball, it was so hot. It almost burnt my finger. I ask Lee, "Why is this ball so hot?" He says, "I had it under my arm for three holes." I ask if that's legal. He said, "Yeah, that's perfectly legal." OK, I hit the ball and it looked like an aspirin tablet with the driver. It went over that creek and I put it maybe 20 to 30 feet from the front of the green. I made a par. Bob Charles had about a 20-footer to tie, and he missed it. I won.

May

Houston Champions International

The tournament at the difficult Champions Golf Club drew a field that included Arnold Palmer, Jack Nicklaus and 54-year-old Ben Hogan. To the delight of the gallery, after 36 holes Palmer led by three shots over Frank Beard, with Hogan four back after shooting a pair of 69s.

By the luck of the draw, Nicklaus was grouped the first two days with Cary Middlecoff and Al Geiberger. Nicklaus had long since established himself as a deliberate player, ever since he was penalized two strokes for slow play at the 1962 Portland Open, which he won by one shot. Middlecoff and Geiberger likewise were notorious plodders, though neither had ever been penalized. It was a perfect storm.

On Thursday, it took the threesome 5 hours to play their opening rounds, but they were not penalized because they stayed close enough to the group in front of them. However, on Friday, when they fell two-and-a-half holes behind, tournament director Jack Tuthill had seen enough and imposed two stroke penalties on all three. Even without the penalties, none of the three were within earshot of the leaders.

Frank Beard was accustomed to Palmer's heat. Just three weeks earlier, at the Tournament of Champions in Las Vegas, Beard had a two-shot lead after 54 holes, with a comfortable eight-shot lead over Palmer. In the final round, Beard shot 71. Nobody challenged him, except for Palmer, who fired a 64 and nearly caught Beard. At 18, Beard nervously faced an 8-foot birdie foot to avoid a playoff. He drained it.

Beard celebrated his TOC win by going to Mass with his wife Pat and their infant son. He had much to be thankful for. After winning the Frank Sinatra tournament in 1963, early in the spring of 1964 he was stricken with encephalitis. He was close enough to death that he once said, "If I wake up tomorrow and can't break 80, I'll still be ahead of the game." He recovered and won the Texas Open in 1965 and the New Orleans Open in 1966.

In Houston, the 27-year-old bespectacled, pulpy Beard was not going to win the affection of the crowd over Palmer, or Hogan, the sentimental favorite who had not won on tour in eight years. Beard was from Louisville, the much younger brother of University of Kentucky basketball legend Ralph Beard. He had graduated from the University of Florida with a degree in accounting. On Saturday, both Palmer and Beard shot 70, so Beard remained three strokes back of Palmer and one behind Billy Casper, who moved into second place with a 65. Hogan fell back with a 72.

On Sunday, Beard and Palmer were paired together. Casper put two balls into water hazards on his way to a 75. Hogan shot 68 to secure third place. It came down to what effectively was match play after Beard made up the three-shot deficit with Palmer.

Frank Beard

In Houston, I got to play with (Palmer). He was leading and I finally caught him on the 14th hole. We get to 15, and it's a short par-4. I hit a driver and a wedge in there about 8 or 10 feet, and he missed the green to the left. He was off the green, but he could putt. So, he putted it up from there to about 6 feet from the hole. But he was putting from off the green, and the putt-out rule was in effect. But he was not away, and he had no right to finish because he was not on the green. If he had been on the green and was putting from outside of me, he has a right to finish, but he was not on the green. So, he putts up and looks at me and says, "I'll just finish that." I knew Arnie, we all knew Arnie, and he was just trying to get at me some way. And he made it, and I made mine to go one up.

And then he birdied, 16, I believe, and we parred 17 and we got to 18. We both got about 25- or 30-footers for birdies, and we're tied. I putted and made mine. And I remember walking by him, and I didn't even want to look at him. And I glanced up and he was looking at me, and he could have shot nails up my ass. I never saw such a look. I went down and got my ball and waved at the crowd. And he missed his.

People remember that more than a lot of other stuff in my career, that I beat Palmer in those two tournaments. My second wife, after I married her, she said, "When that happened, I didn't know who you were, but I loved Arnold Palmer, and whoever that little shit who did it, I hated him." She remembered it but did not remember it was me who beat him.

Frank Boynton

Nicklaus was quite slow. Once, he got paired with Cary Middlecoff and Al Geiberger. I told the guys, "Well, we just picked up two shots on three players, because there's no way they can make it around without getting penalized. And they got penalized.

Photo 63: Ben Hogan in 1966. (Walter Iooss, Jr.)

June

U.S. Open

At the Museum of the Gulf Coast in Port Arthur, Texas are busts of the small city's two most famous former inhabitants, the late singer Janis Joplin and Hall of Fame football coach Jimmy Johnson. In 1967, neither were as well-known as local resident Marty Fleckman, who seemed destined for a Golf Hall of Fame career and his own bust in the museum.

While attending the University of Houston, the soft-spoken Fleckman was on three teams that won NCAA championships, and in 1965 he was the NCAA individual champion. As with Ken Venturi in the 1950s, Fleckman caught the eye of Byron Nelson and became his protégé. Nelson mentored Fleckman on iron play to supplement his exceptional length off of the tee.

At the 1967 U.S. Open at Baltusrol Golf Club in Springfield, New Jersey, fresh off his appearance at the Walker Cup, the 23-year-old Fleckman shot 67 in the first round to take a two-shot lead over a group at 69 that included Arnold Palmer, Gary Player, Billy Casper and Chi Chi Rodriguez.

Rives McBee—he of the record 64 at Olympic in the 1966 Open—probably set another Open record by going through at least seven caddies. On Thursday, while he shot 76, he needed three. The first one assigned by the host club fainted and had to go to the hospital, the second was a spectator who filled in until the third – who had toted a bag for another player – was summoned from the caddie yard.

Fleckman regressed on Friday—when temperatures soared over 90 degrees—with a 73. The amateur's 36-hole total of 140 left him three shots behind leader Palmer, two behind Jack

Nicklaus (who fired 67) and one behind Casper. McBee did not fare better with his fourth caddie, who washed his grips without asking and was summarily discharged. His fifth caddie was Peter Wertz, a golf writer from Spokane who carried McBee's bag for three holes until a sixth caddie—who also had finished a loop—was rushed out. McBee managed a 72 to make the cut and guarantee he would require a seventh caddie on Saturday.

Photo 64: *Arnold Palmer and Marty Fleckman wrestled at the 1967 U.S. Open. (MartyFleckmanGolf.com)*

Temperatures moderated on Saturday. With Palmer and Nicklaus making a dream pairing in the final group that drew the lion's share of the 20,000 spectators in attendance, Fleckman and his playing partner, Deane Beman—who had been an amateur stalwart (winning the 1960 and 1963 U.S. Amateur and the 1959 British Amateur) but who had just turned pro—did not have the pressure of a large gallery. Nonetheless, Fleckman started his third round with a bogey on 1 and a double-bogey on 2. He steadied himself thereafter and went birdie-birdie-par on his final three holes. His 69 gave him a one-stroke lead over Palmer, Nicklaus, and Casper.

Despite being the leader, Fleckman was not in the last group on Sunday. That distinction went to Cesar Sanudo, Jim Ferriell (not to be confused with Jim Ferrier or Jim Ferree) and Chuck Scally, who were at the bottom of the leaderboard after Saturday. Players were sent out in twosomes and because an odd number made the cut, and because the USGA did not want a threesome of stragglers holding up play, they were saved until the end.

Playing with Casper, Fleckman bogeyed the first three holes. Even if he had birdied them, it would not have mattered. Early on, Nicklaus took away all of the drama expected from a pairing with

Palmer for the second straight day. He birdied the third, fourth, fifth, seventh and eighth holes for a 31 on the front side. On the back, Nicklaus—who had set a course record with a 62 in a practice round on Wednesday—shot 34. His 65 gave him a U.S. Open-record 275. Palmer's 69 was one of only six sub-par rounds of the day but still left him four shots back of Nicklaus in second place – his fourth runner-up U.S. Open finish in six years.

Fleckman stumbled in with 80, in a tie for 18th place. He turned pro late in the year. In December, he won his very first event, the Cajun Classic. Fleckman had a decent year in 1968, tying for fourth at the PGA Championship and earning $25,261. But in 1969, he only made 10 of 33 cuts and his winnings dwindled to $3,929. He lost his exempt status and for most of the rest of his career (which ended in 1980) he had to earn his way into tournaments in Monday qualifying. He never won again after the Cajun Classic.

As in 1966, Lee Trevino went through local and sectional qualifying and made the field. He shot rounds of 72-70-71-70 for a 283 total to finish fifth, eight shots back of Nicklaus.

Photo 65: As in 1962, Arnold Palmer (right) congratulated Jack Nicklaus after the 1967 U.S. Open. (United States Golf Association)

Marty Fleckman

I was very fortunate that when I played at the University of Houston, every year either we won, or Oklahoma State won. When I was in college, I was invited to play a practice round at Champions Golf

Club with Ben Hogan. The only thing I remember was he said about two words.

I hit balls almost every single day. I guess I was a grinder. I was very fortunate I had Byron Nelson as a coach. He'd have me to his Roanoke ranch.

I was very quiet. I didn't talk very much. I used to play practice rounds with Bert Yancey and Tom Weiskopf, but I didn't really associate with anybody. I didn't go out at night.

I basically drove to all off the tournaments. One year at the Bob Hope Desert Classic, one of my amateur partners was a head honcho with Dodge. He gave me a Dodge, which I drove to tournaments. The next year he gave me another Dodge.

I'm born again. It happened in the early 1970s. I grew up in a Jewish Reform temple. I was a non-believer. I teach every day but Sunday. I enjoy teaching. The tour is something I've moved on from. I don't think about it very much.

Larry Hinson

I played quite a bit with Marty Fleckman. He qualified, I think, in 1967 and in 1968 I qualified. Buddy, I'll tell you one thing. That man, he could play the game of golf. But I think he got the wrong instructor. He went to Byron Nelson, and Byron, I think, tried to teach him like Byron played. Byron was a real tall man, and Marty Fleckman was short, and he turned his swing into an upright swing. And I'm telling you, he could hit the longest ball, crooked, that you ever seen. You know what I'm saying? Yeah, he would just swing that thing and just knock the cover off of it, but we could never find it. He lost his game.

Charles Coody

Mr. Nelson worked with Marty when he first came on the tour. Trying to help him with the swing and everything. Whether it was on his own or whether Mr. Nelson tried to influence him in this area, Marty started trying to swing the club like Mr. Nelson did. And, of course, the height difference of the two was considerable. Byron, in his youth, *was probably 6-foot-2, 6-foot-3. And Marty was at best 5-foot-10. So, when you're playing golf, that's a big difference. You're talking about 4, 5 inches there and the golf club is swung in a totally different manner for two different heights. I'm not going to say it hurt Marty, but because he didn't have that long a career, you can't say it helped.*

Chuck Courtney

Fleckman was very talented, physically. He got the flinchies with his driver, and you can't play if you're going to have that every day. Great, great looking golf swing, everything looked good, but it's like you get the yips on the 2-foot putts. It's same thing. Marty was a beautiful player. We'd go watch him on the practice tee. God, he could hit it a mile.

Chi Chi Rodriguez

At Baltusrol, the first day, I shot 69. I had a putter that was shiny. So, I went to the USGA official, and I asked if I could put a piece of tape on top of it so it wouldn't shine in my eyes. He said, "Yeah, that's okay, that's legal." So, I shot 69. Then the next day, he was watching me practice putting. I was putting real good. When I was walking to the tee, he told me, "You got to take that tape off." What a nasty guy he was. If he had told me before, I could have got some paint or something and put it on it. He upset me so much that for the rest of the tournament I didn't do very well.

Lee Trevino

At the time, I was a PGA professional, a Class A pro. I wasn't in any golf tournaments. You had to qualify, but I didn't know that and couldn't afford to go out and try to qualify on Mondays. So, when I finished fifth at Baltusrol, I came back to El Paso, I was doing what I do. I would open up the shop in the morning and play golf with the gamblers in the afternoon, and doing the same thing I've always done. All of a sudden, I started getting invitations to play tournaments. The first invitation was to play in the Western Open, and then

I got one to the Canadian Open. So, I said to my wife, "Why don't we go to Minneapolis–St. Paul for the tournament before the Western Open and try to qualify?" That year it was at Hazeltine.

I shot 77 or 78 in the morning. And I had no idea what the criteria was, and I had no idea how many spots were open. So, what happened was, I'm packing my car and Wade Cagle, who was a tour official, comes driving by in a cart, and he says, "Where are you going?" I said, "I didn't qualify. I'm leaving." He said, "What do you mean you didn't qualify? We got 82 spots here. What did you shoot?" I said, "I shot 77 or 78." He said, "Hell, you might be leading."

Sure enough, I made it. Well, the PGA had a rule that if you were a Class A member and you played in a PGA tournament and you made the cut, you were automatically in the next week, if you wanted to play. And so, I made the cut there at Hazeltine. As I said, was invited to play in the Western and I made the cut there. Then the Carling. I think it was at the Board of Trade Golf Course. What a memory, in Canada. And I played in New York and Connecticut. I just kept making cuts. I just stayed out there. I ended up playing like 13 tournaments that year. That's all that was left. And they went ahead and gave me rookie of the year. My money winnings were $33,000. I ended up 47th on the money, and it gave me an exemption for 1968.

July

Canadian Open

Billy Casper beat Art Wall, Jr. in an 18-hole playoff at the Montreal Municipal Golf Course. Jack Nicklaus finished tied for third, one stroke behind. Arnold Palmer finished seventh, three back.

Tony Jacklin

I played with Arnold and Jack in the last round (of the 1967 Canadian Open). We were on the 16th tee and there's this big old TV camera. And they were just (televising) the last three holes. The 16th hole was about 270 yards, a drivable par-4. Palmer's got the honor and he's teeing his ball up.

Jack comes behind me and said, "Watch him when the red light goes on." And he looks up and obviously the camera is in his eye. And he starts with the snorting and grimacing, and then he gives it a smash with that familiar finish and of course the ball goes in the middle of the green, and they all cheered like hell. And that was your example of what he brought to the table. It was the perfect opportunity for him to take the stage and that's what people loved him for. That was the reason we thought we were playing for a lot of money. And it turns out we only thought.

Walter Iooss, Jr.

Arnold Palmer was Arnold Palmer. There was no one ever like him in the history of golf. There's nothing I could say negatively about Arnold Palmer. I would want my children to show the respect Arnold Palmer showed everybody. The way he'd sign his autograph. He was the coolest thing in golf. I think he and Tiger. I mean, swaggering, no hat, smoking. The Army. The periscopes. The swing.

They were unadorned. No hats. You could see the players. Now, everyone's like so covered up. It's ridiculous. I mean, you can't see anyone's face. If I rank all the athletes I've ever met, the greatest person would be Arnold Palmer.

"500" Festival

By 1967, the organizers had moved the tournament from its proximity to the Indy 500 in late May to July, right after the Canadian Open in Montreal, and before the Open Championship. The first round of the Open was the following Wednesday, so Palmer, Nicklaus and Player all were absent from Indianapolis.

Photo 66: Rod Funseth, hoping the putt will not drop. (Historic Images)

After three rounds, Rod Funseth led by two strokes over Frank Beard. Funseth was a long-hitting, quiet but amiable Swedish-American from Spokane. Despite having won the 1965 Phoenix Open and being in contention in other tournaments, Funseth may have been the most comically pessimistic player on the tour. "When I was a little kid I'd pretend that I'd be taking a shot to win the U.S. Open," he once said. "Then I'd stop and think, if I make the putt I'll have to make a speech. So I would two-putt and be second." One year, he was in contention at Augusta National. "I really can't picture myself as Masters champion," he told the press. "They probably don't even have a jacket my size."

In the final round at the 500, Funseth mustered only a 74. Beard shot a 69 to win for the third time in 1967 by one stroke over Funseth and Rives McBee.

Frank Beard

The only thing I really remember about (the 1967 "500" Festival) is I was really getting to the height of my confidence. We used to look at the fields, and I looked at the field and I thought, "You know, I should win this tournament," and that was not my makeup. It was not my ilk. But I really felt like I was going to win it. So, we finished three rounds. Rod Funseth was interviewed. And somebody asked him what were his chances to win tomorrow. He said, "I don't know, but I can't finish any worse than second." And I remember seeing that quote and I thought, "He's done." You know, I mean, what more could I ask for? He was a good player, but he had no confidence in himself. He could have won the Masters twice, but he just couldn't pull the trigger.

I was not a party boy at that time. I was doing a lot of drinking. I ended up drinking myself off the tour, I'm sure you've heard that. But in the '60s was when I was really getting rolling. I'd already started pretty good, but I was drinking pretty good, but not during a round, never during a round. The golfers that drank, if you could play you had a plus in the bag. If you're in the top two or three groups, you always had a 1 o'clock or later tee time. So, you had time to get up in the morning, shake off the old hangover and get some biscuits and milk and get yourself organized for the tournament. You didn't have an early tee time. But I played really good those years.

Rives McBee

My rookie year, I drove all the way around the tour. I didn't fly anywhere except to Hawaii. Of course, you couldn't drive to Hawaii.

Well, you know, you'd get a group of guys taking a pretty long trip and, and rather than do car rentals, we had three guys that had their cars, and we'd buddy up. Our car, Butch Baird was driving. I can't even remember the other dude, but we had some of our stuff in the trunk. And then the car behind us had two guys in it, and they had a lot of the suitcases and the golf bags in that car. And then there was another car behind him, with three guys in it. And we were going to do a little train down to Tucson.

We get to Indio and Butch pulled into this gas station. Of course, back in those days, they pumped the gas for you. Butch had a bad stutter, and he rolled his window down and here comes this big, tall guy. I mean, heavy-set. He got the t-shirt, he got his brogans, he got his overalls, and he walks up and he said, "Ca-ca-can I, can I help ya?" Butch looked up at him and says, "Don't believe so" and he rolled up the window and drove off. And I said, "Well, we need gas." He said, "I'm not-not gonna open my mouth and get my-my-my ass kicked by that guy!"

My wife and baby joined me from Midland, Texas. I had a '65 Pontiac Bonneville loaded down. I had a platform in the back, for my daughter, who was almost 15 months old. She had a place to play and sleep and do whatever she wanted to, and she wasn't cramped at all. We didn't have to have car seats at that time. But we drove all the way around. We even went to Expo 67 in Montreal and then we drove nonstop from Montreal to Indianapolis.

And that's when I went off my rocker, at Indianapolis. I had a reservation at the Speedway Motel and went to check in. They said they couldn't accept it. They could put me up for the night, but I'd have to check for accommodations the next morning. I was first in line and the two ladies that were running the table said, "You're going to have to move to the Holiday Inn." And I said, "Well, my wife and baby are asleep. I'm going to go play a practice round and when I get through, I'll check out."

Well, I went into the locker room and put my shoes on and one of my buddies that I was playing golf with that day, Art Proctor, came in. I said "Well, I can only play 18 holes in the practice round today" because I had to deal with the room. We normally played 36 on Mondays and Tuesdays. And he said, "Well, I just got a room right here at the Speedway." I said, "What room do you have?" He said "101."

I said, "That's the room I'm in!" They're kicking me out of the hotel and putting him in!

Anyway, I walked back to the table. I said, "Ma'am. You please explain something to me. I gave you my room reservation. You kick me out and send me down the road and the gentleman comes in and you give him my room and he didn't have a reservation! How can you do that?" They looked at each other kind of funny and said "Well, that's our decision and we're going to stick by it. I said, "Well, I'll see you when I get in. I will discuss this further," so I went out and teed off.

Hell, I hadn't even got to the green yet and here comes two PGA officials telling me to grab my clubs, go back to the clubhouse. I've been kicked out of the tournament. And I said, "What?" I was just standing up for my rights. I have a right to my room reservation, just like anybody else. And then when they kicked me out and put somebody in who didn't have a reservation. I went back in and said, "Can they do that?," and they said, yes, they can do anything they want to. And I says, "Y'all aren't going to stand up for me?" And these are the two officials. They said, "It's not our business. They're in charge of the hotels. We're not." Well, I said, "OK, if that's the way you're going to be."

So, I started across the parking lot, and I ran into Tommy Jacobs. One of the nicest guys on the tour and he was in charge of the Players Committee. And I said, "Can they kick you out of the golf tournament for complaining about the way they're treating you about room reservations?" He said, "Well, they did me the same way. I had one and they kicked me out and sent me down to the Holiday Inn," and I said, "Well, that's what they did to me." He said, "I suggest you go down there and check into the Holiday Inn." And he said, "Either you play in the tournament, or nobody plays." And I says, "OK."

So, I went down and checked in that afternoon. It was four o'clock or five o'clock. I got a phone call from Tommy, and he said, "Rives, don't leave town. You're in the tournament." He said, "I'm sorry you're not going to get a practice round." Because the next day was

Wednesday and that's the pro-am day and rookies don't play in the pro-am unless somebody gets sick and they need somebody. But I went ahead and stayed and didn't get a practice round. So, I went and played first, second third round. And when I get through, I tied for second place, and Frank Beard won the tournament.

Well, we get up on the podium and the tournament chairman came over says, "I hope you don't say anything about what happened with us. We only did what we thought was, right," and I said, "Well I only did what I thought was right, too." I got my check for the tournament and walked off. It may have been $9,700. It was my biggest check up to that point.

Frank Boynton
Rives McBee was a known hothead on the tour.

The Open Championship

The 1967 Open Championship was held at the Royal Liverpool Golf Club. No PGA Tour event conflicted with the Open. Still, not many Americans traveled to England. Frank Beard – winner the previous week in Indianapolis – opted to play in a 36-hole event in Iowa with a $10,000 total purse, which he won. Recognizing that his status as Masters Champion obliged him to make the pilgrimage, Gay Brewer made his first appearance at the Open. He would miss the cut.

Photo 67: *Roberto De Vicenzo.*
(Creative Commons)

Roberto De Vicenzo of Argentina, age 44, was playing in the Open Championship for the 11th time since his initial appearance in 1948. He was runner-up in 1950 and finished third a total of six times. After a third-round 67, De Vicenzo led by two shots over Gary Player and defending champion Jack Nicklaus.

Player struggled in the final round with a 74 and finished tied for third with Clive Clark and one ahead of Tony Jacklin, both of England. Late in the final round, it had become a match race between De Vicenzo and Nicklaus. Once it became clear that the Englishmen would fall short, the gallery adopted the affable De Vicenzo—who had come close many times without the victory Nicklaus had enjoyed the year prior—as their favorite.

Late in the round, De Vicenzo had a four-shot lead. It was cut to two when Nicklaus birdied the par-5 16th. Playing right behind Nicklaus, De Vicenzo drove right on 16. He decided to go for the green even though the shot required flirting with out-of-bounds on the right side. He hit a wood safely on the green and two-putted for birdie, and held on to win by two strokes over Nicklaus. De Vicenzo became the oldest man in 100 years to win the Open (Old Tom Morris was 46 when he won in 1867).

PGA Championship

For a time, there was doubt as to whether the field at the 1967 PGA Championship would include any top players. Touring pros had been at odds with the PGA of America over the management of the tour, but the immediate source of contention was the PGA's exercise of its veto power to squelch an attempt by Frank Sinatra to hold a high-purse tournament in Palm Springs earlier in the year. PGA President Max Elbin had said the absence of the veto power would bring "a state of anarchy" to the tour.

Arnold Palmer, Jack Nicklaus, Billy Casper and Julius Boros were among the players who threatened to boycott the PGA Championship. They made noises about starting a rival tour. On June 20, the PGA and the tournament players reached a temporary agreement that forestalled a boycott, but assured that there would be continued bickering. The players then were able to turn their attention to playing the 7,436-yard Columbine Country Club course outside of Denver, the longest in major championship history up to that time. As the tournament was played at an altitude of close to one mile, meaning that balls would fly further, the course was stretched to its maximum length.

The first round was played in hot temperatures that were conducive to low scoring. Half a century later, it would not raise an eyebrow for a player to hit an 8-iron from 170 yards, which Dave Hill did from the rough on the 473-yard 14th hole. Hill—who lived near Denver and knew Columbine well—holed the shot for an eagle deuce on his way to a 6-under 66, to take the first-round lead by a stroke over Nicklaus. In third place, at 69, were Boros, Dan Sikes, and club pros Don Bies and Davis Love, Jr.

Despite his good round, afterwards Nicklaus was not complimentary of either the course or of the PGA for holding the tournament, once again, on the heels of the Open Championship. He complained of leg fatigue.

On Friday, Tommy Aaron—with seven second or third-place fin-

Photo 68: Don Bies. (Getty Images)

ishes in his 7-year career but still seeking his first tour win— shot a 65, which included nine birdies, to give him a four-shot lead over Hill, Sikes and Bies. In the third round, a strong wind blew in the afternoon that lowered temperatures but raised scores. Aaron fell back with a 76. Sikes, a lawyer by education and one of the leaders behind the threatened boycott, shot 70 to lead by two over Nicklaus and Aaron. Arnold Palmer was four back.

On Sunday, neither Palmer nor Nicklaus made a charge, Palmer shooting 74 and Nicklaus 71. Bies finished seventh, the best finish ever by a club pro (though Tommy Bolt would finish third in 1971 after he had retired from the tour and had made the field as a club pro). Bies was able to parlay that finish into a successful career on the PGA Tour, and later the PGA Senior Tour.

Teeing off before the leaders, Don Massengale (winner of the Bing Crosby and Canadian Open in 1966) fired a 66 and was the leader in the clubhouse, watching on television to see if Sikes and Don January—in the midst of good rounds—could catch him. Sikes bogeyed 17, then missed a 12-foot birdie putt on 18 to finish one back of Massengale. January birdied 17 to tie Massengale, and then just missed a birdie putt on 18 that would have won. For the first time since the PGA Championship switched to stroke play in 1958, there would be an 18-hole playoff.

After six holes of the Monday playoff, Massengale led by two, but January squared the match on the eighth. January took the lead with a 35-foot birdie putt on 11 and held on to win by two, 69 to 71. It would be the 37-year-old January's only win in a major.

Don Bies

I was a club pro from Seattle. At Columbine, I finished seventh. I think that's the lowest a club pro has finished at the PGA in the history of the tournament. I remember every day at about 3 p.m. a thunderstorm would roll in for about 20 minutes and we'd have to come off of the golf course for half an hour.

It just all kind of happened. I was not really thinking of playing the tour. I had three children at that time and a job at the Seattle Golf Club, which was a beautiful club. I'm still an honorary member now. It was built in 1900. They had the National Amateur there, they had the Walker Cup there.

Finishing seventh at Columbine is really what got me on the tour. At that time, finishing seventh made you exempt from qualifying for the tour for a year. It also got me into the Masters. In 1968 they did some remodeling of the Seattle Golf Club, which shut it down a little bit, so I was able to play on tour. In 1968, I played 16 tournaments and finished 33rd on the money list. And that made me exempt in 1969 for the whole year. At that time, it was the top-60 money winners. So, I quit my job and went out on the tour full-time in January of 1969.

I decided I had to do it. I didn't want to look back and regret not doing it when I had the chance.

August

Greater Hartford Open

The Wethersfield Country Club, an old, leafy course south of Hartford, Connecticut, was a regular stop on the summer circuit.

Charlie Sifford always had good experiences in Hartford. He was welcomed there going back to the 1950s, when his race kept him out of most PGA tour events. In 1956, Sifford missed a 4-footer on the final hole that would have earned him a spot in a playoff with Arnold Palmer and Ted Kroll (won by Palmer). During that time, Wethersfield members pooled money and gave it to Sifford and fellow Black pro Ted Rhodes to make sure they had funds to play at Hartford. One year, a spectator found Sifford's wallet on the course, located him, and returned it the following day.

In 1967, Sifford started the final round tied for 12th place, five shots back. An impressive list stood between he and leader Terry Dill, including Gary Player, Raymond Floyd, Frank Beard, Dave Marr, Dave Hill, Doug Ford, and Kel Nagle. While smoking five of his trademark cigars during the round, Sifford passed all of them. He chipped in for an eagle on the par-5 14th hole. When he came to the 18th, Sifford was among the leaders, with Player, Ford, Floyd and Steve Opperman (a young pro from San Francisco) at his heels and playing behind him. Sifford's approach found a bunker. As he walked to his ball, he was greeted with a prolonged ovation from the gallery, who clearly were behind the stocky 45-year-old veteran. Sifford blasted to within 4 feet and sank the putt. His final round of 64 gave him a 72-hole score of 272.

Player birdied 16 but could only muster pars on 17 and 18 to finish at 274. Floyd's bogey at 17 did him in, and his score also was 274. Paired with Player, Opperman would shoot 68, but bogeyed 16 and

17. Needing a birdie on 18, Opperman parred for 273. Playing in the final group, Ford could only manage a par on the par-5 16th hole and finished at 274. Sifford was the winner. He broke down and wept at the awards ceremony.

In 1957, Sifford had won the Long Beach Open, a 54-hole tournament with a good field but it was a non-PGA event. He likewise won the 1960 Almaden Open and the 1963 Puerto Rico Open when they were non-PGA events. Sifford's 1967 victory in Hartford was the first of his two official PGA Tour wins, and was the first win by a Black golfer in a full-field PGA tournament.

Photo 69: Charlie Sifford in 1968. (Walter Iooss, Jr.)

Westchester Classic

In March 1966, the PGA announced, starting in 1967, a tournament would be held at the Westchester Country Club with a purse of $250,000, sponsored by the United Hospital Building Fund to benefit local hospitals. This would surpass the $200,000 offered by the Carling World Open, then the richest tournament. After the press conference, pro tour founder Fred Corcoran opined the day would come when tournaments would offer total purses of $1,000,000. "In 1945, Byron Nelson won 19 tournaments, 12 of them in a row." Corcoran said. "He was leading money winner with $52,000. If a fellow won 19 tournaments now he'd drag down close to half a million dollars in official earnings."

The four major and semi-majors such as the Canadian Open and Western Open already had been completed when the first Westchester Classic started on August 24. However, the opportunity to win the $50,000 first prize, or even $1,000 for 40th place, was too good an opportunity to pass up. Arnold Palmer, Jack Nicklaus, Billy Casper, and every pro of note appeared, including 65-year-old Gene Sarazen. Even Gary Player, who had skipped the PGA Championship to return to South Africa for an extended stay at home, returned to the United States.

All went well in the first round. Fifty players broke par. Player, who admitted to being homesick, shot 66 to tie for the lead with Mason Rudolph and Jim Colbert. Nicklaus (67) and Palmer (69) were close behind. Playing with Colbert, Sarazen shot a respectable 76.

The fun started on Friday. Torrential rain washed out the second round. Instead of playing 36 holes on Saturday, tournament officials decided to carry the tournament into Monday, to the dismay of the organizers of the Comedians Classic, a one-day pro-am on Long Island for the benefit of blind children, which had been scheduled on Monday and had counted on the attendance of some of the pros.

In the end, it wouldn't have mattered. On Saturday morning, second round play commenced. Rain began to fall again at 10 a.m. and intensified as the day went on. However, almost all of the morning players had completed their round, and all of the afternoon contingent was on the course when play was halted at 1:50 p.m. The bespectacled Rudolph, who looked more like a bank teller of the era than a professional golfer, followed up his 66 with a 69 to nab the lead for the moment.

Dan Sikes, a 37-year-old pro, was one of the more intelligent players on the tour. He held both a bachelor's degree (major in business administration) and a law degree from the University of Florida. Thus, when he followed his even-par 72 on Thursday with a 79 on Saturday morning, he knew he would not partake in any of the bounty, so he checked out of his hotel and headed to the airport.

Needless to say, the sensible course of action would have been to resume the second round on Sunday for the players who were still on the course and allow those who had completed their rounds to sleep in or, for those like Sikes who had no chance of making the cut, get out of town. Except that is not what the PGA did in those days. The second round would be replayed in its entirety by all. Neither Sikes' 79 nor Rudolph's 69 counted. Sikes was summoned from the airport.

If Rudolph was disappointed about this turn of events, he did not show it when he re-played his second round on Sunday, for he shot 67. Eighty-five other players also completed their rounds, with 57 players on the course when thunderstorms struck. Once again, the round was washed out. "I don't think I can continue playing this kind of golf," Rudolph said glumly.

Finally, on Monday the second round was completed. Rudolph shot 68, which tied him with none other than Sikes who, given a second chance, fired a 62. Close behind was Roberto De Vicenzo, who had gone 69-67-67-67, which would have been a 72-hole course record, but only one of the 67s counted.

Even with the field finally cut, and the Carling World Open starting on Friday, the PGA did not opt for a 36-hole finish on Tuesday.

In the third round, Rudolph stumbled to a 75. Nicklaus fired a 65 to take a three-shot lead over Player, Sikes, and De Vicenzo. Palmer was one behind. Ordinarily, having all of the Big Three in the top five for a final round would make for a gripping conclusion. However, golf tournaments are not supposed to end on Wednesday. Before a sparse gallery, Nicklaus held on for a one-stroke victory over Sikes. Many of the exhausted pros—some of whom had played 108 holes over the prior seven days—headed to Toronto to play in the Carling, now the second richest tournament.

September

Carling World Golf Championship

Billy Casper defeated Al Geiberger on the first hole of a sudden-death playoff at the Board of Trade Country Club outside of Toronto to take home $35,000.

Doug Sanders was disqualified from a tournament for the second time in 18 months. This time, unlike at Pensacola in 1966, he signed his scorecard after a third round of 69, but was barred from the final round for "unbecoming conduct." He requested that he be allowed to take a free drop when his ball rolled close to a television cable but was denied relief by tour official Steve Shabala. After his round was completed, he had a verbal altercation with Shabala regarding the ruling and used "abusive language" that resulted in his banishment.

Thunderbird Classic

The tour returned to the New York metropolitan area for the second time in three weeks. In the opening round of the Thunderbird Classic in Clifton, New Jersey, Bob Benning shot either a 72 or a 74. He was not quite sure and sought clarification from tournament officials. Benning, 35, was the pro at nearby Plainfield Country Club and had qualified for the tournament on Monday.

On the par-5 12th hole (Benning's third of the day), he chipped his third shot into a water hazard. His caddie plucked a ball out of the water. Benning placed his ball after his required three drops all rolled into the water, and then chipped it to within 3 feet. He then discovered he had hit the wrong ball, so his caddie went back to the hazard and found his original ball. Benning hit another good chip and knocked in the putt after picking up his marker for his original chip. He wrote down a triple-bogey 8 for his score, and proceeded to birdie 13, 16 and 18 to give himself 38 for the nine. On the front nine, Benning shot 36 for a 74, not bad all things considered.

However, things unraveled for Benning when, prior to turning in his card, he wanted to make sure he was required to take an additional two-stroke penalty for hitting the wrong ball. While he was telling his story to reporters in the locker room, none other than Arnold Palmer—who shot 71—walked by, stopped, and listened intently to the tale of woe by the unknown club pro. "Why, you have to be disqualified for something like that, but don't take my word for it," Palmer said. To his chagrin, Benning learned Palmer was right. Had Benning simply putted the ball found in the water, he would have been entitled to take a 6 if he had made the putt. Under the rules (at least at the time), if a player hit a ball into a hazard, he was entitled to drop another ball with a one-stroke penalty, even a ball found in the hazard. However, picking up the ball he unknowingly had properly dropped made Benning's score for the hole incalculable, requiring his disqualification.

Palmer was told Benning said he wished Palmer had not stopped by. "Imagine how he'd feel if he picked up a check here and then found out he should have been disqualified," Palmer said. "Bob's too nice a guy to be that way." Thanks to Palmer, Benning did not have that moral dilemma.

On Sunday, Palmer put on one of his patented charges. He started the day five shots back. With nine holes to play, Palmer was three behind Billy Casper. The stakes were much smaller than in their duel the previous year at Olympic, but Palmer knocked in a 10-foot birdie on 18 (which television viewers did not see because he finished before the start of the telecast) and watched the Giants-Cowboys game in the clubhouse while waiting to see if anybody would catch him. Casper folded down the stretch, with five bogeys on the final nine holes. Charles Coody and Art Wall Jr. both missed birdie putts on 18 that would have tied Palmer. Finally, Jack

Nicklaus came to the 18th hole needing a birdie to tie. His 9-foot putt missed, giving the 38-year-old Palmer his 51st tour win. The $30,000 first prize was the largest check of his career at the time.

Chi Chi Rodriguez

One of the greatest stories that I can tell you is there was a guy named Bob Goetz. He was a pretty good player. We were playing in St. Paul, Minnesota (and Goetz was in contention). And on the 17th hole, the second day, he shot the ball in the left rough. And he found a ball and he hit it about a foot from the hole. He had that for a birdie. And it was the same number, the same type of ball that he was playing. And he said, "this is not my ball." What a man, huh? He went on and found his ball and he made a 7. He never won, but he won the respect and admiration of all of us.

1968

January

Kaiser International Open

Photo 70: *A scholarly Kermit Zarley as a member of the University of Houston golf team. (Courtesy of Kermit Zarley)*

Kaiser Industries presumably added the word "International" to its new tournament in California's Napa Valley just to provide some pizazz, insofar as there were no more non-Americans in the field than usual.

On the 11th hole of the second round, Bob Duden hit his second shot into water and found a partially submerged ball. After three unsuccessful swipes, he picked the ball up, looked at it, and discovered it was not his ball. A tour official ruled that because Duden was not trying to hit his own ball, he was entitled to a drop behind the hazard with only a one-stroke penalty. From there, he got up and down for an unusual bogey. In the end, it did not do Duden much good as he missed the cut.

Kermit Zarley was the 1961 NCAA individual champion while attending the University of Houston. A devout Christian, in 1965 he founded the PGA bible study group with fellow pro Babe Hiskey. His unusual name caused Bob Hope to label him "the pro from the Moon." Zarley beat Dave Marr by one stroke at the Kaiser for his maiden tour victory.

March

Greater Jacksonville Open

In 1967, Tony Jacklin decided to make a go of it on the American tour. He had won seven professional tournaments in Great Britain and Australasia. At the 1967 Dunlop Masters at Royal St. George's, he made history by scoring the first hole-in-one captured on live television.

Jacklin—23 years old, handsome, and stylish—was drawn by the purses on the PGA Tour, which were exponentially larger than those offered in Europe. In October, he and wife Vivien made their way to Florida for the 144-hole qualifying tournament and the classroom work required of aspiring pros. Jacklin passed both tests.

The move paid immediate dividends. Jacklin started 1968 with a 10th-place finish at the Crosby, earning him $1,840, more than first prize at most British tournaments. He took in $2,950 for eighth-place in Tucson, and $5,347.50 for fourth at the Florida Citrus Open in Orlando. With a chance to win at Pensacola, Jacklin faltered but tied for second and earned $7,800.

The next week in Jacksonville, Jacklin shot rounds of 68, 65 and 69 to tie him for the lead with Doug Sanders, one stroke ahead of Arnold Palmer. In the final round, in a pairing with Palmer, he shot 71 to win by two strokes, the first Englishman to win on tour since Ted Ray's victory in the 1920 U.S. Open. First prize was $20,000.

Tony Jacklin
When I look back at those times, the most significant thing of all was the prize money. In Britain for example, we were playing for no money. At Wentworth, they had the Daks tournament, which was a men's clothing company. Into the late '60s, it was 5,000 pounds total

purse, 1,000 pounds for the winner, on probably the best venue in the U.K. We were playing for nothing. In America, first prizes were $20,000, total purses were $100,000.

The great players, Nicklaus and Johnny Miller and Trevino, those guys were fine. If you think you can play, bring it on, was their attitude. But there were a number of mean-spirited players who weren't very pleasant to be around. Dan Sikes, Gardner Dickinson, Bob Goalby, Doug Ford, Howie Johnson. Miserable old sods. They made our lives as miserable as they could. They wouldn't speak to you. Anything they had to say to you they would say through the scorekeeper.

I remember playing with Dan Sikes in 1968 at Doral and I was in the lead. I was teeing the ball up, minding my own business, on the ninth hole there, the short par-3 surrounded by water. And he announced out of the blue, "I was playing with Tommy Aaron last year and he went in the water here." And I went into the water, double-bogeyed, cost me a lot of money. All that being said, it toughened me up. I became mentally stronger for that.

To get drawn with these individuals, no doubt it affected the outcome for me. Half the time you were wondering what they would say next. It was tough. It was not an ideal environment. You didn't have to deal with it when you were playing with Nicklaus.

I played with Palmer in 1968 when I won at Jacksonville. I played with him and Don January in the last round. And dealing with the Palmer gallery, it was as big a deal as there was, because you were a fool if you thought that anyone was out there watching you. That being said, to survive it and come through and win, that win was bigger than just a win. It was a win in the toughest environment that there was. That was a steppingstone for me, (and helped me) to be able to handle the pressure of winning an Open.

Ultimately, this is a mental game. It's being as tough as nails. And I understand those guys. They came up through the 1950s driving around with no air-conditioning. It was tough for them, too. You learn to avoid these miserable people. My wife (Vivien) was my companion in the late '60s. We had no family, so we traveled together for three years. And there was Harold Henning and his wife Pat. We were close friends.

April

Greater Greensboro Open

On April 4, 1968, after the completion of the first round of the Greater Greensboro Open, Martin Luther King Jr. was assassinated in Memphis. Friday's second round was rained out, and play was curtailed on Sunday for a National Day of Mourning. The tournament was completed with a 36-hole finish on Monday. Billy Casper won.

Frank Beard

When play resumed on Monday, I was playing with Bruce Crampton and Charlie Sifford. The first hole of the Sedgefield Country Club is beautiful, with tall trees along the fairway, almost like a cathedral. It was early in the morning and there were maybe 20 people. All of a sudden, this voice echoes through the trees, "Hey Charlie, what do you think about what we did to that nigger?" Bruce starts to run back to the clubhouse. Charlie grabbed his driver and raised it like a samurai and starts to move towards the voice. I was friends with Charlie. I put my hand on his shoulder and said, "Charlie, we're not going to do that." I'd never heard anything like that in my life.

I was on the tour's player's committee. There was a meeting, but little talk of postponing or canceling the tournament, and we never took a vote. It's not like postponing a basketball game, where you can just reschedule. People in Greensboro had invested a whole year in the tournament. I was at the Cajun Classic in 1963 when Kennedy was assassinated, and they didn't even cancel for that.

The Masters

Torrential rains in advance of the 1968 Masters softened the course and almost guaranteed that scores would be low. However, winds on Thursday kept scores reasonable. Billy Casper's 68 was the low round of the day and put him one ahead of Jack Nicklaus and Tommy Aaron, as well as three international players: Tony Jacklin of England, Bruce Devlin of Australia, and Roberto De Vicenzo of Argentina.

On Friday, Casper skied to a 75 and was a non-factor for the remainder of the tournament. Gary Player fired a 67 and Don January a 68 to tie for the 36-hole lead at 139, one ahead of Nicklaus, Bob Goalby and Frank Beard (whose 65 was the low round of the day).

Devlin made the turn in 33 on Friday and had a three-shot lead when he arrived at the 455-yard, par-4 11th. He hit a nice drive in the fairway before hitting his second shot into the pond abutting the left side of the green. After a drop, his fourth shot failed to clear the pond and was caught in mud. With his next shot, Devlin failed to extricate his ball from the mud, before finally reaching the green with his sixth stroke. Two putts gave him a quadruple-bogey 8. He maintained his cool and finished with a 73, three shots back and tied with De Vicenzo, Jacklin, Raymond Floyd and Bert Yancey.

After a first-round 72, Arnold Palmer was on the periphery of contention when he hit his tee shot on the short par-3 12th into Rae's Creek and made double-bogey. On the par-5 15th, Palmer's second shot failed to clear the pond that fronts the green, and neither did his fourth. Palmer made a triple-bogey 8 on his way to a 79. He missed the cut at Augusta for the first time.

In Saturday's third round, it appeared that there would be a six-way tie for the lead until Player sank a downhill 25-foot putt on 18 to take a one-shot lead over Beard, January, Devlin, Floyd and Goalby. De Vicenzo was two back, tied with Miller Barber and Lee Trevino. The stage was set for one of the most dramatic final rounds in golf history.

On Sunday, the conditions at Augusta provided for optimal scoring. Those who did not go low fell by the wayside, including Player (72), Beard (70), January (73) and Floyd (71). Yancey posted a 65 for 279, which would be good for third place.

De Vicenzo started his final round in dramatic fashion, holing a 9-iron from 125 yards for an eagle on the par-4 first hole. The gallery responded by singing "Happy Birthday" (De Vicenzo turned 45 that day). He followed up with birdies on the second and third holes to take a share of the lead at 8 under with Devlin, who started birdie-birdie-birdie. Devlin followed with nine consecutive pars and would finish in fourth place at 8 under for 280, ruing Friday's snowman on the 11th hole.

Goalby was 3 under for the day through 12 holes on a mild, overcast afternoon, before matching De Vicenzo's feat of gaining four strokes in only three holes. He birdied 13 and then, after De Vicenzo sank a 15-foot birdie putt on 15 to take a two-shot lead, Goalby drained a 20-foot putt from off the green at the 14th hole for a birdie. Goalby then hit a perfect 300-yard drive on 15, followed by a 4-iron to the green to within 9 feet, with a chance for eagle. Soon thereafter, De Vicenzo's 9-iron on the par-4 17th landed 4 feet from the hole. Minutes later, almost simultaneously, both sank their putts. They apparently were tied at 12 under. On 18, De Vicenzo hit the fairway with his drive, while Goalby's iron on 16 was safely on the green, 30 feet to the left of the hole. He two-putted for par.

De Vicenzo pulled his approach well to the left of the 18th green. Although he was about 30 feet off the green, in an area where the gallery had been standing, he used a putter and hit to within 7 feet. His par putt slid just below the hole. Television viewers were informed that the bogey dropped De Vicenzo one shot behind Goalby. A few moments later, viewers of the CBS broadcast saw De Vicenzo and his playing partner Aaron conversing at the scorer's table behind the 18th green as they reviewed their scorecards. De Vicenzo did not notice that Aaron had marked him for 4 instead of 3 on 17. After signing his card, De Vicenzo walked toward the clubhouse while acknowledging the gallery's applause.

Goalby pulled his drive on 17 to the right side of the fairway, in the vicinity of pine trees that would affect his approach. He managed to catch the right front of the green. Goalby's lag from 50 feet stopped 4 feet below the hole. He pushed his par putt and missed. De Vicenzo and Goalby were tied again. Or so everybody thought.

Doing commentary for CBS, Cary Middlecoff informed viewers that on 18, Goalby was faced with the decision of whether to hit driver to give him a reasonable approach for a possible birdie, but flirt with fairway bunkers that could spell disaster, or play for par with a 3-wood. Goalby paced nervously as he decided, while his playing partner, Raymond Floyd, prepared to hit his drive.

Photo 71: Roberto De Vicenzo (right) after being told by Tommy Aaron (left) of the latter's scorecard error. (Getty Images)

De Vicenzo had maintained a cheerful demeanor during his round, which continued even after his bogey on the final hole. Now, television viewers saw that he had returned to the scorer's table behind the 18th green. His expression was not what would be expected if he was there just to see what Goalby would do. Instead, it was grim. He shook his head and gestured as if frustrated. A minute later, viewers saw Aaron sitting beside him. In retrospect, this was odd, because Aaron finished at 6-under par in a tie for seventh and no longer had a dog in the fight, but the CBS commentators offered no opinion on what might be going on.

Goalby chose 3-wood off the 18th tee. His choice to play

safe appeared to backfire as his drive went right, into the trees. However, a fortunate kick placed his ball in the fairway, but so far back that instead of a 5- or 6-iron Goalby had to go with a 3-iron for his approach. He hit the green but went past the hole to the right.

When Goalby reached the 18th green, in his mind, and in the minds of everybody but De Vicenzo, Aaron and a few tournament officials, he faced the prospect of having to get down in two putts from 45 feet, downhill and with two breaks, just to salvage a tie. De Vicenzo nervously gnawed at his fingers, knowing the reality that his only chance was if Goalby three-putted to force an 18-hole playoff on Monday, which CBS repeatedly was touting.

Goalby's putt broke sharply and slowly rolled down the green, stopping 4 feet away. Not a ripple of applause could be heard from the knowledgeable gallery. He was left with a putt that had an imperceptible break, one that foiled unwary competitors over the decades. As he surveyed it, a loud murmur is heard from the gallery. Floyd, who had previous experience with major championship drama as Ken Venturi's playing partner for the final 36 holes at the 1964 U.S. Open, raised his putter high above his head in a gesture to quiet the crowd.

During his round, De Vicenzo repeatedly conferred with his caddie. Goalby did not confer with his caddie, known as "Marble Eye." He was on his own. As he carefully looked at his putt from all angles, Marble Eye took a posture on one knee off of the green, looking away and appearing to pray. Adding to the drama, Goalby called Floyd over to look at a spot midway between his ball and the hole, and then proceeded to repair a ball mark. Goalby finally stepped to his ball and took out the break by dead-nailing his ball into the center of the cup.

"We have a tie," intoned Pat Summerall, doing his first Masters broadcast for CBS. "That has to be one of the greatest clutch putts of all time."

Goalby looked relieved, not happy.

Several minutes later, after two groups behind the Goalby-Floyd pairing had finished, Summerall solemnly announced that there appeared to be a problem with De Vicenzo's scorecard. Holding an umbrella to shield himself from light rain that had started to fall, De Vicenzo was seen talking to Gary Player, who was in the final group. Player nodded sadly. Goalby's expression likewise was solemn, though he knew he was the Masters champion. Minutes before, Middlecoff, had climbed out of the broadcast tower and walked over to him. "Bob, you won," Middlecoff whispered. "De Vicenzo screwed up his card."

In the Butler Cabin, Goalby and De Vicenzo sat for the custom- ary interview ahead of the green-jacket ceremony. The late Frank Chirkinian, the longtime producer of the CBS Masters telecasts, hated the Butler Cabin interviews with a passion because usually Augusta National co-founders Bobby Jones and Clifford Roberts, not professional commentators, presided and would ask (often stupid) questions. "I would watch this with my face in my hands," Chirkinian wrote in 2007, "but the club wouldn't have it any other way." Roberts' wrinkled, stern, bespectacled face was made for radio, and his reedy voice was made for the silent movies.

In 1968, Augusta National member and former USGA President John Winters filled in for Jones, who was ailing. He informed the television audience that because De Vicenzo had inadvertently recorded his score on the 17th hole as a 4 instead of a 3, under the Rules of Golf there was no choice but to accept that as his score. Thus, Goalby was the winner and De Vicenzo the runner-up.

Bearing out Chirkinian's complaint, Winters did not ask the obvious question every viewer wanted to know (what happened at the scorer's table, Roberto?), but instead went into a soliloquy about the galleries and missed chances and the now inconsequen- tial eagle De Vicenzo made on the first hole and mindlessly asked if he had any comments on the course and the play.

To his credit, De Vicenzo answered the unasked question. "I can't forget what I do on the first hole and what I do on the last," he said. "I am a professional for many years and never think what a stupid I am. Because when you play in a tournament, you have to check the scorecard very carefully. And I make the wrong thing today. I looked at the scorecard and, to tell the truth, I don't see anything, I don't see any numbers. I feel sorry for myself."

Roberts interrupted and babbled about a round Bobby Jones and De Vicenzo played in Buenos Aires 20 years before. He then said that he and Jones were "going to be busy trying to figure out some way to have two winners in place of our winner and runner-up. In our hearts, we will always regard you as one of the two winners of this tournament, without taking anything away from the new Masters champion."

During the too-brief exchange with Goalby, Winters asked if there were any shots he would have liked to hit differently, which was pointless given that Goalby had won the tournament. Goalby sincerely expressed his regret to De Vicenzo. "It seems like it's not really the way to win the golf tournament," he said.

For Goalby, it was a bittersweet victory. His final round of 66 was one of the greatest in Masters history. He made clutch putts on 14, 15 and 18 to nail down the win. But he was not going to come out ahead no matter what. If he had failed to get up-and-down on 18 and won a playoff the next day, history would still note that De Vicenzo's error gave him a big assist. If he lost a playoff, he would have been deprived of his only victory in a major championship to go along with his 10 other victories. Goalby was one of the finest, if underappreciated, golfers of the 1960s. He died in January 2022 at age 92.

Bruce Devlin

In the second round, I had a three-shot lead going into 11 and hit what I thought was a perfect second shot. Unfortunately, it landed a little short and hit the down slope of a mound in front of the green and kicked left and went into the water. Then if my memory serves me correctly, I hit it in the water again. Then, I went into the water to play it out, and to cut a long story short I made 8. Funny enough, I played rather well after that. I think I made three birdies the balance of that round and had two three-putts, and I still was in convention right up until late Sunday afternoon.

Bob Goalby

I was playing a half-hour behind Roberto De Vicenzo, so I did not know what was going on. When I got to 18, I thought we were tied. I had a 40-foot putt that had about 15 feet of break and hit it to within 4 feet. That was a hard putt I had left. I had three-putted 17, and as I stood over the putt I said to myself, "You choking so-and-so. Stand up good like a man and hit the goddamn thing." And I hit the most perfect putt you've ever seen. Good putts don't always go in. But this one did, at the right time for me.

After I made it, I was standing behind the 18th green talking to Sam Snead and Cary Middlecoff. Middlecoff whispered to me, "Bob, you won. De Vicenzo screwed up his card."

It was unfortunate for Roberto, but it was unfortunate for me as well because I didn't get the credit I deserved. I shot the fourth-lowest (72-hole)] score ever at the time. I won within the rules. But I guess if we had a playoff it would have been better.

In the same round, I had caught an error I made on the card I was keeping for Raymond Floyd.

Tommy Aaron

De Vicenzo had hit his ball real close on 17. I mean, he could have gone up and putted out. It was so close, and I was on the back of the green. I played way past where his marker was, and I was working pretty hard to get my putt in for a par. I did. And he stepped up quickly and just tapped his very short putt in for a birdie. He played very quickly. And so, we walked very quickly to the 18th tee. I usually write scores down after the hole is finished, but I didn't have time then.

Roberto hit his drive to the right, behind the trees on the right. And I had a pretty good drive, hit my second shot on the green. And then his second shot, he had hit a big slice around those trees to get to the green and he didn't slice it enough. He missed the green on the left and it rolled down the bank. I'm on the green watching him play. He putts up the bank, past the hole and misses the next putt. My thinking was, "It was too bad that he didn't make 4 here. He may have won the tournament." So, when we sat down at the scorer's table, I put a 5 at 18 and just without thinking, I put 4 at 17. Because in my mind, I was thinking, "Too bad he didn't make 4."

At that time, the scorer's table was out in the open. People are leaning over the rope, trying to see what you were doing, trying to talk to you while you're trying to check your scorecard. And I'm sitting there checking mine. I would check it three or four times. I think maybe I finished in the top 10. A member stuck his head underneath the rope. It was Charlie Coe. He was a member. He said, "They want you in the press room." And Roberto just jumped up quickly, scribbled his name and left. I saw quotes from Charlie Coe. He said that he said something like, "Be sure to check your scorecard." He didn't say that. He just said, "They want you in the press room." That's all he said to Roberto. I've never told anybody who it was because I thought, "Well, why bring him into it?" but it was Charlie Coe. With that, Roberto just bolted out of his chair and left. And my first thought was, well, "He didn't check his scorecard. I hope to hell it was right."

I'm still sitting there with this elderly gentleman whose job it is to collect scorecards, and I look at the 18th-(hole) leaderboard and I thought, "Something's not right." I looked at his card and I went right to the 17th, and I thought, "Oh my God, he made 3 there, and I put down 4." The guy sitting there at the table says, "What's wrong?" I said, "Is Roberto around here somewhere?" He said, "No, he's been in the press room for 5 minutes." I said, "Well, you better bring him back." He said, "Why?" I said, "He signed an incorrect scorecard."

So, he comes back. I said, "Roberto, I don't know what to say, except I'm sorry, but I put down 4 on 17, you made 3. Roberto said, "Let's change it." I said, "We can't do that, Roberto." And you are one of the few people I've ever told that, because it sounds so bad. "I said, no, we can't do that." He accepted that. He just sat in a chair with his head in his hands. And I stayed there too.

There were two or three groups who finished while we were still sitting there. Goalby's group, they didn't have a place to sit down and check their scorecards. There were only two chairs there and Roberto was sitting in one and I was sitting in the other. Eventually I got up, so a player could sit down and check the score. But they saw that issue. Now, they put a trailer out there. Well, they used to. They may take you in the clubhouse now, I don't know, to check your card. But it's very unfortunate. If I'd had a chance, if I just stopped Roberto, but he jumped up so quick, he was just sitting there, with his head in his hands thinking, "Well, I just lost the tournament."

My thought was, "How can you not check your scorecard?" That's so irresponsible, not to check your scorecard. But he had a history of doing that, not checking his card.

Anyway, I felt sorry for Roberto, you know, I just feel terrible about it, but it's just one of those things that happens. I was getting ready to say to him, "Be sure to check your scorecard," because I knew he hadn't looked at his card. Everybody felt so sorry for Roberto, and nobody blamed him. I guess they blamed me, which was ridiculous, because right in the rules book it says the player himself is responsible for his score, and no one else.

After the last round of the Masters in 1973, when I won, Johnny Miller put down a 5 for me on 13. I made a 4. We sat down at the table. I went through my card, and I said, "Johnny, don't you remember I hit a driver and an iron on the green and I two-putted for a 4?," and he said, "Oh yeah, yeah. I forgot that." He eventually changed it to a 4. That's the way the rule works. I made a casual comment about it in the press room. Johnny said to me, "What are you trying to do to me?" I thought, "What the hell is wrong with you? I'm not trying to do anything to you." He thought I was trying to blame him. I didn't blame him for anything. We just changed it. That's the way it works. Johnny thought I was trying to throw him under the bus.

May

Houston Champions International

Lee Trevino arrived at the Houston Open ready to win. In 1967, he was named Rookie of the Year by *Golf Digest*, despite only playing half a year. He was doing well in 1968, with top-10s at Los Angeles, the Bob Hope, and Pensacola.

After three rounds, Trevino was one shot back of Dan Sikes. On Sunday, he was paired with Roberto De Vicenzo. There was a great outpouring of sympathy for Roberto De Vicenzo after his Masters debacle. Sikes was done in by a double-bogey and two bogeys on the front. Trevino led De Vicenzo by three shots at the turn, but De Vicenzo birdied 12, 13, and 15. After Trevino bogeyed 17, the two were tied.

On 18, Trevino pushed his second shot into the crowd, while De Vicenzo hit his approach 35 feet from the hole. Trevino chipped to within 4 feet. De Vicenzo missed his birdie chance and putted out for par. After Trevino missed his par putt, De Vicenzo would be the winner, after the mere formality of signing his scorecard.

Like at the Masters, De Vicenzo made things hard on himself. He left the scoring area without signing his card. Tournament director Jack Tuthill was on hand, just as he was in 1966 at the Pensacola Open, where he disqualified Doug Sanders for leaving the scoring area without signing. Tuthill was in a quandary. The letter of the rule was that the penalty was disqualification, just like for Sanders. However, not having the stomach to see De Vicenzo again be the victim of his own carelessness, Tuthill went after him, brought him back, sat him down, went over the scorecard with him, and watched him sign to confirm the victory.

"You young," De Vicenzo told Trevino after the round. "You got a chance to win many tournaments. How old you are, 28? This may be my last." In fact, Houston was De Vicenzo's last of seven PGA tour wins. He also was right about Trevino.

Tommy Aaron

At Houston, I think, De Vicenzo won. He almost did the same thing, but Jack Tuthill stopped him from leaving the scoring area and went over the card with him. There was an error on his card, but they changed it, which is the way you do it. But nobody ever talks about that.

Lee Trevino

I played extremely well there, at Champions.

You've got to understand where I came from. I'm not an educated guy. I don't have any options. I had to make it playing golf. When you've got no options, you can't complain. If you have options and complain, you can go do something else. All I could do was play golf and I was good at it. And the good Lord gave me a hell of a talent. It came easy to me, and I never got discouraged, wherever I finished. It never bothered me, not one little bit, where I finished. The most money I ever made in my life working was $100 a week. So, if I finished dead last in a tournament, I was going to make more than a hundred.

So that was the one attitude I had. It didn't bother me. Disappoint me? Maybe, but only for a short period of time until I could get to the practice tee and get ready for next week. In other words, where I could kick your ass. That's how I played the game. But I never got disappointed. I made bogey at 18 and lost to Roberto. I go from there to Atlanta and Bob Lunn beat me by a couple shots. I finished second again.

Greater New Orleans Open

Rives McBee appeared for Monday qualifying and was paired with Bill Garrett, who was his teammate when they played at North Texas

State. Things were not going well for McBee. He was over par and told Garrett that he did not care if he qualified because he could use the time off. On the 13th hole, he mis-hit his 3-iron and angrily smacked it against the tee marker, bending the club. On the 15th hole, after missing a short birdie putt, he snapped his putter in two.

McBee was 4 over and looking forward to finishing his round so he could go home to Texas for the weekend. On his way to the clubhouse, he placed his second shot on 16 on the green. From 50 feet, putting with his bent 3-iron, he somehow got down in two for a par. On 17, he sank a 12-foot birdie putt with the broken club and on 18 made birdie from 6 feet. As a result, McBee's 73 was good enough to make the field.

In Thursday's first round, McBee shot a 1-under-par 70 at the Lakewood Country Club in New Orleans, presumably with repaired clubs, six behind leader Bob Stanton and one ahead of Jack Nicklaus. By Friday evening, McBee wished he had not qualified. He had injured his wrists the day before and had to withdraw in the middle of the second round, and was required to take time off from the tour to recuperate.

George Archer won by two shots over Bert Yancey.

Rives McBee

I hit one of those cypress roots that are everywhere on that golf course at Lakewood. I was over at the edge of the rough and I hit a cypress root and jammed both of my wrists. I went out later that day to hit some golf balls and I was shanking them. I was worried about it because my wrists were hurting. I called my doctor and he said, "You've evidently damaged the tendons in your wrists. I suggest you ice them down tonight, and then tomorrow, before you play, tape them up." So, that's what I did. I iced them all night long, got up the next morning, went out to the golf course, went to the nurse's station and had them tape my wrists.

On the front nine I shot even par. At the 10th tee, I looked at my fingers and they were twice the size of what they should have been.

I took the tape off, and on the eleventh hole, a par-5, I was right in front of the green in 2. I went completely around that green with shanks. I mean, right, right, right. I was back in the same spot lying nine as I was in 2. I said, "Guys, I'm through." I withdrew.

June

U.S. Open

Lee Trevino headed to the Oak Hill Country Club in Rochester, New York for his third U.S. Open. His opening round of 69 left him tied for second with Charles Coody, two strokes back of Bert Yancey. On Friday, Yancey shot 68 for a 36-hole score of 137 to maintain his two-shot lead over Trevino, who also had a 68. Coody was at 140, tied with Bruce Devlin, Don Bies, and club pro Jerry Pittman.

In the third round, Trevino and Yancey were paired. Yancey shot 70, Trevino 69 as they separated themselves from the rest of the field. On the 11th green, Trevino asked Yancey to move his coin marker. After Trevino putted, Yancey placed his ball down, picked up his coin and prepared to putt. "Did you put your coin back?," Trevino asked. Yancey had not. Yancey re-marked his ball to the correct spot. Trevino's headiness and sportsmanship saved Yancey a penalty and possible disqualification. "One of these days I'm going to win a big one," Trevino told the press after the round. "Maybe I'll even win this one tomorrow, but I wouldn't want it because Bert had to take a two-stroke penalty."

Paired again on Sunday, both Trevino and Yancey bogeyed the first hole. It was to be Trevino's only blemish. Yancey was to have seven more bogeys on his way to a 76. Trevino birdied the 11th and 12th holes and parred the others. His 72-hole score of 69-68-69-69 for 275 was four shots better than Jack Nicklaus, whose final-round 67 passed Yancey for second place. Trevino was the first player in U.S. Open history to shoot four rounds under par.

Trevino would win the Hawaiian Open in November and in Tucson the following February. His career really took off in the 1970s and he became a gallery favorite for his regular (some would say nervous) chatter. In all, he would win 29 times on the regular tour. Trevino won another U.S. Open in 1971 (beating Nicklaus in an 18-hole playoff), consecutive Open Championships in 1971 and 1972, and two PGA Championships (in 1974 and 1984).

Photo 72: Lee Trevino. 18th hole, 1968 U.S. Open (Walter Iooss, Jr.)

Lee Trevino

I took off a week and went to visit my friends up in Stamford, Connecticut, and played a little golf and watched Little League baseball and just relaxed. And then I drove up on Saturday to Rochester, New York, and started playing practice rounds. I played Sunday, Monday, Tuesday, Wednesday, and I played all four rounds with Doug Sanders, and Doug Sanders told me that he was going to place a bet in Vegas on me. I don't know how much he bet, but he won, I can tell you that.

I was playing extremely well. I tried to dissect where I messed up a little bit, and my problem was being a little bit too aggressive, and it didn't work out. If I wouldn't have been as aggressive on two or three holes, I probably would've won both (Atlanta and Houston), but that's just not the way I play. But I use percentages also. I look at a shot and I know if it's dangerous, (I'd think), "If I put down five balls, how many of these balls are going to go on the green, and how many are going in the water?" If it's 50-50, I'm not messing with it. It's got to be 70-30 before I go for it.

I didn't (think about being the first player to break par all four rounds). You have to understand, I'm a golfer who never knew who Sam Snead, Ben Hogan, Sarazen, Jones were until I went on tour. I had no idea who these people were. I started playing golf when I was 22 years old. When I got out of the Marine Corps is when I got serious about it. I caddied a little bit as a youngster, but I never played golf. I didn't do anything like that. I'm like Larry Nelson, who took it up when he was 22, when he got out of Vietnam. I came up in a house with no plumbing, no electricity, we didn't have televisions, we didn't have radios, we didn't have newspapers. And golf wasn't one of my deals, so I sure wasn't watching anybody.

I probably could tell you more about Mickey Wright, the lady golfer who had the sweetest swing of anybody—male or female—in the history of the game, and the only reason for that is because our little four-room house with no paint on it was next to the seventh fairway of the Glen Lakes Country Club, where they had a ladies' tournament every year. So, she's the only one I watched play golf. I didn't know anything about them making money, playing professional. I had no idea. I thought they were playing for trophies. You know, those trophies don't cook good in an oven. You can't eat them.

Don Bies

In 1968 I qualified for the U.S. Open at Oak Hill in Rochester, New York, and finished fifth. I was pretty much in awe, being a club pro and playing in the Open and playing good. I was a pretty good ball striker and hit the ball pretty straight, good for major golf courses at the U.S. Open and the PGA, with narrow fairways and high rough.

Walter Iooss, Jr.

I always had problems with the officials, the hierarchy of golf. I was always trying to push the limits to get photographs. And I've had my credentials ripped off. I was thrown out of the 1968 Open, when Lee Trevino won at Rochester. I was in a sand trap. (USGA Executive Director) Joe Dey and I didn't get along very well. He stripped me and I had to call the magazine. I did get the cover. He would walk around in that blue flannel jacket in the middle of the summer. It wasn't a good match.

July

The Open Championship

The Open Championship returned to Carnoustie, Scotland for the first time since Ben Hogan's historic victory in 1953 in his only attempt to win the Claret Jug. At 7,252 yards, the course was the longest Open test to date.

The first Greater Milwaukee Open ran opposite the Open, a $200,000 purse with a $40,000 first prize, as opposed to about $43,500 (with $7,200 for the winner) offered at the Open. Thus, U.S. Open champion Lee Trevino and other tour stalwarts again skipped the Open and headed to Wisconsin.

Temperatures plummeted into the 50s during Wednesday's first round. British Amateur champion Michael Bonallack and Brian Barnes, both of England, led at the end of the day by one stroke over two other Englishmen, Maurice Bembridge and Peter Mills. A fifth English golfer, Tony Jacklin, was at 72 along with Paddy Skerritt of Ireland, Bob Charles of New Zealand and Californian Billy Casper, who was playing the Open for the first time.

On a windy Thursday, Casper shot a remarkable front nine of 32 and finished with 68 to take a four-shot lead at 140 over Jacklin, Charles and Barnes. Gary Player, Skerritt and Jack Nicklaus (who shot 69) were at 145. For the 72 holes, nobody other than Casper and Nicklaus would break 70 on the par-72 course.

Cold conditions continued for the third round. Casper's lead was cut to one as he shot 74 for a 54-hole total of 214, 2-under par. Charles was one back, and one ahead of Player. After a 73, Nicklaus was four back, one ahead of Bembridge, Jacklin and Gay Brewer. At 220 and six back was Arnold Palmer, who recovered from an opening round of 77 with rounds of 71 and 72.

On Saturday, Casper quickly dipped below even par for the tournament with a succession of bogeys. He would close with a 78 and finish fourth. Charles hovered at par longer but shot 76 to finish tied for second. Nicklaus started well, but on the sixth hole drove out of bounds on the left and uncharacteristically showed his disgust by kicking his bag hard enough that it fell out of the hands of Jimmy Dickinson, his regular caddie when he played in Britain. Nicklaus calmed down after that outburst and stayed in the fight.

The championship was decided on the par-5, 485-yard 14th hole, called "Spectacles" for the twin circular bunkers short of the green that seem to peer at players as they hit their approach shots. In Friday's third round, using a 3-iron for his approach, Player eagled 14.

On Saturday, Player hit a good drive in the fairway while Nicklaus—with whom he was paired—drove into the rough. Player could not see Nicklaus' second shot, but the cheer from the gallery near the green told him that Nicklaus had hit a good recovery shot. Player decided not to play safe. With the wind in his face much stronger than the day before, he pulled out his 3-wood and hit the greatest shot of his career. His ball soared over the Spectacles and stopped 2 feet from the hole. Player's eagle gave him a lead he would not relinquish. He closed with a 73 and a 72-hole total of 289, 1-over par. His two-shot victory over Nicklaus and Charles was his second at the Open Championship (he previously had won in 1959), and he would win a third in 1974.

Mohammed Said Moussa of Egypt, who was most accustomed to playing sand courses and would win the Egyptian Open 24 times, made both the 36-hole and 54-hole cuts and finished tied for 39th.

Gary Player

Carnoustie may be the toughest golf course in the world. It's certainly right up there. And when the wind blows there, I'm telling you, if you break 290 you've had a career tournament. Going into the 14th hole, five of us were within one shot of each other. I'm playing with

Nicklaus. Let me tell you that Jack Nicklaus is the greatest gentleman I ever played golf with in my life. Billy Casper, Bob Charles, Maurice Bembridge, and somebody else was one shot back. At the 14th hole, known as the Spectacles, I hit a 3-wood into the wind 10 inches from the hole, and went on to win by two. When you win a tournament at Carnoustie, you've played your heart out.

PGA Championship

The 50th PGA Championship was played at the steamy Pecan Valley Golf Club in San Antonio. Playing on a dusty Texas course in the middle of July—the week after some of the top pros had competed at chilly Carnoustie—never was a good idea but was a terrible idea for 1968. Moreover, the touring pros were at the height of their bitter fight with the PGA of America, the tournament's sponsor.

Almost every international star (including Gary Player and Tony Jacklin) skipped the event. By one count, the field consisted of 112 club pros and only 56 touring pros. Jack Nicklaus, who was at the forefront of the fight with the PGA over tour management, missed the cut and termed the field "ridiculous." Budding star Tom Weiskopf (who won twice in 1968 and would finish third on the money list) also missed the cut (77-82) and angrily left the course. "This is not as good as a local public links tournament," one prominent pro told a reporter, adding, "If you use my name, I'll strangle you." For a major, the 1968 PGA seemed very minor.

Yet, Pecan Valley provided drama on as well as off the course. Arnold Palmer, 38 years old, presumably had long given up on his quest for a calendar-year Grand Slam and had lowered his sights on winning the PGA, the only major he had failed to win. His first round 71 put him five shots behind Marty Fleckman. Palmer followed with a 69 that left him two back of Fleckman and Frank Beard.

On Saturday, the temperature topped out at 102 degrees. Palmer departed from his usual habit of going hatless and wore a baseball cap, and shot a 2-over-par 72. Fleckman and Beard maintained their two-shot lead. Palmer, Miller Barber, Lee Trevino, Doug Sanders and 48-year-old Julius Boros, were in a five-way tie for third.

Palmer played well in another 102-degree cauldron on Sunday. He came to 18 one stroke behind Boros, who was 3 under for the day and in the group behind Palmer. The 18th hole was 488 yards, an unusually long par-4 for the time. Palmer hooked his drive into a buried lie in deep rough but got a huge break when he received a free drop from an overhanging television cable. With a clean lie, he hit one of the greatest shots of his career, lashing a 3-wood onto the green to within 8 feet of the cup. His birdie putt just missed. Palmer watched Boros get up and down from off the green, making a 3-foot putt for par to become the oldest player to win a major championship, a record that stood for 53 years until Phil Mickelson's 2021 victory at the PGA Championship.

At the 1968 PGA, Boros also helped pave the way for pros to make additional money. During the tournament, he donned a baseball cap he had picked up when he played at the Amana Corporation's yearly corporate outing. Affluent television viewers saw the Amana logo atop Boros's head in the torrid Texas heat. Amana manufactured and sold air conditioners and other appliances. Lou King, who then worked for Amana, had the idea to pay pros to wear its hat. Previously, pros would wear hats bearing the names of golf equipment companies who sponsored them, but Amana was the first non-golf business to use pros for advertising purposes. Amana initially paid pros $50 per week to wear their hats. Today, pros receive up to $100,000 per year just to display a company's logo on their attire.

Chuck Courtney

The PGA of America was famous for picking courses that weren't ready. Pecan Valley. The National Cash Register Club in Dayton. They didn't have a lot of money in those days, and whoever gave them the best deal, that's where they'd go.

Julius Boros, a wonderful guy and a very sweet man and a wonderful player. I, still, when I teach people, I try to get them to swing like Julius Boros. An ageless, old-fashioned golf swing. It never went wrong. He'd amble up to the ball like Bob Jones and just hit. Fluid.

He was living down in south Florida, somewhere by Miami, in a place called Coral Springs. We're playing an event down there and I'm playing with Julius the first two days. I had the flu something godawful. I felt like shit. I probably shot 160 and missed the cut by a mile. And my ass was dragging around. We finished on Friday, and he came over and put his arm around me and said something like, "Don't worry, kid, you'll get well," something like that. He said, "I'll tell you what. Get a courtesy driver, here's my address, get the courtesy car to bring you over to my house and I'll cook you a steak and get you a great big glass of scotch and you'll feel better." He sat me down in his own big easy chair and gave me a scotch and barbecued a steak. He was just a nice guy, very empathetic. He was a terrific guy. A very quiet man. He never said very much of anything, but when he opened his mouth, you listened.

Frank Boynton

I skipped a tournament to come to San Antonio early and get used to the weather, because I knew how hot and humid it would be down there. So, I spent a week getting acclimated. And fortunately, that was the first year they had brought out Gatorade. So, I think getting used to the weather, plus Gatorade, helped me.

(In the final round) I was paired with two fellows that were known for being tough to play with, Dan Sikes and Bob Goalby. Goalby could hear a mouse peeing on cotton from 20 feet, so it was almost impossible to stay still enough. Dan Sikes, if you made too many putts he started chastising you. "Jesus Christ. Are you going to make every damn putt!" So, it was their stature, and if they got on you, it was hard to play. But they were just delightful to play with that day. They were just like mother hens getting me in, and we all tied for eighth. And I got to go to the Masters the next year as a result, but they were very helpful, which was very surprising because they were known for being very tough to play with.

Jack Nicklaus

I don't think (what was going on with the PGA Tour) had anything to do with my play. I just played crappy.

Marty Fleckman

About the only thing I remember is if I birdied the last hole I would have tied, but I bogeyed.

Tony Jacklin

As far as the PGA Championship is concerned, for me it was the least important of the four (majors). It was hard for me to get excited about it, if that makes any sense.

August

American Golf Classic

While he was dominating the United Golf Association—which is where African-American players competed before the PGA dropped its "Caucuasian race" clause—Lee Elder also caddied for his friend, Billy Maxwell, winner of the 1951 U.S. Amateur and seven PGA tour events, in order to supplement his income. Elder qualified for the 1966 U.S. Open and made the cut. In 1967 he went to Q-School and earned his playing card.

Under the radar, Elder was having a successful rookie year. In 18 tournaments, he had cashed checks in all but four, and had earned about $15,000 when he arrived in Akron. Elder opened with a 68—the same score as another tour rookie, Hale Irwin—three shots behind John Schlee.

In the second round, there was a surprise leader, William C. Campbell, a 45-year-old amateur and insurance executive from West Virginia. Campbell, who had won the 1964 U.S. Amateur and was in Ohio to prepare for the 1968 edition in Columbus, followed an opening round 70 with a 67 to take a one-shot lead over Elder and George Knudson of Canada. Jack Nicklaus—who won the Western Open the week before to break a victory drought that had extended back to the Sahara Invitational in October 1967—was two back of Campbell.

On Saturday, Don Bies, the Seattle club pro who was taking advantage of his exemption earned by his finish at the 1967 PGA Championship, shot a course-record 64 to take a two-shot lead over Campbell and Arnold Palmer. Nicklaus started his third round strong but a double-bogey on 15 (where he required two shots to dislodge his ball from under a bush) set him back. His 72 put him five back of Bies and one behind Elder, who also shot 72.

A tournament record crowd of 23,331 came to Firestone for the final round. There were no scores among the leaders lower than Nicklaus's 69. Campbell soared to 77. Palmer was in the thick of it until bogeying 13 and 14, and he then hit into the water on the long, par-5 16th hole and suffered a triple-bogey.

Nicklaus sank an 8-footer for birdie on the 18th hole for a 280 total and waited. Frank Beard shot 70 to tie Nicklaus. Elder could have won with a par on 18, but he found two bunkers and bogeyed for a 70 to join Nicklaus and Beard. Bies faltered with a 75. He could have tied Nicklaus, Beard and Elder but bogeyed the 18th to finish one shot back in fourth place.

On the first playoff hole—the 16th—Beard drove into a bunker, blasted out, hit a 3-wood over the green, narrowly missed chipping in and settled for a par. At the time, with the existing club technology, the 625-yard hole was unreachable in 2, and Elder and Nicklaus were on the green in 3. Elder rammed in a birdie from 30 feet to eliminate Beard. Nicklaus then rolled in his birdie putt from 15 feet to stay alive. Nicklaus and Elder went on to 17. Elder was in a position to win when he hit his second shot to within 7 feet while Nicklaus could get no closer than 30 feet in 3 after blasting out of a greenside bunker. However, Nicklaus nailed his putt for par and Elder lipped out on his putt that would have won.

On the third playoff hole (the 18th), both Nicklaus and Elder traded two-putt pars. The duo went back to the 16th hole. There, Elder hit his third shot into a bunker, while Nicklaus had a 14-foot putt for birdie. Elder's shot from the sand landed 6 feet from the hole. After Nicklaus missed his putt for a win, Elder calmly stroked his ball into the cup to stay alive.

On the fifth playoff hole, Elder split the fairway while Nicklaus found the left rough. Both hit good approach shots, Elder to within 15 feet and Nicklaus 8 feet. After Elder missed his birdie putt, Nicklaus made his to end what still is commonly regarded as the greatest sudden-death playoff in tour history. "I'm satisfied," Elder said afterwards. "I gave it my best and it wasn't enough. But that's not too bad against the best player in the world."

Elder used the epic playoff as a springboard to future success. He would win four times on the regular tour and in 1975 became the first African-American to play in the Masters. Eight victories on the PGA Senior Tour followed. Elder died in November 2020, several months after he was honored in the opening ceremony at the Masters.

Don Bies

Lee Elder was a good friend of mine. I shot a 64 at Firestone to set the course record. At the time it was about the hardest course on tour. I still have the scorecard. It's hanging in the furnace room down in my basement.

September

Robinson Open

Photo 73: Dean Refram. (Ralph Walters, The Chicago Sun-Times)

The Robinson Open was a little tournament played in southern Illinois for a few years, for the first time in late September 1968. Its purse was $25,000. The adjective "little" often preceded Dean Refram's name, as he was about five-and-a-half feet tall. However, Refram came up big, winning by five shots over Mike Hill and an unimpressive field to take home $5,000 for his only regular tour victory.

Chi Chi Rodriguez

Dean Refram was a good guy. He used to smoke like a chimney. He bet that he could throw a golf ball on the green on a par-3 hole that was 100 yards long. One time he bet me that he could swim the length of a pool in Oklahoma, under the water, back and forth. "I bet you $50," he said. I told him, "You're going to drown." Well, he did it and then he came out and said, "If you bet me another 50, I bet I can go one, two, three times underneath." I told him, "No, Dean, I can't do that." What he used to do, Refram could drink a six-pack and eat three hamburgers in less than a minute.

One time, Ken Still and I were in La Costa and we didn't have anything to do and they had a poker game going. I said, "Kenny, I always carry two silver dollars in my pocket. You fill up a bucket of ice and put it in the corner and we can bet money that I can throw a coin in there." So, they started giving me 3-1 odds. And bingo, boom, right in. Two to one, boom, right in. Even money, boom, right in. All the guys who were playing poker, we took all their money.

I'd take a silver dollar, if the green was wet, and bet I could throw it from 50 feet within 6 inches of the hole. One time I bet Doug Sanders out of $1,000 doing that.

Steve Opperman

I played with Ken Still a few times. I remember seeing him at the L.A. Open. He said, "You want to bet on the Super Bowl? Fifty dollars." I said OK. I won my bet. Next year I see him at L.A. and he wants to bet another $50. I won again and he gave me another $50. That was the last time. Fifty dollars wasn't too bad in those days. He liked to bet a lot.

November

Caracas Open

During the 1960s, the PGA sponsored the Caribbean tour, a series of unofficial events. Wes Ellis Jr. was in his element there, particularly in the Venezuela tournaments.

Ellis attended the University of Texas, where he played golf and graduated in 1953 with a degree in zoology. Ellis turned pro and had success, winning the 1958 Canadian Open, then the 1959 Texas Open. In 1965, he beat Billy Casper in a playoff to win the San Diego Open. All the while, he held club pro jobs in the New York metropolitan area. In 1967, he landed the plum head job at the Westchester Country Club.

Photo 74: Wes Ellis in 1961.
(Metropolitan Golf Association)

Ellis' arrangement with Westchester allowed him to play tour events during the winter. In March 1968, he won the Maracaibo Open, after finishing second there in 1965 and 1967. In November, he shot a 62 in the second round of the Caracas Open and came in second, one behind Bert Weaver.

In February 1969, the PGA Tour announced Ellis had been suspended until April 1 for a rules violation that occurred the previous fall at a tournament in the Caribbean. The tour was circumspect as to the reason. "That is a matter between the

Association and Ellis," said PGA President Leo Fraser. "We have no intention of divulging it." Another official, who would not give his name, said "Ellis was guilty of repeated infractions of a rule outlining procedures for marking the ball on the greens."

Fraser understated Ellis' violations, which amounted to blatant cheating. Ellis would put a magnet on the bottom of his putter, mark his ball on the green with a coin and, when his playing companions were occupied, place his putter on top of the coin and move it. It was a clumsy scheme that was not going to go undetected forever. Eventually, fellow players had suspicions and a camera was set up that confirmed the cheating. It was a testament to Ellis' affability that not only was he was given such a short suspension, but the Westchester Country Club also renewed his contract. He worked at Westchester into the 1970s and continued to occasionally play tour events.

Ellis suffered from alcoholism and died of a kidney ailment in 1984 at age 52.

Bert Weaver

Ellis was suspended and I think it's because he was caught in the Bahamas. That was the next week after Caracas. Somebody had said something, to watch him, I guess, and they put a camera on him, caught him doing that. We played in a tournament two years before that where you had couples playing as partners. He was on the green and moved it about 3 feet, his coin. When it was our turn to putt, I said, "What are you doing?" He said, "Oh, I wasn't thinking," or something like that. And then if it didn't happen to him again. It caught up with him. That's something else. I'll never forget that.

You're talking about interesting stories. Wes Ellis and his wife, Tom Nieporte and his wife, and me and my wife, we rented a house at Wrightsville beach one year when we played the Azalea Open. I'm going to say 1964. We had a three-bedroom house, with a bathroom in between the bedroom Wes had and ours. We were in our room one night and Wes knocked on our door, the bathroom door. And he said,

"Now y'all, don't listen. I really gotta go. So don't pay us any mind." Everything was real quiet. This was about 11 o'clock at night. All of us were asleep, or supposed to be. And all of a sudden we heard this noise like you're taking a leak in your commode, and it went on and on and on. Hell, it must have been an hour. My wife and are in bed listening to this, him just taking a pee in there.

After a while, it stopped. And the next morning we had the biggest laugh in the world when we found out that Wes had taken an enema bag and filled it up with water. A big enema bag which had a hose on it. And he took that in that bathroom and held it up and put the other end down in a commode and then turned a little spigot on, to make that sound. That was one of the funniest things that's ever happened to me.

Chuck Courtney

Wes Ellis had that club job in New York, and won everything in the Met Section for a few years. He was a good player. He was a weirdo. He had an ocelot in his house. A pet. That's what I heard.

Today – I'm sitting right now watching the Honda Classic – the greens are dead perfect. You should have seen the stuff we were playing on. First of all, everybody was wearing spikes, so there's spike marks and by late in the afternoon they're just a mess. There's little holes on the green, so the ball bounces and isn't going to roll as good. Moving the ball just an inch can help you. Half an inch. A quarter of an inch. Just to get it out of a little depression. These days, there's no such thing. The greens are dead perfect, and the guys are all wearing smooth shoes. It's a whole different world.

December

PGA and APG Dispute

From the time of its inception in the early 1930s through most of the '60s, the PGA tour had a loose structure. For most of its history it was run by the PGA of America. The PGA's primary constituency was the club pros, who gave lessons and sold equipment at golf courses throughout America. The tour was viewed as a showcase for the best professionals to display their skill, all for the purpose of increasing interest in the game of golf. The club pros would teach people how to play golf, and when the tour came to town the weekenders could go watch the very best pros practice their craft. Almost all of the touring pros were affiliated with a club some place, to which they periodically would return during the year and, if not actually give lessons, at least hobnob with members.

However, by the mid-1960s most touring pros were, well, full-time touring pros who had little in common with the club pros. Still, the PGA of America was calling all of the shots for the tour. By 1966, Arnold Palmer, Jack Nicklaus and others had launched a renaissance in golf, and it was a much more popular sport than it was in 1960. Television dollars brought a dramatic increase in purses. Agent Mark McCormack—who represented Palmer, Nicklaus and Gary Player—created a template for players to earn money through endorsements, corporate sponsorships, and exhibitions, more than they could have dreamed of just a few years before.

However, second and third tier pros—who, unlike the Big Three, often were car-pooling to tournaments and sharing rooms in cheap motels—may have felt the game was passing them by. In 1966 and 1967, three things happened that added to the tension between the PGA of America and the touring pros. One involved the replacement of the tour's on-site manager, Jim Gaquin, who resigned. Although the on-site manager was not near the top of the PGA of America hierarchy, to the players it was the most crucial position, as he was responsible for the orderly functioning of the tour from week to week. The players lobbied for Gaquin's deputy, Jack Tuthill, to replace him. Tuthill—a former FBI agent—was popular with the players, who valued his competency, not just as an arbiter of the rules, but also as a fixer of the everyday concerns of the pros, such as finding local accommodations each week. The PGA replied that they would allow it, if Tuthill would work from their office at Palm Beach Gardens, not on-site, which would defeat the very purpose for why the players wanted him. Instead, the PGA installed their own man, Bob Creasey, to replace Gaquin.

Two, Frank Sinatra wanted to sponsor a tournament in 1967 near Palm Springs with $175,000 in prize money. Naturally, the pros were all for having an event with such a high payout. The PGA vetoed the Sinatra tournament, viewing it to conflict with the Bob Hope Desert Classic, which was held annually in Palm Springs with a much smaller purse.

Three, the PGA of America wanted 20 percent of the $250,000 purse at the new Westchester Classic to be used to fund a pension plan. The players did not object in principle to having a pension fund, but the PGA intended that the fund would be for both the touring and club pros, the latter of which overwhelmed the former in numbers. The PGA acceded to the players objections and tabled the pension idea.

By the summer of 1968, the long-simmering dispute between touring pros and the PGA of America was brought to a boil. The pros threatened to start their own tour, separate from the PGA, called the Association of Professional Golfers.

During the PGA Championship at Pecan Valley, the PGA announced that Creasey—whose removal had been demanded by the players—had been rehired for a three-year term. The PGA then also discharged the players' tournament committee, consisting of Jack Nicklaus, Gardner Dickinson, Frank Beard and Doug Ford. That was the last straw.

On September 4, 1968, Billy Casper—who had been named treasurer of the APG—sent letters to 72 pros requesting they pay $250 for an initiation fee and dues. Frank Beard was the first to sign up and many followed. The APG demanded that the PGA pay what amounted to back royalties for money generated by the players.

In October 1968, both the PGA and the APG conducted qualifying schools. Grier Jones finished first of the 79 players who opted to play at PGA National in Palm Springs Gardens. Martinus Roesink of the Netherlands topped the 39-player field at APG qualifying at the Doral Country Club. He and 20 other aspirants were presented with APG player's cards by Jack Nicklaus.

Photo 75: Gardner Dickinson.
(Creative Commons)

On November 30, APG president Gardner Dickinson announced it had signed contracts for 28 tournaments in 1969—many of them existing PGA tour stops—with total purses exceeding $6 million. That induced a quick end to the dispute. On December 13, 1968, the PGA and APG announced that a settlement had been achieved. From thenceforth, the touring pros would be a governed by an entity known as the Tournament Players Division, with a 10-member board comprised of four tour players, three PGA executives, and three outside businessmen with golf backgrounds. The commitments to the APG tournament sponsors would be honored. Having achieved its purpose, the APG disbanded.

Don Bies

The tour players had a meeting at the American Golf Classic in Akron, and I think that's when they decided to split from the PGA of America and start the APG tour. I remember someone was talking about $300 dues. For some of the guys like myself, that was a lot of money. Gardner Dickinson and Dan Sikes were two who were really strong. And Frank Beard. Jack Nicklaus was in the background a little bit. He certainly was there.

I was pretty neutral. I still really wasn't playing full-time and probably didn't know a lot about it. I really was not involved in the politics of it, of why we were breaking from the PGA of America, because I really was a club pro. They got Joe Dey to be the first commissioner of the tour.

Frank Beard

I was right in the middle of it. The tour had been loosely run since the 1940s. The PGA of America sort of, very loosely, had their sections run the tournaments that were in their area. There was a schedule, and it was called the PGA tour, but it was very loosely done and of course there was no money.

In the old days, the sponsor would have a $20,000 purse, and he was responsible for everything. The PGA didn't have to do anything. Players showed up, the sponsor would give the PGA tour official who was in charge that week $20,000 in checks, and off he would go. There wasn't much going on between the PGA tour and the tournaments and the players because there was nothing involved except the tournament itself, which was run by the sponsors and paid by the sponsors, and the money went to the players.

Then all of a sudden, Palmer comes along, and it's going to be a big, big business. There were some TV contracts getting ready to be signed, or talked about. I think Mark McCormack probably got it started. Palmer and Nicklaus were involved, and said, "Look, we ought to be running this tour. The players ought to be running the tour. We're doing all the work, we're doing all the planning and we're collecting all of the money."

The PGA of America, all club pros, don't know anything about television, they don't know anything about the tour, because they'd never been around it. They ran their shops, and taught the lessons. The players wanted to run their own show. But the PGA stood up and said, "It's been our tour all these years." Which hypothetically, and in a very loose manner, was correct. It had been their tour.

So, we said, "Look, either we get to run the tour the way we want to, or we're going to leave." We eventually wound up with all of the players behind us, all the TV sponsors behind us, all the TV networks behind us. And they said, "We're no good without you, so we'll follow you wherever you go." The PGA Tour dug a trench and said, "You're not going anywhere. This is our tour."

We never got to court, but it was a dirty, dirty, bloody battle, names called, bad press. It was just godawful. But Nicklaus and Palmer, being a little smarter than the rest of us, especially Nicklaus, and Mark McCormack said, "You all settle this or I'm going to take Palmer, Nicklaus, Player and Casper, and I'll take another 15 or 20 guys and we'll just start our own tour. How do you like that? We don't really want to do that. We want to leave it the way it is, but you better get this settled."

So, the next thing you know, we've got an agreement. The PGA Tour is going to stay under the PGA of America. If you look at it like a corporate graph, and you go down the different sections of a corporation, down in this corner over here on the right, it's one section called the PGA Tour. But it was set up so that our board called all of our shots. We had like four players on the board, we had one or two PGA of America members on the board, and one or two outside businessmen who we selected. So there never was any problem on voting on something that we wanted to do, including TV contracts, all that.

Of course, the funny thing about all of it was that we said, "You keep your PGA Championship, and you can go ahead and keep the Ryder Cup." The Ryder Cup wound up being the biggest money-maker besides the Masters and the U.S. Open. Maybe the biggest money-maker of all when you get right down to it. But it was OK. And it's been that way ever since.

Kermit Zarley

The American pro tour was created by the PGA of America in the 1920's and 1930's. Pros who had club jobs in the north had a few months off during the winter. Wanting to play some competitive golf, they trekked south and created a few tournaments. In those years, it was not feasible to make a living playing pro golf full-time on the fledgling tour. Pros who competed in such tournaments needed to have club jobs during the remainder of the year to make a living.

Late 1968 was the most chaotic period in the history of what is now called the PGA Tour. During those days, emotions ran high among professional golfers on both sides regarding the tour's break away from its parent organization.

When I started in 1964, there wasn't any qualifying school, which was instituted in 1966. In the late 1960s, the PGA Tour was growing every year. Many of its tournaments were televised nationally on major networks. Wherever a tour event was held, many local club pros wanted to test their skills by teeing it up against the tour pros. But these club pros were being shoved out of tournaments they regarded as the creation of their own organization—the PGA of America.

Monday qualifying was getting tougher. The non-exempt tour players—those who had to qualify on Mondays to get in a tournament—understandably complained the most. They complained too many club pros were being allowed to take up spots in the qualifying field. I agreed. About 50-150 fulltime tour players were being turned away every Monday. It didn't seem fair that several club pros, most of whom had club jobs that they could depend on for their living, would take up spots. Tour players were spending hundreds of dollars per week in expenses, and oftentimes they weren't qualifying to get in the tournaments. Of course, we all agreed that a few of these club pros should be allowed to play because they were fine players.

Many club pros were angry. They thought of the touring pros as a bunch of prima donnas. Even on tour, there were players who objected to going independent of the PGA of America. Sam Snead was one who voiced his disapproval of the split. But then, Sam never had to worry about qualifying to get into any tournaments. Plus, Sam reportedly had a lot of loot stashed away in a bunch of tomato cans in his backyard! He didn't have our worries.

I was chosen as a young player to an advisory players committee that would oversee the new tour. During the summer of 1968, one of these committee meetings was held in which we discussed what we would name the new organization. I can't remember all the players who were present, but they included Lionel Hebert, Gardner Dickinson, Bob Goalby, and Dan Sikes. I suggested the name that was chosen—the Association of Professional Golfers (APG). But this break-away organization would not last long because the matter was settled by having a tour largely independent of the PGA of America, without totally breaking away at that time.

Our players' committee decided that we needed a commissioner to help lead and operate this new tour. Our members felt that since our reputation was on the line, this new commissioner should be a man of impeccable integrity. About this time, we were playing an event. The tour bible study was held earlier than usual one evening so its member pros could attend a players' meeting regarding the breakaway tour. The players' committee frequently held meetings to inform the players of developments and allow for open discussion. Sometimes, tempers flared.

A small number of pros attended the PGA tour bible study earlier that evening. Some of us bible toters also were split on this matter. Jim Hiskey and Dave Ragan opposed the split, but Babe Hiskey and I favored it. As Babe and I stood up to leave for the players meeting, Jim and Dave said, "We're going to stay here and pray that God works this thing out." They said they would pray God "raises up someone to settle this dispute."

Well, Joe Dey became our first commissioner. He didn't exactly settle the dispute; but as the former director of the USGA, he certainly *had impeccable credentials. I think he was the right man for the job at a crucial time in the history of the PGA Tour.*

Martinus Roesink

I was allowed to play on the Tour. They honored the APG qualifier.

Frank Boynton

Until we got Jack Tuthill, they would make different rulings for the stars rather than the journeymen. They would always lean toward forgiveness for the real stars, the Palmers and the Nicklauses and the Players and what have you. So, we were kind of glad to get somebody out there. Tuthill would get everybody in the same room and ran it the way it should have been run. We didn't have any kind of retirement plan when the PGA of America ran it. I never got to take advantage of that retirement plan. But now, I think they've got a beautiful retirement plan.

Life Begins at 40 Pro-Am

On December 11, Mason Rudolph boarded Trans World Airlines Flight 496 from Nashville to Miami. The 34-year-old native of Clarksville, Tennessee had had a down year, earning $24,429 in 28 tournaments, with no better than a fifth-place finish. He had not won since the 1966 Thunderbird Classic, when he beat Jack Nicklaus by a stroke. Rudolph was headed to play in the Life Begins at 40 Pro-Am, a non-tour 54-hole event. Touring pros Paul Bondeson and Bob Shave Jr. also were entered.

On the way, the plane made an unscheduled stop in Havana, Cuba. This was during the airplane-hijacking craze, before such actions were viewed as acts of terrorism. The hijackers were a man with a trumpet and his girlfriend. Also aboard was country musician Tex Ritter. When the plane landed in Havana, the passengers were allowed to walk around the airport and were given refreshments and propaganda material. "It was not bad at all," said Ritter. "I think most of the people rather enjoyed it." Indeed, it was a simpler time.

According to Rudolph, a Cuban soldier "came around and took down your names, addresses and occupations. I had a hard time getting over to him what a professional golfer was." Eventually, the passengers reboarded, and Flight 496 completed the trip to Miami. Rudolph won the tournament, taking home $750 for his adventure.

1969

1969 was a good year for pro golfers. They were free of the PGA of America's governance. One result of the settlement with the PGA was that purses increased, by 39 percent between 1967 and 1969.

However, overall, 1969 was not necessarily a good year for fans of pro golf. For the first time since 1957, none of golf's Big Three (Palmer, Nicklaus, and Player) won a major. In fact, all four Grand Slam events were won by first-time major victors.

February

Phoenix Open

The Phoenix Open was staged at the Arizona Country Club, a short, 6,389-yard, par-71 course. With an unimpressive course and a now very ordinary $100,000 purse, the biggest names skipped the event. Jack Nicklaus had won the Andy Williams-San Diego Open two weeks prior. He, Arnold Palmer and Billy Casper had completed 90 holes at the Bob Hope Desert Classic 250 miles west the week before (won by Casper). Gary Player was home in South Africa.

Photo 76: Dutch pro Martinus Roesink with admirers, 1967. (Liverpool Echo)

Their absence gave second-level players the chance to shine. After the opening round, seven tied for the lead with 65s: Lee Elder, his friend and mentor Billy Maxwell, John Jacobs (brother of Tommy), Larry Ziegler, Miller Barber, and 58-year-old Dutch Harrison (whose first of 18 tour victories came at the 1939 Bing Crosby Pro-Am). Two back was Martinus Roesink, the exceptionally long 29-year-old rookie from the Netherlands, who had had a modicum of success overseas. In all, 82 of a field of 150 broke par on the kitten of a course.

The assault on par continued in the second round. Maxwell, 39 years old, whose last of seven tour victories was at the 1962 Dallas Open, shot 66 to tie Frank Beard for the lead at 131. The cut was 2-under par. On Saturday, Gene Littler fired a 9-under 62 to take the lead. Roesink continued to impress, even though he lost ground on the leaders with a 69. His measured drives averaged 273 yards, the longest in the field.

In Sunday's final round, Littler shot 66 for a 72-hole total of 263 to win by two shots over Maxwell, Barber and Don January. It was the 21st victory for the 38-year-old Littler.

Martinus Roesink

Even though I had my card and was allowed to play on the tour, you still had to qualify on Mondays for the tournament. We weren't totally exempt. Of course, if you qualified, you could tee it up on Thursday and Friday, and if you made the cut you could play the last two days. So basically, you would play three tournaments in one. Mondays—qualifying—then you had to try to make the cut, and then you'd try to make some money. So, it was pretty tough.

In 1969, the first tournament I played in was the San Diego Open. I qualified on Monday, and I got in as an alternate on Tuesday because somebody couldn't make it or whatever. I made the cut, so I played all four days and was exempt for the next tournament in Phoenix. I played in Phoenix and I made the cut there. I shot 67, 67, 69 and 68, and I finished eight shots behind Gene Littler, who won the tournament. So, now I was allowed to play the next week at the Tucson Open, and I made the cut there, and from there we went to the Doral Open.

I couldn't afford to fly, so I drove to Florida. I was traveling with another guy by the name of Ed Davis. We roomed together and shared costs. I missed the cut at the Doral by one shot. And then after that it was tough to qualify. So, I started out pretty decent and then it went downhill.

When I played on the tour, I asked Jack Nicklaus a couple of times to play a practice round. He said, "Sure, any time." So, every time I qualified, Jack wasn't playing. One time, I saw him and he said, "I thought we were supposed to have a practice round together one of these days." I said, "Jack, every time you play in a tournament, I don't qualify. And if I qualify, you don't play." So, the next week we played at Pebble Beach. I saw Jack and he asked, "How are you hitting them?" I said, "Man, I'm hooking them so bad." He said, "What time are you playing?" I was playing at 10 o'clock or so at Pebble Beach, and he was playing around the same time at Cypress Point. He said, "If you want to, I can meet you at the range after we finish and maybe I can help you a little bit." I said, "That's fantastic. I would love that."

So, after I finish my round, I went right to the driving range. I was waiting for maybe a half an hour, and there comes Jack. He spent about an hour with me on the range, trying to help me. That evening, he said, "What are you doing this evening?" I said nothing special, so he said, "Why don't you have dinner with us at the lodge." So, that evening we met at the lodge at Pebble Beach, and we had king crab. That's the first time I ever ate king crab. It was Jack Nicklaus, his wife, and a couple other of his friends. I thought that was the nicest thing for him to do. He was on top of the world, had won all of the majors already, and he was taking interest in a rookie, trying to help him. I thought that spoke an awful lot of him.

April

The Masters

CBS televised the Masters as usual, and on Sunday narrowly avoided a fiasco similar to that experienced by NBC the previous November during the infamous "Heidi Game." Then, with the New York Jets leading the Oakland Raiders 32-29, at 7 p.m. Eastern Time NBC chose to break away from the AFL game to broadcast the previously scheduled family movie "Heidi." Viewers in the eastern half of the country missed out on seeing the Raiders rally with two touchdowns in the game's dying moments to win 43-32. The NBC switchboard was jammed with angry callers.

On the afternoon of April 13, 1969, CBS was televising Game 2 of the Eastern Division Stanley Cup finals between the Boston Bruins and Montreal Canadiens. Weeks before, the CBS brass made the decision that if the hockey game went past the 4 p.m. scheduled start time of the Masters broadcast, the network would switch to golf. CBS had a year-to-year contract with Augusta National to tele-vise the Masters and was not going to jeopardize the relationship, even for a Stanley Cup contest. The Bruins-Canadiens game went into sudden-death overtime. Exactly 45 seconds before the switch from hockey to golf would have been made, Mickey Redmond of the Canadiens saved CBS's switchboard from exploding by scoring the game-winning goal.

The Big Three never were in contention over the weekend. Billy Casper led by one shot at the start of Sunday, but went out in 40 and bogeyed the 10th hole. The final round was a war of attrition. Five of the six players in the last three twosomes were within one stroke of the lead late in the round, but none made a push on the final two holes. Charles Coody got to 8 under with an eagle on 13 to take the lead, but bogeyed the last three holes. Tom Weiskopf had a chance but was done in by a bogey on 17.

Photo 77: George Knudson.
(Getty Images)

Playing with Weiskopf, George Archer, a six-and-a-half foot tall 29-year-old from the San Francisco Bay area, bogeyed 14 to fall out of sole possession of the lead, and then parred in to finish at 7-under par 281. George Knudson, a 31-year-old Canadian from Winnipeg who had won six times on tour, was slim with dark hair, smoked constantly, and wore dark glasses that gave him an air of mystery. He birdied 16, and on 18 just missed a birdie putt that would have got him to 281.

Casper birdied 11, 13 and 15 to get back in contention. Playing in the final pairing, he arrived at 18 needing a birdie to finish at 281. However, he pushed his approach to the right of the green and ended with a par. Thus, Archer prevailed by one stroke over Casper, Weiskopf, and Knudson.

Archer's victory at Augusta was the highlight of his long, successful career. He won 13 times on tour, the last in 1984 when he was 44 years old, and he had 19 Senior Tour victories. Towards the end of his time on the regular tour, he sported a full beard that gave him a professorial look. However, after Archer died in 2005 at the age of 65, his wife Donna revealed something about him of which few were aware: because of a serious learning disability, her husband was functionally illiterate. He could read only at the third-grade level and lived in fear that his disability would be revealed. Donna Archer founded the George Archer Memorial Foundation for literacy, which runs an annual fundraising tournament in the San Francisco Bay area.

Photo 78: George Archer. (Getty Images)

Charles Coody

I always hate to say that maybe I should have won a tournament, or that the person that won shouldn't have won. So, I never say that. Billy Casper had the lead and was really playing well, but he didn't have a really good day the last day. And he brought several players into the fold. George Archer was one, I was one, I think Tom Weiskopf was one, and George Knudson was one. Anyway, I birdied 15 and I stand on the 16th tee with a one-shot lead. So, as it turned out, had I parred the last three holes, I would've won. But I hadn't been there before in that position, especially in a tournament like that. And I just didn't handle the situation real well and I made three straight bogeys, and obviously did not win.

Did you ever see Bill Murray in "Groundhog Day"? When I got to the 16th tee in 1971, the pin was in the same position, the yardage was the same, and I benefited from my mistake two years before. And, as it turned out, I birdied 16 and then parred 17 and 18. I have no feelings that I got away with something in winning in 1971. My philosophy has always been that it's a 72-hole tournament and at the end of the tournament, the guy that has the fewest strokes that he's the winner.

I played with George Knudson in the last round. George was a big admirer of Ben Hogan. He tried to emulate Hogan as best as he possibly could, not in his dress, but just in his play. I don't know how many tournaments he won on tour, but he was a very good player. And unfortunately, shortly after playing his first tournament on the Senior Tour he was diagnosed with throat cancer. He was a big smoker. He passed away probably within a year, a year-and-a-half after that.

Chuck Courtney

George Archer was illiterate. Everybody always wondered why Donna was always right by his side every minute. He couldn't check into a hotel because he didn't know where to put his name. She was a real sweet girl. She really took care of him. He was a real nice guy. You'd never know because he was real chatty, real verbal, but he couldn't read or write. Great putter. Practiced his putting night and day. It was beautiful, even, kind of a mechanical putting stroke. Most of all, he was real sure of himself. He'd make those 5- or 6-footers like they were gimmes.

Frank Boynton

I played in the Masters one time, in 1969. I'll tell you one thing about that tournament. Trevino asked me to play a practice round on Monday, with Bruce Fleischer and Gene Sarazen. And we played and just had a wonderful time. Gene loved to tell stories, and I ended up playing Monday, Tuesday, and the Par Three tournament with Gene Sarazen. It was a wonderful memory, and I loved his stories.

It was wonderful to be there and be part of it. I think I was too awe-inspired to play well. I missed the cut. But as I've said, I played in half a Masters.

Byron Nelson Golf Classic

One of the storylines at the Preston Trail Golf Club was whether Arnold Palmer, who was in the midst of a long slump, would play well enough to make the U.S. Open field without having to go through qualifying. The top-15 money winners over the previous year would get into the Open. Palmer was 15th going into the Nelson, and had a lead of $5,133.51 over Frank Beard, but did not fall within any other exempt category. Beard would finish tied for second to overtake Palmer, who tied for eighth and would have to decide whether to go through sectional qualifying for the Open.

Bruce Devlin of Australia regularly appeared on leaderboards in the major championships and had won three times on tour, but none since 1966 when he won the Colonial and the Carling. In 1967, he fell off of a cliff, earning only $12,726. On Sunday at the Nelson, Devlin was leading when, on the 16th hole, he was stymied by a tree. He hit the ball backward through his legs onto the fairway, then got up and down for a par. On 18, Devlin sank an 8-foot putt for par to beat Beard and fellow Aussie Bruce Crampton by a stroke.

Bruce Devlin
It was nice to win that because I had previously won the Colonial. In those days, they had a champions dinner at the Byron Nelson. It was always nice to go to dinner the next few years and sit and chat with Byron about himself and his game, and the game of golf. And of course, Mr. Nelson was just the sweetest man. I don't know if a person ever said a nasty word about him.

May

Greater New Orleans Open

Larry Hinson came from Douglas, Georgia, in the southern part of the state. As a boy, he was afflicted with polio, resulting in a permanently withered left arm. When he took up golf, his handicap limited his driving distance, but also meant that he could not turn over his left arm, eliminating the possibility of a duck hook. Hinson had a good, but not great, junior career. He attended East Tennessee State, where he won the NCAA College Division Championship; in the parlance of the day, the "small-college" championship.

Photo 79: Larry Hinson. (The Times-Picaynue/The Advocate)

Hinson qualified for the PGA Tour in 1968, when he was 24 years old. In 1969, he finished second at the Magnolia Classic, a small-purse event run opposite the Masters and cashed checks in several other events. He was blond, handsome, 6-foot-2, pencil thin, polite, and devoutly Christian.

At New Orleans, Hinson started the final round five shots behind leaders Frank Beard (who had won the tournament in 1966 and would win it again in 1971) and Dave Hill. Hinson finished his closing 67 while Beard and Hill were still on the course. Hill struggled to a 73 and Beard struggled as well, but when he came to the par-3 17th hole, Beard was up by one. He put his tee shot on the green. However, he three-putted, missing a 3-foot putt for par. When Beard parred 18, he and Hinson were tied.

On the third playoff hole—the 17th—Beard again missed a putt for par, again from three feet. Hinson two-putted from 18 feet to win. "Everyone back home just thought I'd never make it," he said afterward, "because I didn't make good in my studies—a C average going through college—and they said, 'He's not bright and he can't knock the ball far enough and his handicap will probably keep him out.'"

In 1970, Hinson finished second twice and earned $115,397, and continued to make a decent living on the tour through 1975, after which he faded away. His win at New Orleans would be the only one of his career.

Larry Hinson

In all the time I've had to think about it, I've felt like Frank Beard gave the tournament to me. He missed a putt he wouldn't normally miss. I had to make one behind him. I was a little closer to the hole. Instead of thinking "I'm something," I think Frank gave it to me.

I think it was just a sure blessing to be able to get to the tour. I truly do because I had polio and my arm didn't move for two-and-a-half years. It was a struggle, but I still felt like the Lord could get me there and let me do it. And He did.

Look what they're playing for (today). It's unreal. I don't know that I would want to play for what they play for today. You win a tournament, and you just start thinking about spending it. Money didn't motivate me.

Frank Beard

First I gave the tournament away and then gave the playoff away. I could have won that tournament five years in a row.

June

U.S. Open Qualifying, McKeesport, Pennsylvania

On June 3, 4,500 turned out on a chilly Tuesday at the Youghiogheny Country Club in McKeesport, Pennsylvania, for U.S. Open qualifying. Almost every one of them were members of Arnie's Army. Their hero—the face of golf for the last decade, but now 39 years old and in a deep slump—was reduced to trying to qualify for the Open.

The USGA's decision not to give Arnold Palmer a free pass through a special exemption did not sit well with many, including his long-time on-course nemesis, Jack Nicklaus. "After all that man has done for the game, after all he's won, I just can't see how they can leave him out." Nicklaus said. Palmer easily qualified at McKeesport, as did Tony Jacklin, along with the likes of Andy Berkovich, John Felus, Norman Rock, and Chuck Scally, with a ticket to the U.S. Open and a guaranteed $300 (the sum awarded to those who would not make the cut).

U.S. Open

Texas boasts a golf history unsurpassed by any other state. U.S. Open winners from the Lone Star State include immortals Ben Hogan, Byron Nelson, Lee Trevino, and Lloyd Mangrum. Every year in the 1960s, Texas hosted three, four or even five tour events. Yet only three times has the state hosted a U.S. Open, and none since 1969.

A disappointing crowd of about 8,500 turned out on June 13, 1969, for the opening round at the Cypress Creek Course of the Champions Golf Club in Houston. The small attendance may have been the impetus for the USGA to decline to return to Texas.

Temperatures reached 90 humid degrees. The early leaders who broke par of 70 included Bob Murphy, Miller Barber, Deane Beman, George Archer and Dean Refram. After the second round, Beman's 68-69 led Barber and Murphy by a shot, and Bob Rosburg by two. Jack Nicklaus fired a 67 to follow his opening 74 and was four back. At 143, Arnold Palmer was six behind. Defending champion Trevino missed the cut by one stroke.

Rosburg, age 42, was on the back end of a successful career, playing the tour part-time. He grew up in San Francisco, the son of a physician who belonged to the Olympic Club. As a boy, he beat baseball immortal Ty Cobb in a club match, 7 and 6. It is noted that in 1938, when Rosburg was 11, he and 51-year-old Cobb thought enough of their games to enter an open match-play tournament in San Francisco, along with the likes of Ben Hogan, Byron Nelson, and Sam Snead. In the first round of qualifying on a windy day, Cobb shot 98, Rosburg 107.

As a graduate of Stanford University, Rosburg was smarter than the average pro and appeared so, bald and bespectacled. "He looks like a doctor who makes house calls," wrote Jim Murray. Rosburg won six times on tour, including the 1959 PGA Championship and in 1972, when he was 45, the Bob Hope Desert Classic, before embarking on a long second career as the first on-course golf television commentator.

On a sweltering Saturday, Barber shot 68 to take a three-stroke lead over Orville Moody, a 35-year-old who 15 months earlier had left the U.S. Army. His 14-year military career consisted mostly of working on base golf courses and playing golf (he won the Korean Open three times). Moody had to go through local and sectional qualifying to make the field. Rosburg was five back of Barber.

In the final round, in brutal, windy conditions, Barber bogeyed five of the first eight holes to surrender the lead, on his way to a 78. He finished tied for sixth with Palmer. Rosburg had a good round and came to the 71st hole tied for the lead with Moody. He put his second shot into a greenside bunker and hit an excellent shot to within 5 feet. He holed the putt. On the last hole, he again found a bunker with his approach and hit an even better sand shot, to within 30 inches of the hole. However, he missed the putt.

Moody (who claimed to have never taken a lesson, and to rarely practice; "I hit about 20 shots, but only to loosen up," he said) shot a 2-over 72, parring the last four holes. With nobody else making a charge, his 72-hole total of 281 (1-over par) gave him a one-stroke victory over Rosburg, Beman and Al Geiberger to become the most unlikely winner of a major tournament in the 1960s. It would prove to be Moody's only victory on the regular tour, although he would have much more success after turning 50, winning 21 times on the PGA Senior Tour.

Photo 80: Orville Moody during the 1969 U.S. Open.
(United States Golf Association)

Lee Trevino

I went in Wednesday evening to talk to the press there for the U.S. Open. I was the last player in the press room. Once we did the whole interview they asked me, "Who do you think is going to win the tournament? Who are you picking? I said, "I'm picking Orville Moody." This guy in the back of the room says, "Orville who?" I said, "No, Orville Moody." So, he wins it.

Larry Hinson

It was a mighty long golf course. I remember having to hit 2-woods to some of the par-4s. I felt like that was a tough, tough way to check my skills. I didn't play as well as I would have liked to. I got humbled because of how hard that golf course was.

July

The Open Championship

The 98th Open Championship was held at the Royal Lytham & St. Annes Golf Club near Liverpool. In the preceding 17 Opens, the tournament had been won by Australians six times, Americans five, South Africans four, and golfers from New Zealand and Argentina once apiece. However, no player from the British Isles had won since Englishman Max Faulkner in 1951.

As the 1960s had progressed, more and more Americans had chosen to make the transatlantic trip in hopes of adding the Open Championship to their résumés. In 1969, the PGA Championship was moved to August, away from its proximity to the Open Championship. As a result, Americans Raymond Floyd, Orville Moody, George Archer, Lee Trevino, Gardner Dickinson and Miller Barber made their first appearances at the Open, to join Jack Nicklaus, Bert Yancey, and Gay Brewer, among other returning Americans. Citing business commitments, Arnold Palmer withdrew in advance. Other top Americans, such as Dan Sikes, Bob Goalby, Frank Beard, Charlie Sifford, Dave Hill, and Mason Rudolph, chose to stay stateside and play at the Minnesota Classic, which was won by Beard.

Photo 81: *Tony Jacklin, December 1969. (Creative Commons)*

In Wednesday's opening round on July 9, the 1963 Open winner, Bob Charles of New Zealand, shot a 66 to take a two-stroke lead over Englishmen Tony Jacklin and Hedley Muscroft. Barber's 69 made him the top American by one over Billy Casper and Davis Love Jr. Charles' 69 Thursday gave him a one-shot lead over Irishman Christy O'Connor, who shot a 65, with Jacklin three back. At 140, Casper was five behind and one ahead of Moody.

On Friday, Nicklaus followed rounds of 75-70 with a 68 to put him back in the picture. He was the low American at 213 by one over Love. Roberto De Vicenzo shot 66, the low round of the day to put him at 211. Among the late finishers, Charles (75) and O'Connor (74) were at 210. O'Connor was a frequent winner in Europe who rarely traveled off of the continent and declined 20 invitations to play in the Masters.

Jacklin was poised to run away with the Open after going out in 34. On 15, he drove right, then hooked a 3-wood into trouble. His third shot landed in a greenside bunker, but he was able to get up-and-down for a bogey. After a birdie on 16, he had more trouble on the par-4 17th, where he again was in a greenside bunker in 3. Again, Jacklin got up-and-down for a bogey. On 18 he yet again was bunkered near the green, but miraculously blasted close enough to save par. His adventurous 70 gave him a two-stroke lead at 210.

In Saturday's typically cool and overcast Open final round, Jacklin went out with a 2-under 33 and held a three-shot lead over Charles. On the 11th green, play was delayed for 2 minutes while a martin landed next to Charles. Jacklin chased away the bird and play continued. As on Friday, Jacklin bogeyed 15 and 17. When Charles birdied 17, Jacklin arrived at the 18th tee with a nervous two-stroke lead. But Jacklin hit a spectacular drive on 18, followed it with just as good an approach and two-putted for the win before a delighted gallery of 10,000 of his countrymen, to break the long British drought at the Open Championship.

Tony Jacklin

At the beginning of the week, the R&A was inspecting clubs. They were looking at grooves. In order to be safe, I was using this sand wedge—I can't remember what make it was—I put it in front of them, and I said, "Tell me about the grooves on this wedge." And they said, "Well, they're borderline," were the words they used, "borderline wide." Of course, the last thing I wanted was to infringe any rules. So I went into the tented village, and I got a sand wedge off the Dunlop stand. I think it was a Roberto De Vicenzo sand wedge, and I left the other one in the car.

The upshot of it was, I was in 11 greenside bunkers over the four days, and I got up-and-down every time. That was the making of my score basically. To be competitive in an Open you have to be well-rounded out. You've got to scramble. It's a big part of what links golf is. Imagination. It was all part of the examination, as it were, so I took care of it.

The 15th was notoriously difficult, I think the hardest par-4 on the golf course. It always was into the wind. About 20 years ago they filled in six or seven bunkers that ran across the fairway on that hole. And 17 ran in a similar direction. It was against the wind. The wind would come in from the west. The third-round wind was part of the battle. I was just fighting to maintain the lead.

In the final round I was playing with Bob Charles. He won the championship in 1963, and he was a good friend. As everybody knew, he was an unbelievable putter. I had my head down doing the best I could to stay in front.

There was an interesting incident on the final hole. Charles had the honor. Being left-handed, he pulled his tee shot and it was heading for a bunker that was on the right-hand side. I watched his ball the whole way, and I saw it just miss the bunker and run into light rough beyond it. I remember him giving his club to his caddie and saying he thought his ball might be in the bunker. I always wondered—I never asked him—if that was an effort to make me relax and not give it 100 percent. Anyway, I saw it finish and I knew it wasn't in the bunker, and I made one of the best swings of my life.

My drive on the 18th on the final day is what cemented the win for me. It was a notoriously difficult drive. There was no lay-up. There *was a cross-bunker on the 18th hole. You couldn't clear it with a one iron, or I couldn't. If you were going to hit 3-wood, you might as well hit driver. There's deep bunkers left and right, any of which if you got in you couldn't get on the green in 2. So, it was a commitment to hitting driver. Henry Longhurst was doing the commentary, and his comment was, "What a corker." He said it was the longest drive of the day, and of course it was in the dead center of the fairway. So that really got it done for me. It was a game changer, and a life changer.*

Canadian Open

A vestige of the APG-PGA dispute the prior year was two top-rate tournaments going on at the same time in late July 1969.

In 1968, prior to the settlement between the touring pros and the PGA, the sponsors of the American Golf Classic at Firestone had chosen to jump from the PGA to the APG. One of the stipulations of the settlement was that commitments to the APG sponsors would be honored, and in fashioning the 1969 schedule the AGC was slated to be held the same week as the Canadian Open. The latter tournament always was part of the PGA Tour calendar, but while the dispute was raging in late 1968, the Royal Canadian Golf Association made plans to hold its Open independent of the outcome of the dispute.

Thus, the 1969 Canadian Open does not appear in the record books as an official PGA Tour event, but the AGC does. Both tournaments had stellar fields. Jack Nicklaus chose to defend his title in Akron, and Arnold Palmer, Lee Trevino, Raymond Floyd, and Chi Chi Rodriguez were among the many top names who joined him. Floyd would win by one stroke over Bobby Nichols, who in addition to being a tour stalwart also was the host pro at the Firestone Country Club.

North of the border at the Pinegrove Country Club in Montreal, Billy Casper, Sam Snead, Tony Jacklin, Doug Sanders, Bob Charles, and Roberto De Vicenzo were among the headliners. Snead shot

67 to take the first-round lead. Afterwards, he made mention of Tommy Aaron, who was four shots back after a 71. "He's got to have led more tournaments than Arnold Palmer," said Snead. "But he hasn't won one yet, and I can't understand it. He swings as well as anyone on tour."

In the second round, 57-year-old Snead shot 68 to maintain a one-stroke lead over 46-year-old De Vicenzo. In Saturday's third round, Snead added a 70 in wet conditions to expand his lead to five shots over Takaaki Kono of Japan, who won numerous times in Asia, had tied for 13th at the Masters earlier in the year and would play four more times at Augusta, but never in the other majors.

On Sunday, Snead birdied four of the first five holes and appeared certain to win a fourth Canadian Open title (his first was 31 years earlier, in 1938, his latest in 1941). However, Aaron—who started the day six shots back of Snead—went on a run. Even par after four holes, Aaron played the last 14 holes in 8-under par and finished with a 64. After bogeys on 13 and 15, Snead had fallen one stroke back of Aaron when he arrived at the par-5 18th. He later admitted to being tired, but summoned the energy to knock his second shot 30 feet from the hole. Snead left his putt for an eagle and a win 2 feet short, and sank the putt to tie Aaron. An 18-hole playoff would follow on Monday.

In a close match, Snead again came to the final hole one behind Aaron. Snead birdied, but only after Aaron sank a 25-foot putt for an eagle to win by two. Thus, in his 10th year as a pro, Aaron finally shed the label of the best player never to win. In 1970, Aaron would win the Atlanta Classic for his first official PGA Tour event, and the Canadian Open returned to being recognized on the PGA Tour calendar. Aaron would win only one more event on the regular tour, the 1973 Masters. He would play in the Masters 31 more times and in 2000, at the age of 63, would make the 36-hole cut.

Tommy Aaron

I remember that Sam Snead had, I think, a five-shot lead, and six-shot lead over me starting the last round. I think most of the gallery and maybe the Canadian sponsors wanted Snead to win. It was a difficult 18-hole playoff, which I won. I shot 69 and Snead shot 71. So, it was an exciting win for me, with a lot of pressure involved.

The fact that it was unofficial, I knew that before I ever went up to play. It was opposite the American Golf Classic. That was when the friction was going on between the tour players and the PGA. I think it was made not official to try to keep players from going there and playing. I wasn't really aware of all that friction that was going on. I wasn't privy to all of that. And I had just made my decision to play there, and the fact it was unofficial did not really deter me any. They still were giving Ryder Cup points.

In the final round, the ball seemed to be going in from everywhere on the green. It was just one of those days. It was difficult conditions. The wind was blowing very hard. Just one of those days where everything goes right for you, with putts going in, and I shot 64. I'm sure that before the last round started, if someone had said to Sam, "You'll shoot 70 today," with a five-stroke lead, he would have bet everything he'd win the tournament. But that's just golf for you. It's very unpredictable.

One thing about the playoff I remember, through about 11 holes, I think we were pretty much even. The 12th hole or the 13th hole, one of those holes, there was a long par-3, well over 200 yards, and to the right, there was a was a great big drop off with a bunch of trees and bunkers on the right. And to the left, there was a road that was out of bounds.

Well, I hit my shot, I think I hit a 4-wood or a 1-iron or something like that. And I hit it to the right down to those trees on the bank. I tried to play up on the green, and I put it in the bunker. And then I played out the bunker about 7 feet past the hole. And I'm looking at best a bogey. Snead is on the left side of the green, not on the putting surface. He plays a chip that's inside me. He goes up to hole out and he's thinking, "If I get this 3, I make his putt for 4 a lot harder for him." And the official stopped him because he can't hole out or whatever the situation was. That was little gamesmanship on Snead's part. He wasn't above doing that. So, I putt and made mine for a 4 and he missed his and made 4. It looked like there was going to be a two-shot swing, but there wasn't. That was a big hole for me.

And then, we halve a number of holes and there was a par-3, maybe 14 or 15, and I made a birdie. Then we kept tying holes, 16 and 17, and then 18, it's a par-5 that was reachable, and I made a putt for an eagle and Sam made 4. So that's basically what I remember about the playoff.

Chuck Courtney

We're playing at Charlotte one year in a practice round. Tommy Weiskopf, who was another good buddy of mine, and I played against Sam and somebody else. It was like a $5 Nassau. Not a big deal. I think we beat them three or four ways. At Quail Hollow. And Sam came in there and threw the money down on a bench in the locker room. He was so pissed off that he lost 15 or 20 dollars to two whippersnappers. It was hilarious. Oh, God, he hated to lose. But what a dreamboat of a player. I still like the way Julius Boros swung the club better than Snead. But both of them were spectacular.

I saw him in the basement of the Sedgefield Country Club in Greensboro. This was either '64 or '65 or '66, I'm not sure which year. In those days the players' lounge was some place in the basement, with a great big galvanized bucket full of ice and beer. And we're all sitting down there drinking beer and smoking cigarettes. Sam walks in. He only won that thing like 10 times. He came in and put his heel on the top of the door jamb. He's so flexible in his hips and his legs. And he's fifty-some years old when he did that. It's probably a 7-foot door and he's 6 feet tall. He's got his heel a foot over his head resting on the door jamb. He used to say, "I play my best when I feel oily."

August

Westchester Classic

Frank Beard's goal was to earn money, which he pursued with the mindset of a savvy gambler. If he won, that was great, but given a choice between laying up on the 72nd hole to guarantee a second-place finish or trying an unlikely miracle shot for the win where a fifth-place finish was the more likely outcome, he would lay up every time. With this philosophy, Beard arrived at the Westchester Classic on a hot streak. In his previous five appearances on tour, he had won in Minnesota, placed second at the Buick Open, fourth in Cleveland, fifth in Philadelphia, and eighth at the American Golf Classic. Beard also was writing a book (with Dick Schaap), "Pro: Frank Beard on the Golf Tour," a diary of his 1969 season, which would be published in 1970.

On Sunday, Beard was tied with Bert Greene, who was in the final pairing behind him, when he came to the par-5 18th. Beard hit a good drive, but did not consider going for the green in 2. Instead, he laid up with a 4-iron and landed in the rough short of bunkers guarding the green. He benefited from a fluffy lie and hit a perfect pitch-and-run to within 2 feet, which he knocked in for a birdie. Needing a birdie to tie, Greene went for the green and instead went into a bunker. Greene was unable to get up-and-down, and Beard was $50,000 richer as a result.

Beard would win the money title for 1969, his best year on tour. He would win three more times in 1970 and 1971, and then his career quickly was derailed by alcoholism. At the 1975 U.S. Open at Medinah near Chicago, he resurfaced to lead after 54 holes by three strokes. He was unable to control his drinking the night before the final round, showed up hung over and shot 78 to miss a playoff by one shot. In 1981, Beard had his last drink and has been in recovery ever since.

Frank Beard

The night before the final round (of the Westchester Classic), of course I'm drinking like a fish. I was with Dick Schaap and we went to a show, "Oh Calcutta" that had nudity, then ate at the Stage Deli. Next morning, I went to Mass at St. Patrick's Cathedral. The whole New York experience. And then I won the tournament.

I was the leading money winner (in 1969) but I played in more tournaments. It was a nice honor. Don't get me wrong. It was one of the few that I had. There was a time when the money really meant something. I mean, they play for so much now. We knew how much each tournament was worth. If you were going to take off a tournament, you always took off the ones with the lowest money. And they weren't all the same.

They're all basically the same now. I bet if you asked (a player today) how much he plays for each week, he couldn't tell you. He'd take a stab, you know, 5, 6, 7 million, something like that. We knew almost to the penny. Of course, the way it was measured, it was the money list. We didn't have any FedEx Cup or anything like that. So, the leading money winner was really the player of the year, unless you won a couple of majors.

PGA Championship

From August 14 to 17, the 1969 PGA Championship was played at the National Cash Register Country Club outside of Dayton. It was held in the aftermath of the historic Apollo 11 moon landing, the tragedies of the Charles Manson murders and Chappaquiddick, and contemporaneously with the Woodstock Music and Art Fair festival in Upstate New York. It would have been hard for a mere golf tournament to match the drama of the time. The PGA Championship did its best.

For the most part, the tour had been sheltered from the tumult of the 1960s. Early in the decade, the "Caucasian race" clause had been removed, and by the end of the decade Black pros Charlie Sifford, Lee Elder, and Pete Brown were tour mainstays who, for the most part, were accepted by their peers and appreciated by fans.

Many established pros, such as Arnold Palmer, Julius Boros, Phil Rodgers, Orville Moody and Lou Graham, had served in the military during the 1940s, '50s and early '60s and had fulfilled their obligations and/or were too old for service when the Vietnam war began to sow divisions in America in 1965. Bud Allin delayed his golf career while he earned decorations for combat in the early days of the war. Cliff Harrington, who excelled on the United Golf Association while he served as a career Army paratrooper, lost his chance to prove himself on the PGA Tour when he was killed in action in Vietnam. Steve Eichstaedt earned his player's card in 1967 and entered five tournaments in 1968 before he was drafted. After service as a combat medic in Vietnam, he briefly played the tour (finishing second to Bruce Devlin at the 1970 Cleveland Open). But, for the most part, golfers who came of age during the war were able to use college or family deferments, or service in the reserves, to stay out of Vietnam.

However, cultural upheaval and pro golf intersected at the last major championship of the decade. Before the PGA Championship, a group known as the Dayton Organization threatened to disrupt the championship unless a list of 27 demands were met, including 3,000 free tickets, access to all private clubs, a donation to the poor equal to the $175,000 purse, and an end to the Vietnam war. According to a leader of the coalition, they were disturbed that the Dayton area Chamber of Commerce had devoted more resources toward promoting the tournament than attempting to assist with problems in the community. Needless to say, the PGA was unwilling or unable to meet the demands. Sifford, Elder, and Brown rejected the coalition's overtures that they boycott the tournament, and all played.

After the first round, there was a nine-way tie for first place at 69. None of the leaders were known other than by hardcore golf fans. However, their scores were overshadowed by the 82 shot by Arnold Palmer, who, citing a hip injury, immediately withdrew, saying that he did not intend to return to competitive golf until he had recovered. Palmer was less than a month from turning 40 and the press immediately speculated that his career might be over.

One of the nine first-round co-leaders was Raymond Floyd, a 26-year-old from North Carolina who had won twice in 1969, most recently three weeks earlier at the American Golf Classic on the other side of Ohio. On the tour, he was known as much for being a party boy and a baseball fan (of the Chicago Cubs) as for his golf, and for his ability to play well after a night of carousing.

Floyd was grouped with Herman Keiser and Jim Ferrier, an odd threesome given that both Keiser and Ferrier were 54 years old. Ferrier, an Australian, was in the field by virtue of his PGA Championship win in 1947. In 1960, Ferrier nearly won the PGA, but by the end of the decade he was taking up space in fields by virtue of the lifetime exemption granted at the time to all former PGA champions. In 1969, he entered 19 tournaments and won a grand total of $1,172.

Photo 82: Jim Ferrier (above) and Raymond Floyd were not friends. (Historic Images, Wilson Sporting Goods Co.)

Less than half the age of his playing partners and at the top of his game, Floyd was displeased having to go out with two old-timers who had little chance of making the cut, let alone winning. Keiser shot a 41 on his first nine on Thursday and did not turn in his card at the end of the round. Floyd, who often had a sour disposition on the course, was annoyed that Ferrier took forever to line up his putts, though Ferrier did manage a respectable 74.

Floyd and Ferrier played as a twosome in the second round. Still, the round took 5 hours to complete as Ferrier gave no quarter as he slogged to a 79 to comfortably miss the cut. Floyd was able to channel his anger during the round to shoot 66 and take a one-shot lead over Gary Player, who shot 65.

However, after the round Floyd erupted. "I was irritable teeing off," he said. "For one thing I knew I was going to play with a man that I absolutely loathe. We couldn't have said four words all day. Herman quit Thursday. He said he couldn't take it anymore and apologized to me for leaving me in a twosome." Of Ferrier, Floyd continued his rant. "He's not a considerate player with those he's playing with. I guess it's because his nerves are gone. I can't say nothing to a guy like that. He's an old man."

After Ferrier complained to PGA commissioner Joe Dey, Floyd apologized for his intemperate remarks. The third round offered more unwanted drama. The two of the Big Three remaining in the field—Player and Jack Nicklaus—were paired. They started the day one and three shots, respectively, behind Floyd.

On Saturday, the Dayton Organization dramatically aired their unmet grievances. As Player prepared to tee off on the fourth hole, a man threw the 250-page tournament program in his direction. The demonstrator was taken away by security. On the ninth hole, a protestor yelled, "Hey!," as Nicklaus prepared to putt. While walking to the 10th tee, somebody threw ice cubes in Player's face and yelled, "Racist!" On the 10th green, while Nicklaus was lining up an eagle putt, several demonstrators ran on to the green. One ran through a bunker toward Nicklaus, who raised his putter in self-defense. The demonstrator stopped, but another picked up Nicklaus's ball on the green and threw it into a trap. On the 13th hole, as Player prepared to putt, a woman threw a ball onto the green and was arrested. In all, 11 demonstrators were arrested and charged with misdemeanors.

After the round, Player was diplomatic. "I wasn't touched," he said. "I tried to be a peacemaker." According to Player, a shaggy-haired young man being led off in handcuffs said to him, "We have nothing against you and Jack, Gary, we're just against the PGA." Despite the distractions, Player managed a 71, while Nicklaus struggled to 74. Floyd, who also was harassed by demonstrators, but to a lesser extent, shot a 67 for his third sub-70 round to give him a commanding 5-shot lead over Player, Bunky Henry and Bert Greene.

In the final round, 100 police officers and gallery marshals surrounded Floyd and Player in the final group, and there were no further disturbances. Floyd struggled for most of the round. After bogeys on 13 and 15, when Floyd arrived at the 16th tee his lead over Player had been reduced to one. However, Floyd knocked in a 35-foot birdie on 16 while Player bogeyed to extend the lead to three. Player birdied 17, and Floyd bogeyed 18. Then, Player's 40-foot birdie putt on 18 fell short and Floyd escaped with a one-stroke victory.

Photo 83: *Raymond Floyd after winning 1969 PGA Championship.* (Associated Press)

Winning the PGA meant that Floyd would represent the United States in the World Cup in Singapore in early October, which did not entirely please him. "I was hoping to see the Cubs in the World Series in October," he lamented. It was a real dilemma because the Cubs then held an 8-game lead over the New York Mets in the National League East. Floyd would withdraw from the World Cup, citing other commitments, and was replaced by Lee Trevino. The Cubs would crash and burn, leading the way for the Miracle Mets' world championship. Not until 2016, 30 years after Floyd won his fourth major championship at the 1986 U.S. Open at Shinnecock Hills, and when he was 73 years old, would his beloved Chicago Cubs play in (and win) the World Series.

Gary Player

They threw telephone books in my back swing. They threw ice in my eyes. They charged me on the green. They threw golf balls between my legs when I was putting. They screamed on my backswing, and they threatened to kill me. And I lost by one. I certainly would've won if I never had any of that, without a question. But ifs don't mean a thing. There's so many ifs in golf. I could write a book on ifs.

Frank Beard

Raymond was a great player, and to us he was a good guy. He never caused any problems. He was class, he wore nice clothes. We weren't social friends, he lived in another world from what I did. He was arrogant. He was like Nicklaus. He wore the arrogance. He'd walk up to the tee and you didn't even want to look him in the face. He was like, "I'm going to kick your ass today." You see it in other sports. It was appropriate arrogance. They earned it. You don't hear it out of their mouths. He didn't care. He had business to do and he had golf to play.

Ron Cerrudo

I played well for a couple of rounds, but shot a 76 on the final day. I wasn't going to win, but I missed a chance to make the top 10. I remember the protests. They weren't near me, but I heard about it on television.

I went through qualifying school in the same class that had Tony Jacklin, Deane Beman and Gibby Gilbert. A lot of good players. When I got my card, that just gave me the opportunity to qualify for tournaments. Only the top-60 players were exempt from qualifying. To try to get exempt, I had to play every week, sometimes 15 weeks in a row.

Today, they play three weeks in a row and they're exhausted. Some weeks, the last thing I wanted to do was play golf, but I had to. I was traveling with my first wife. All of the young players would graduate, get married and join the tour. That's just what everybody did, get married, and not always for the right reason. It must have been hard on the wives. There wasn't anything for them to do on tour.

Chuck Courtney

Jim Ferrier was slow. I was a slow player, too, but compared to him I was like Superman. His wife's name was Norma, and Norma never, ever, ever missed a hole. She had a shooting stick like you'd have at the racetrack, with the leather thing you'd stick your butt on. Norma Ferrier. She never missed a hole.

September

Michigan Golf Classic

What happens if you put on a golf tournament, and nobody comes? The promoters of the 1969 Michigan Golf Classic learned the answer.

"We feel and have felt that there should a major professional tournament in metropolitan Detroit," spokesman Marshall Chambers—a local advertising agent—said when the tournament was launched in January 1969. Chambers added that $100,000 had been placed in escrow for the prize money and $40,000 for operating expenses. The organizers overlooked the fact that an earlier Detroit tourney—the Motor City Open—failed to get legs in the 1950s and early '60s and was discontinued after the 1962 edition. Moreover, the Buick Open was a longtime popular tour stop and less than an hour's drive from the new tourney's site at the Shenandoah Golf and Country Club in Walled Lake, close enough for Detroit fans to get their annual golf fix.

Also, the assigned calendar slot put it in conflict with the World Series of Golf, a popular television event. Even though the 1969 World Series did not feature any of the Big Three, Palmer, Nicklaus and Player were absent from Michigan, along with just about every other top name. Word had got around that the Shenandoah course was in terrible shape. Commissioner Joe Dey had implored Chambers (unsuccessfully) to move the tournament elsewhere.

Deane Beman and Tom Shaw were the only pros among the top-20 money winners who showed up, hardly names that were going to move the needle. Thus, spectators needed all the help they could get just to identify the competitors. However, none of the $40,000 in operating expenses went toward the purchase of caddie bibs or scoring standards for each group, the norm for even the most minor tour events. Furthermore, the scoreboards on the course were not operational.

"What's the difference?," Chambers snapped when asked about the lack of basic spectator aids. "There aren't enough people out there to make any difference." In fact, total attendance for the four tournament rounds was only about 15,000.

Larry Ziegler did not even want to play. His wife was home near St. Louis expecting their first child, and he thought he had to go through Monday qualifying. However, he learned he had been given a sponsor's exemption, so he decided to play. After barely making the cut, he shot a final-round 64 to tie Homero Blancas. Ziegler won the sudden-death playoff. Then, he, Blancas and the other contestants who made the cut got some

Photo 84: Larry Ziegler after winning the first and last annual Michigan Classic in 1969, perhaps being told not to cash his check. (Historic Images)

bad news. "Receipts at this time are insufficient to write checks to pay the fund," said a statement issued by the organizers even before the playoff was completed. "Payment must be deferred until all of our receivables are in."

If players went to Dey seeking reassurance, he did not provide any. Dey said he hoped "they don't go out and buy some stock or a new house before they find out what happened." It took some time, but eventually, the players were paid, and nobody went to prison. Not for another 50 years would a regular tour event return to Detroit.

Grier Jones

If I remember correctly, it was only a $100,000 tournament. We played for so little money in those days.

Somebody ran off with the money. I know it was a brand new tournament. I remember there weren't many people there. I remember finishing tied for fifth, and I remember that we didn't get paid until sometime later on in the year. The PGA Tour itself made good on everybody's money. I do remember having enough money in my column to make the top 60, which was just as important as getting the money. So, I remember not being too upset about not getting paid right away.

I was one of those guys who, the minute I was done, made a mad dash to the airport to get to the next tournament, or to go home. When I walked off the 18th green, it might have taken me, at the most, 20 minutes to get to my car. I had my bag packed, I paid my caddie, and I was gone. So, if the players knew we weren't going to be paid, I wouldn't have known about it until the next day.

There were some guys who were living from tournament to tournament, so after the tournament was over you could actually pick up your check. I never did. I had sponsors. I had a dad who was smart and knew what he was doing. I had enough money to play for the year. So, the checks went directly from the PGA to an account. But I knew a lot of guys who picked up their check the night of the tournament, or they got it the next week. When you went from Phoenix to Tucson, maybe you got there on Monday and went into the tour office and the checks were there for the week before.

Almost all of the players got along, with the exception of a few guys. Everybody stayed in the same motel, everybody ate in the same places. But it was pretty damn competitive in those years. There was so little money, that you had to play really well to make a living out there. It was crowded. There were a lot of guys playing who probably weren't quite good enough who were trying to qualify each week.

When you went to the winter tour—L.A., Phoenix, San Diego, the Crosby—the qualifying fields were usually full. There were over 100 guys, but a lot of them were PGA pros that worked in a shop that were off for the winter. They were from northern clubs, and those clubs weren't open in the wintertime, so they were in the southern part of the United States, and they were trying to qualify to play a little bit. So, it was pretty tough going. I mean, you had to play pretty damn well week to week, unless you were in the top-60.

The Ryder Cup

As we approach the end, mention must be made of the biennial Ryder Cup. Prior to the 1969 edition, there simply is nothing interesting to report during the decade. The U.S. team led Great Britain & Ireland, 14-3, overall, in the series going back to 1923. In the '60s, none of the matches were competitive: U.S. won 14½-9½ in 1961, 23-9 in 1963, 19½-12½ in 1965 and 23½- 8½ in 1967.

Players on both sides of the Atlantic coveted positions on their respective teams. For the Americans, being picked for the Ryder Cup was like making the All-Star team. Back then, the honor was more important than actually playing. In addition, the autumn matches held little importance to the sporting public either in America or Britain, who were interested primarily in their versions of football. Whereas British golf aficionados were well-aware of the likes of Arnold Palmer, Jack Nicklaus and Billy Casper, few Americans had even heard of Peter Alliss, Neil Coles, Harry Weetman, and Malcolm Gregson.

The better British-Irish golfers occasionally were enticed to play in the Masters but otherwise were content to play for small purses on the weather-challenged Continent for six months per year. By contrast, American pros were hardened by a tour that stretched for 11 months annually, for money their counterparts from across the Atlantic could only dream of. It was if the Notre Dame football team were required to play Columbia University every two years. For the American pros, it was more of a social event, an opportunity for the best to get together for a few days of food and drink at night, in between usually friendly matches with players who shared with them golf and a common language, but little else.

The 1969 version broke the mold. It was played September 18-20 at Royal Birkdale in Southport, England, and provided a temporary detour from the U.S.'s dominance that lasted until the Britain-Ireland side was expanded to include all of Europe a decade later. The catalyst was Tony Jacklin, who had distinguished himself on the American tour the previous two years and achieved worldwide prominence with his victory in the Open Championship two months earlier. Other than Jacklin, the British-Irish team was comprised mostly of veterans who were battle-tested, if not well-known outside of Europe. On the American side, only Casper and Gene Littler had ever played the Ryder Cup. Arnold Palmer did not qualify for the first time since 1959. Among the 10 U.S. rookies was Jack Nicklaus, who missed out on earlier editions because he had not completed the apprenticeship required for full membership in the PGA of America.

There was unusual acrimony during the matches. Britain-Ireland captain Eric Brown instructed his players not to help the Americans search for golf balls. On the second day, a four-ball match between Americans Ken Still and Dave Hill, and Welshman Brian Huggett and Scot Bernard Gallacher, almost resulted in fisticuffs. It was left to Brown and American captain Sam Snead—neither known for their diplomatic skills—to calm their players. At one point, Still berated the gallery for their unsportsmanlike behavior.

Jacklin played in six matches in 1969 and was on the winning end in four, with the other two halved. Fellow Englishman Coles won three matches and halved one. In singles, on the final day Jacklin beat Nicklaus, 4-and-3, in the morning. Going into the afternoon session, the U.S. trailed Britain-Ireland by two points. Americans Littler, Hill, Miller Barber and Dan Sikes won their matches, while Gallacher and Peter Butler won for Britain-Ireland to square the competition. The penultimate match was between Casper and Huggett, with Nicklaus and Jacklin meeting again in the last match.

Trailing by one, Jacklin holed an impossible 50-foot eagle putt on 17. When Nicklaus missed his eagle chance from 15 feet, their match was squared. At the same time, Huggett sank a 4-footer for par on 18 to halve his match with Casper.

On 18, Jacklin and Nicklaus put their approaches on the green, both with makable putts. Both missed. Nicklaus hit his first putt 4 feet past the hole. Jacklin left his short. Nicklaus calmly stroked his second putt into the hole. In the same motion, he took his ball out of the hole and picked up Jacklin's marker to concede the putt. Their match, and the whole competition, ended in a tie. Because the U.S. had won in 1967, it kept the Ryder Cup.

Snead was unhappy with Nicklaus's act of sportsmanship. "When it happened, all the boys thought it was ridiculous to give him that putt," he said. "We went over there to win, not be good ol' boys."

Tony Jacklin

I played a lot of golf with (Brian) Huggett. He was a damn good player. We used to refer to him as the Welsh bulldog. He had a face like a bulldog. But he was a tenacious competitor. He didn't travel that much, similar to his close friend Neil Coles. They traveled everywhere together. They used to stay in these wonderful country hotels, small hotels where the food was fantastic.

I holed a putt on the 17th green to tie with Nicklaus, and Huggett was on the 18th green at the time. I think he was playing Billy Casper and he had this 4-footer. He heard this roar and he thought I had beat Nicklaus, and he thought he had this 4-footer to win the Ryder Cup. Anyway, he makes it and Huggett breaks down on the ground thinking he's holed the winning putt in the Ryder Cup. And captain Eric Brown says, "No, no that was just Jacklin getting even." But that was an example of his competitiveness. (Huggett) was a tough competitor.

Nicklaus, on that last hole, as we walked off the tee, I was racing on ahead of him. He hollered at me, and I stopped. He said, "Are you nervous?" and I said, "I'm bloody petrified." And he said, "I thought you might be, and if it's any consolation I feel just the same way you do."

When (Nicklaus) hit his 20-footer (on 18), he hit it four-and-a-half or 5 feet past. It was too far past for me to say "good-good." It wouldn't have been right to do that. I don't think it would've been right for him to give me a 3-foot putt. (My first putt on 18) was 2 feet short. It was in if I had hit it. Some people say it was 3 feet, but it wasn't 3 feet. It was 20 inches to 2 feet. And that was (Nicklaus') reckoning, not mine. We've talked about it 100 times. And then when he picked up my marker so I didn't have to putt it, it was a mixture of shock and relief. He said, "I don't think you would've missed it, but I wouldn't want to give you the opportunity."

It's not a position you want to be in, to be honest, with the outcome dependent on your result. I was tremendously relieved that I didn't have to putt. But having said that I knew when I stood there, I was saying to myself, "T.J., whatever happens you're going to have to make this putt."

I think any player who has played Ryder Cups will tell you that the pressure for a Ryder Cup is about as big as it can get, when your teammates are all sitting around the green and the outcome is dependent on you. You feel it if you're playing for yourself in a major. It's just you, I mean it's bad enough. You battle to try to win, but in the Ryder Cup it's all magnified, and it's a hell of a responsibility.

Frank Beard

I was excited about it. Sam Snead was the captain. We had one team meeting. It lasted about 15 minutes. Snead said, "I want you to write down who you don't want to play with."

When one of the Americans missed a putt, (the gallery) cheered. It was really unnerving. Bernard Gallacher and Dave Hill both were hot-tempered alcoholics. They argued about mud on a ball and had to be separated. We picked up on the negative vibe and really wanted to beat them.

When Nicklaus and Jacklin were on the 18th green, Kenny Still and I were on our knees watching. I asked, "What did he do?" Kenny said, "He gave him that putt." I was upset but, as usual, Jack was smarter than any of us. "We kept the Cup," he said. "These guys are trying to build golf. If they get a tie, it's a big deal."

Tommy Aaron

I was standing there watching, and there were a number of other players there, too. I was shocked that Nicklaus had conceded Jacklin's putt. They both had short putts, but very difficult putts, as I remember. And I had the impression, just probably my impression—I never discussed it with anyone else—that Nicklaus was so happy making his putt he picked up Jacklin's coin. This was like something he hadn't planned, but it just happened very quickly because he was so happy about making his putt. You know, he couldn't have planned that. He didn't know how that was going to play out. It must have been a spur of the moment thing. He hadn't thought about all the consequences. You can't plan that. When you're playing, you just have to concentrate on playing. That was my take on it. I never discussed that with any of the other players.

We were standing out by the green and I remember a lot of them just all kind of gasped, like "What is all this about?" They wanted to see Jacklin putt it. But that concession made Nicklaus a hero in Europe.

Alcan Golfer of the Year Championship

The Alcan was sponsored by the Canadian bauxite mining company. It was restricted to 24 players and had a first prize of $55,000, the richest in the world. In 1969, it was played in Portland, Oregon.

The process for selecting the field was strange. Tournaments were chosen in the United States, Canada, the United Kingdom, the rest of Europe, South Africa, Australia, and Asia to determine who would qualify. The four PGA tournaments were the Western Open, the Greater New Orleans Open, the Greater Hartford Open, and the Philadelphia Classic. Also, the top three PGA money winners got in. The result was that none of the winners of the four majors qualified for the Alcan, but Bert Greene, Grier Jones and other less-known players were in the field.

In the final round, after eagling the 15th hole Lee Trevino had a comfortable 6-shot lead over Billy Casper. In an outcome reminiscent of his final round rally at the 1966 U.S. Open, Casper birdied the last four holes, while Trevino bogeyed the 16th hole and then, on the par-3 17th, hit his tee shot into a bunker, took two to get out, then three-putted for a disastrous triple-bogey. As a result, Casper beat Trevino by a stroke.

In dead last of the no-cut tournament was Kel Nagle of Australia, with a 72-hole score of 324, 25 shots behind Brian Barnes of England, who was next-to-last. This was due to his score of 105 in the second round. On the ninth hole, Nagle was credited with a 35. He actually made a par 4, but inadvertently penciled in his nine-hole score of 35 in the square reserved for the ninth hole. Nagle signed his card, so he was stuck with a 105 instead of the 75 he actually had. The error did not hurt him financially, because even if he had been credited with a 75 for the round and 294 total he still would have won $2,000, the sum awarded to each of the seven bottom finishers.

Lee Trevino

I went to Singapore and won the World Cup. I won the individual. Things don't bother me. Like I say, you have to understand where I came from. Whatever happens to me is a hell of a lot better than what I had. I came in second. If it was winner-take-all, that would bother me.

November

Heritage Golf Classic

In September 1969, *Sports Illustrated* ran a story titled "Farewell to an Era: Arnold Palmer Turns 40". The cover photo shows Palmer with his chin resting on his hands. His forehead is furrowed. He looks sad.

The decade that started with wins at the Masters and the U.S. Open and talk of a Grand Slam did not end well for Palmer. He had not won since the Kemper Open in September 1968. In 1969, Palmer only had eight top-10 finishes, none higher than third. His only top-10 in a major was a sixth at the U.S. Open, after suffering the humiliation of having to go through qualifying.

Palmer's nadir came at the PGA Championship in August. He shot 82 in the first round, his highest round ever as a pro, anywhere. Citing a hip injury, Palmer withdrew and said he intended to stay on the sideline for the remainder of the year and attempt a comeback in 1970. "However," the Associated Press reported, "many observers believe that this may mark the end of a career."

Three weeks later, Palmer was in Akron, Ohio, doing television commentary for the World Series of Golf. For the first time, neither Palmer nor Nicklaus nor Player were in the field. Many who tuned in were more interested in seeing their hero behind a microphone than George Archer, Orville Moody, Tony Jacklin and Raymond Floyd battle for the $50,000 first prize. Palmer was asked if he had read the stories saying he might be through. "Every one of them," he answered. "I save 'em all." Asked how they made him feel, Palmer paused. "It made me feel like I want to show everyone I can still play."

By mid-October, Palmer's hip improved enough for him to enter four successive fall events. At the Sahara Invitational in Las Vegas, he tied for 34th. The following week, in San Francisco, he finished 27th. Then, at the Kaiser International, he placed sixth. In Hawaii, he was 28th. Even though Palmer was not doing much more than making cuts, after the disaster at the PGA he was encouraged.

After a week off, in late November Palmer headed to Hilton Head, South Carolina for the inaugural Heritage Golf Classic at the brand new Harbour Town Golf Links. A year earlier, the tournament was slated to be part of the APG tour. After the rapprochement between the tour pros and the PGA, the Heritage was added to the schedule.

Palmer and Jack Nicklaus were the headliners. Although Nicklaus won three times in 1969 (including recently at the Sahara and the Kaiser), like Palmer he considered it to be a down year. He did not come close in any of the four majors, and in fact had not won a major since his 1967 U.S. Open victory at Baltusrol. Yet, Nicklaus was third on the money list, $37,000 behind Frank Beard (who was not playing at Hilton Head), and he had designs on winning the last two events to overtake Beard. Nicklaus had a decided advantage because he had designed the Harbour Town course with Pete Dye.

In the first round, held on Thanksgiving Day, Palmer grabbed the lead with George Archer, both shooting 68. Palmer drove impeccably on the narrow course and missed seven putts less of less than 8 feet. Host pro Wallace Palmer (no relation to Arnold) could not keep his ball in the fairway and signed for a 97. Nicklaus shot 71. On Friday, in a cool drizzle, Palmer maintained a share of the lead with Tom Weiskopf after a 71. Nicklaus' 72 left him four shots back. In the third round, Palmer took sole possession of the lead by three shots with a 70. On 18, Nicklaus put his second shot on the beach and was able to advance his third shot only 4 feet on his way to a double-bogey that left him five shots out.

On a sunny, chilly Sunday, Palmer struggled to a 74. His 72-hole score of 283 was only 1-under par. However, it was good enough for a three-shot victory over Bert Yancey and Dick Crawford. Nicklaus' 75 clinched the money title for Frank Beard.

The following week, Palmer won again at the Danny Thomas Diplomat Classic in South Florida, closing with a 65 to beat Gay Brewer. Thus, the golfer who, more than any other player, defined pro golf in the 1960s won the final two tournaments of the decade.

In 1970, for the first time since turning pro, Palmer failed to win on his own (though he and Nicklaus won the National Team Championship). He returned in 1971 with one last great year, winning three times, plus repeating with Nicklaus in the team event, and making the Ryder Cup team for the final time. At the 1973 Bob Hope Desert Classic, Palmer won for the 62nd and last time on the PGA Tour. In 1975, he won the Spanish Open. He did not win again until 1980 when, at age 50, he beat Isao Aoki of Japan by one shot and Gary Player by two at the Canadian PGA Championship.

Thereafter, Palmer focused most of his competitive energy on the new PGA Senior Tour, where he won 10 times between 1980 and 1988. However, on the regular tour, at the 1983 Glen Campbell–Los Angeles Open he found himself one shot behind the leaders after 54 holes, which spiked attendance for the final round. After sinking a 30-foot putt for birdie on the fifth hole, he took the lead, and was tied for the lead after eight holes. He stumbled down the stretch and finished tied for 10th. After he putted out on 18, thousands of the 26,000 in attendance left.

Palmer had one last moment of glory on the tour, in the first round of the 1989 PGA Championship, when he was one month shy of 60 years old. Looking splendid in a fedora on a sunny day at the Kemper Lakes Golf Club near Chicago, he birdied five consecutive holes to briefly ascend to the top of the leaderboard one last time.

After Palmer died on September 25, 2016, his ashes were scattered over the Latrobe Country Club. Shortly after, a rainbow appeared above Latrobe.

Photo 85: *Arnold Palmer after winning the inaugural Heritage Golf Classic.*
(The State)

Acknowledgments

I owe deep gratitude to the retired pros who took the time to share their experiences. This book is dedicated to all of them: Tommy Aaron, Frank Beard, Don Bies, Frank Boynton, Ron Cerrudo, Charles Coody, Chuck Courtney, Bruce Devlin, Don Fairfield, Marty Fleckman, Bob Goalby (1929-2022), Larry Hinson, Babe Hiskey, Tony Jacklin, Grier Jones, Rives McBee, Bobby Nichols, Jack Nicklaus, Steve Opperman, Gary Player, Chi Chi Rodriguez, Martinus Roesink, Bob Shave, Jr., Jerry Steelsmith, Lee Trevino, Tom Watson, Bert Weaver (1932-2022), Kermit Zarley, and Bob Zimmerman. Also, thank you to Doc Giffin, Walter Iooss, Jr., Cindy Samartino, and John Maples.

Much of the historical information comes from accounts published via the Associated Press and United Press International. Newspapers.com was an invaluable resource, as was the USA *Today Golfers Encyclopedia* (2009). I gratefully acknowledge the assistance of the United States Golf Association in providing photographs.

Thank you to Jim Nugent, Steve Eubanks, Jeff Barr, James Dodson and Barbara Ivins-Georgoudiou at *Global Golf Post* for giving me a stage to pursue a second act as a golf writer, and to Gordon McClellan, Suanne Laqueur, Mark Hobbs, and Simona Meloni at DartFrog Books and Canoe Tree Press for putting this all together.

Thank you to my father, Edward Hand, for introducing me to the game of golf, and to my mother, Alice Ann Hand, for encouraging me to write.

To my brother, Brian Hand, thank you for all of your help. You're the best.

Finally, to my wife Katie, you have my eternal love and appreciation for all things, including your support as I undertook this project.

About the Author

Patrick Hand was born in Jacksonville, North Carolina. He is a graduate of Catholic University and Fordham University Law School. In addition to practicing law, he has written for *Washington City Paper*, *The Washington Post*, *LA Weekly* and other magazines. Since 2020, Hand has been a regular contributor to *Global Golf Post*. This is his first book. He lives in Rapidan, Virginia, with his wife, Katie, and children.

Photo Index

Index

Row 1, left to right: George Knudson, Harold Henning, Jacky Cupit, Julius Boros.

Row 2, left to right: Ken Venturi, Larry Hinson, Larry Ziegler, Martinus Roesink.

Row 3, left to right: Marty Fleckman, Marty Furgol, Orville Moody, Paul Bondeson.

Row 4, left to right: Pete Brown, Phil Rodgers, Raymond Floyd, Rives McBee.

Row 5, left to right: Tom Nieporte, Tommy Jacobs, Tony Jacklin, Tony Lema.